WHAT'S IN A NAME

WHAT'S IN A NAME

NAZIR RAZAK

Hardback ISBN 978-1-913532-60-4
Trade paperback ISBN 978-1-913532-94-9

Also available as an ebook
ISBN 978-1-913532-61-1

Typeset by seagulls.net
Cover design by kid-ethic
Project management by whitefox
Printed and bound by CPI

To my mum, Rahah,

who passed away on 18 December 2020,

for her unconditional love and selfless

dedication to everything family.

'This is a book that needed to be written and must be read by all Malaysians who care about the country. No one who has family disagreements could not be moved by the terrible choices one has to make between loyalty to family, honour and dedication to the nation. When one is a member of the family at the leadership and founding of Malaysia, these choices are fateful because they decide not just the direction of the family, but also the nation. I salute therefore Nazir Razak for writing what must be very painful to write, but necessary to explain why very difficult choices face the nation and each and every one of us. I commend this book not only for its lucid analysis, but also constructive ideas that recognise that it is in our inner strength and will to change and exchange ideas that we will forge a stronger nation.'

Tan Sri Andrew Sheng, chairman, George Town Institute of Open and Advanced Studies, Wawasan Open University, Penang, and former chairman of the Securities and Futures Commission of Hong Kong.

'When a country's most accomplished deal maker puts pen to paper, its most compelling passages would usually be the account of businesses built, pivotal deals struck and even grand scandals unfolding. Thrilling as these stories are, the book's main contribution lies elsewhere; in Nazir's lifelong quest for the deeper truths and values left by his late father. When Tun Razak told his young son to "jaga nama baik", Nazir rightly concludes that this means a duty to "jaga *yang* baik", to uphold what is true and proper. What's in a name? Quite a lot in fact: Mohamed Nazir linguistically means the good overseer or the good warner. In Malay and Muslim tradition, when parents name a child, it is both a name and a prayer. This book may just be a fulfilment of both. Malaysians would do well to give it serious consideration.'

Tan Sri Azman Mokhtar, former managing director of Khazanah Nasional Berhad

'I could not and would not put down What's in a Name when I started reading it, and was riveted to its pages, reading it cover to cover in two days over Christmas Day and Boxing Day. It is a story of Malaysia, Tun Abdul Razak and Nazir Razak. I would recommend this book to anyone who is interested in Malaysia, its history, politics or economics. In fact, it should be compulsory reading in our universities. This book provides an intimate look and insight into key events which shaped Malaysia in the last fifty years. It is a book providing a glimpse of the past, present and future of Malaysia.'

Dato' Lim Chee Wee, senior partner of Lim Chee Wee Partnership and former Bar Council President

'A gripping account of the emergence of the Malaysian financial sector into global prominence, from before the Asian Financial Crisis through the drama of 1MDB. Nazir Razak saw it all at first hand and relates the story with verve and a heartfelt plea for good governance as the solution for stability and growth. Not just a book for bankers, this is essential reading for anyone interested in the modern history of Malaysia. An outstanding book.'

Professor Eugene Rogan, director of the Middle East Centre, University of Oxford, and author of *The Arabs: A History*

'A three in one insight on the Razak family history, values and legacy. This book is a tour de force reference for corporate values and good governance. It provides a page-turning account of CIMB's success by design and brings to light the untold story behind 1MDB. A mesmerising read indeed.'

Dato Hussamuddin Yaacub, publisher, SinarHarian/Karangkraf Group

'*What's in a Name* is a first-hand story of Malaysia's fascinating development journey and the transformation of a small merchant bank to a major ASEAN financial institution. This book reflects on what it takes to build economies, societies and institutions that can take on the challenges of the future. At the same time, it highlights a few enduring lessons – that context really matters when making decisions; even the best solutions don't last a lifetime; there is real power in diversity; first movers are not cautious, considered people; conduct matters far more than words, and hindsight is indeed twenty-twenty. Ultimately, this book is on the importance of legacy and the enormous responsibility borne by inheritors to recognise, preserve and enhance. An insightful read.'

Joydeep Sengupta, senior partner, McKinsey and Company

'Paradoxically, both poverty and privilege can be challenging. I suffered poverty. Nazir suffered privilege. And privilege can be more corrupting, undermining key values of determination and diligence, integrity and compassion. This elegantly written and charming book describes well how Nazir overcame it all while hewing faithfully to the values that his father, a great statesman, bequeathed to the family. This memoir provides invaluable insights into contemporary Malaysia. It will also play a critical role in the rejuvenation and revitalisation of Malaysian society.'

Kishore Mahbubani, founding dean of the Lee Kuan Yew School of Public Policy, NUS, and the author of *The ASEAN Miracle*

'I did not just read this book; I dived into it! As someone who served under Tun Razak, Nazir's excellent account of life in Seri Taman and description of his late father stirs vivid memories of a golden time of political leadership in the country. Nazir's stories about building CIMB are fascinating; his assessment of what ails our nation are astute and his ideas about the way forward must be given serious consideration despite being very challenging. Almost no one is as enthusiastic and determined as Nazir to put into reality his ideas for bringing Malaysia forward. This book deserves encouragement and support.'

Tun Musa Hitam, former deputy prime minister, Malaysia

'This splendid book gives you a seat in the cockpit, as one of the largest banks in Malaysia is built. The audacious deals and the setbacks make gripping reading. Nazir Razak's journey is both personal and national, and so too are the lessons he draws.'

Professor Ngaire Woods, dean of the Blavatnik School of Government, University of Oxford

'What's in a name? Evidently, a lot. This book is about a family at the heart of the Malaysian project. It familiarises us with Tun Abdul Razak from the perspective of his youngest son. We learn of his childhood, his values and the challenges he faced. These values come to shape the life of Nazir Razak – and end up getting him into direct conflict with another member of the Razak household, Najib Razak. But what's more than a name? Beyond being a story of legacy and family, it is a deep insight into corporate Malaysia through the lens of Nazir Razak in CIMB. As we follow his journey with CIMB and how they've grown over the decades, we see the evolution of a corporate leader and his lessons learned. But we also learn about the many conflicts, power-plays and battles behind the scenes that only few have known about. Fundamentally, these stories really tell us a tale of nation building. What we got right, where we went wrong and most importantly, how do we get back on track. A must read for all Malaysians.'

Tharma Pillai, co-founder of UNDI18

CONTENTS

LIST OF ABBREVIATIONS

AEC	ASEAN Economic Community
AFC	Asian Financial Crisis
AMD	Annual Management Dialogue
ASEAN	Association of Southeast Asian Nations
BCB	Bumiputra Commerce Bank Berhad
BCHB	Bumiputra Commerce Holdings Berhad
BMF	Bumiputra Malaysia Finance
BN	Barisan Nasional
BNM	Bank Negara Malaysia
BOC	Bank of Commerce
BOT	Bank of Thailand
CDRC	Corporate Debt Restructuring Committee
CEO	Chief Executive Officer
CEP	Council of Eminent Persons
CIC	Capital Issues Committee
CIMB	Commerce International Merchant Bankers
CLSA	Crédit Lyonnais Securities Asia
DAP	Democratic Action Party
DRS	Dividend Reinvestment Scheme
EES	Employee Equity Scheme
EPF	Employee Provident Fund
ESOS	Employee Share Option Scheme
ETP	Economic Transformation Plan
FELDA	Federal Land Development Agency
FPTP	First-past-the-post (electoral system)

GDP	Gross Domestic Product
GFC	Global Financial Crisis
GLC	Government Linked Company
GLCT	Government Linked Companies' Transformation
GLIC	Government Linked Investment Company
GMC	Group Management Committee
GTP	Government Transformation Programme
IMF	International Monetary Fund
IMP	Independence of Malaya Party
IPO	Initial Public Offering
KL	Kuala Lumpur
KLCI	Kuala Lumpur Composite Index
KLIA	Kuala Lumpur International Airport
KLSE	Kuala Lumpur Stock Exchange (later renamed Bursa Malaysia)
KMUK	Kesatuan Melayu United Kingdom (Malay Society of the UK)
KWAP	Kumpulan Wang Persaraan (Retirement Fund Incorporated)
MACC	Malaysian Anti-Corruption Commission
MAS	Malaysian Airlines
MBSB	Malaysian Building Society Berhad
MCA	Malayan Chinese Association
MCKK	Malay College Kuala Kangsar
MESDAQ	Malaysian Exchange of Securities Dealing and Automated Quotation
MITI	Ministry of International Trade and Industry
MOF	Ministry of Finance
MoF	Minister of Finance
MP	Member of Parliament
MRI	Magnetic Resonance Imaging
NBMC	National Bond Market Committee

NCC	National Consultative Council
NEAC	National Economic Action Council
NEM	New Economic Model
NEP	New Economic Policy
NKRA	National Key Results Area
NOC	National Operations Council
NRP	National Recalibration Plan
OCBC	Oversea-Chinese Banking Corporation
OJK	Otoritas Jasa Keuangan (Financial Services Authority, Indonesia)
OKIS	Orang Kaya Indera Shahbandar (Nobility title in the Pahang Sultanate)
PAC	Public Accounts Committee
PAP	People's Action Party
PAS	Parti Islam Se-Malaysia (Malaysian Islamic Party)
PH	Pakatan Harapan (Hope Coalition)
PKR	Parti Keadilan Rakyat (People's Justice Party)
PM	Prime Minister
PNB	Permodalan Nasional Berhad
PSA	Prostate-Specific Antigen Test
QE	Quantitative Easing
RFP	Request for Proposal
RHB	Rashid Hussain Bank
RTM	Radio and Television Malaysia (Department of Broadcasting)
SBB	Southern Bank Berhad
SME	Small and Medium Enterprises
SOE	State Owned Enterprises
SVP	Senior Vice President
TIA	Terengganu Investment Authority
UEM	United Engineers of Malaysia
UMNO	United Malays National Organisation

PREFACE

I remember it clearly: at 3:15 p.m. on 19 December 2018, as scheduled, my wife Azlina and I walked up the stairs to the consultant urologist's office to be told the results of the biopsy that had been conducted one week earlier. I was sure it would be bad news. There were no symptoms to speak of, only a high PSA score spotted during a random blood test and a suspicious discoloration on the MRI scan. But everything seemed to be going against me, and I had no doubt this would prove to be the same.

Over the course of the previous few months, I had been: forced out of CIMB, the bank I had led to become one of the biggest in ASEAN (Association of Southeast Asian Nations) and where I had worked for twenty-nine years; faced the ignominy of being stopped at airport immigration because I had been banned from travelling overseas; interviewed by the police and the Malaysian Anti-Corruption Commission (MACC). There were constant rumours that I was on a list of people who were about to be arrested by the government that had just come to power. My family name was being dragged through the mud following my brother, former Prime Minister (Dato Sri) Najib Razak's, sensational fall from power amid allegations of corruption. Distressingly, my eighty-five-year-old mother's house had been searched by a squad of about twenty policemen while she was at home alone. Everything was awry and out of joint. Why would my health be any different?

The consultant's office was on the first floor of a grand Georgian house in the Harley Street terrace. High-ceilinged and imposing, it was a stone's throw from the London Clinic, where my father, (Tun) Abdul Razak, had died forty-three years earlier. Behind the desk was Professor Prokar Dasgupta, one of the UK's leading urologists and the pioneer of robotic prostatectomy. If there was a time to treat yourself to the best, this was surely it.

I had been to see Prokar a couple of times before and we got on well. We joked that we were 'twins from different parents' because we were born on the same day. He was one of the most self-assured people I've come across (and as an investment banker I met more than my fair share), always convincingly able to substantiate anything he said. He was direct and didn't like to dance around the topic. I knew his first words would be definitive, and so it proved.

'I am sorry,' he said, 'but it's what we feared and probably slightly worse. There is a malignant tumour in your prostate, and it's aggressive, which means we don't have much time. We should remove it as soon as possible. The risk of spread is high.' We had only just sat down on the other side of his desk. I've seen this on television: the moment a patient is told he or she has cancer. It seemed oddly less dramatic in real life. Perhaps I was taking consolation from the fact that I knew recovery rates for prostate cancer are high so long as it is detected early enough.

I was certainly becoming accustomed to dealing with bad news. I had learned that the best approach was to stay calm and immediately think about what I should do next. It did not help to be distracted by emotions. I had to focus on the next step, whatever that was. As ever in a crisis, Azlina was very calm. She reached over from her chair and squeezed my hand. Now that we understood what we were dealing with we swiftly moved on to talk about the surgery itself: what it would involve, where I should have it, and when.

In the days that followed, I reflected on the situation I found myself in. I'd had a stressful career and had perhaps neglected my health. Cancer ran in the family; both Abdul Razak and his father had died of it at roughly my age. In fact, I found it easier to respond to the cancer than some of the other things that had not gone my way that year.

It was probably naive of me to have expected different treatment from the new Pakatan Harapan (PH) government. In the run-up to the country's fourteenth General Election held on 9 May 2018, my sympathies had plainly been with PH rather than ruling Barisan Nasional (BN) party, despite the fact that the latter had been created by my own father and was being led by my eldest brother. My public opposition to the 1MDB financial scandal and other shenanigans that had gone on in Najib's government – at the rural development agency the Federal Land Development Authority (FELDA), for example – had often been used as good fodder for opposition attacks. In private I had been helpful to several senior PH figures. Nevertheless, I was the brother of Najib, the coalition's main enemy, who was the *raison d'être* of the most unlikely partnership of old foes – former PM (Tun) Dr Mahathir Mohamad and (Dato' Seri) Anwar Ibrahim, his former deputy PM, whom he had sacked and imprisoned back in 1998. And as chairman of CIMB, I was a senior figure in the ruling nexus of politics, government and business. None of the senior PH figures whom I helped were going to risk their political capital to keep me in my job.

It was certainly naive of me to believe that my position at CIMB was secure. I had earned my position by working my way up and building the bank from a mid-tier Malaysian merchant bank to an ASEAN financial powerhouse. (Along the way we became a Government Linked Company or GLC.) As a non-executive director at national institutions, Khazanah Nasional and the Employee Provident Fund (EPF) I had done my bit to keep them on the straight and narrow. Yet once the new government had decided to treat the leaders of all GLCs as having been complicit with BN, my career achievements became irrelevant. I had assumed the incoming government would want to work with experienced heads of GLCs, but instead removing many of us became an early priority.

Feeling sorry for yourself is never a good look. As I mulled my own *'annus horribilis'* I realised I was seeing life from the wrong perspective. I needed a longer lens. CIMB, my life's work, had far exceeded my expectations. I was so proud of what all the CIMBians, as we called ourselves, had achieved. My kids were doing well. My immediate family was financially secure. My country had an opportunity for reform that once seemed inconceivable. I had been fearful of what life would be like with more years under a BN government that would have buried the huge financial mess at 1MDB at all costs. I had become convinced that the whole system needed an overhaul, and this could finally happen. I had built a public mosque to honour my mother, Masjid Ar Rahah, in Bangsar South, Kuala Lumpur and I had stood up for my father's legacy, of which I was immensely proud. That's when the penny dropped. There was just so much more to be proud of and grateful for. It was a challenging time, but challenges pass. It was time to pick myself up, move on, overcome whatever setbacks came my way and grasp new opportunities.

The surgery in February 2019 was successful – 'as near-perfect as possible, even if I should say so myself', as Prokar so humbly put it. I adapted to life after CIMB more readily than I had expected, focusing on my new private equity fund, Ikhlas Capital; a visiting fellowship at the Blavatnik School of Government at Oxford University; and writing this book. I am by nature a fairly sunny character; my default mode is to look forward.[1]

This is not a regular autobiography. This book is about my family, business, and politics in Malaysia – and how they are intertwined. *What's in a Name* is firstly about my father's legacy and how I have tried to live up to the towering surname with which I was born.[2] (In Malay custom someone's last name is typically the father's first name by virtue of the naming convention that uses 'bin' or son of.) Over the course of getting to know the father I lost at such a young age, I realised that his legacy came in two parts: an obvious, public part (the institutions and government programmes he created) and a personal part (the values and principles he upheld). The growing tension between these two aspects to his legacy helped to shape my life and career and ultimately left me with fateful choices to make, over which of the two to honour. This book is also about how I led CIMB to become a leading ASEAN bank while navigating the complexities of business and politics in Malaysia. I have been lucky enough to observe the events of the last half-century from a very privileged vantage point, scion of a political family and a leading banker. I hope the perspectives and insights I have to share will be valuable to my children and the next generation of Malaysians as a whole as they navigate an uncertain future.

At the end of this book, as I reflect on the past and future of Malaysia, I find myself in the year 2021 more convinced than ever that Malaysia needs to do what it did in 1970: undergo nationhood recalibration, a thorough re-examination of what it means to be Malaysian and how its democracy, government, economy and society works. If we fail to do the hard work of thinking about what we did wrong, what no longer works and what we need to thrive in the twenty-first century, we will remain trapped in a failing system. The challenges and opportunities are daunting – the Fourth Industrial Revolution is upon us and US-China tensions may escalate, Covid-19 has brought devastation, and climate change is a daily reality. If we are at our best we can be a nation that leapfrogs others; if we carry on as usual we will sink to new lows. I know which I choose.

Nazir Razak
Kuala Lumpur
March 2021

SECTION ONE

REMEMBERING MY FATHER

GROWING UP
A RAZAK

Your family name is one of the most important cards you are dealt when you are born. As Shakespeare's Juliet said: 'What's in a name? That which we call a rose by any other name would smell as sweet.' Juliet was pleading to be seen as herself rather than as a Capulet. A name, she argues, is no more than a superficial marker; it tells you nothing about who people really are. The tragedy is that she and Romeo were not allowed to escape being Montagues and Capulets. Their family names defined them in the eyes of others, where they belonged, whom they could talk to; much less fall in love with.

When your name is well known, for better *or* for worse, it will shape how people react to you before you've even said a word. Your name connects you back to your family and goes before you, placing you, telling people where you come from, perhaps what you stand for. That can be both a help and a handicap. As the youngest son of Tun Abdul Razak bin Dato' Hussein, I have had to be conscious of my name every step of the way in Malaysia. I did not have a choice: I am and always will be a Razak and proudly so.

I was born into the Razak family on 19 November 1966 at Kuala Lumpur's General Hospital, the youngest son of Abdul Razak and his wife (Tun) Rahah Noah. My father did not attend the birth. In those days it was not expected; he was at a dinner at his favourite haunt, the Lake Club, a sports and social club established by the British and after independence frequented by expatriates and government officials. Since the birth of their first child, thirteen years earlier, my parents had been hoping for a daughter. I was their fifth son. With each son they grew more desperate, but my father was a great believer in probabilities. He thought that by the time they got to the fifth, the chances of having another boy were pretty slim. When he was told of my arrival, he is reported to have exclaimed, 'Oh no, another boy!' I assume my parents gave up relying on probabilities after me because I spent my first few months wearing the baby girl's clothes they had kept expectantly for years.

My parents named me Mohamed Nazir. This was meant to be my brother Johari's name, but when he was born, in 1954, General Nasser had just overthrown President Mohamed Naguib in Egypt. Since my eldest brother was already named Najib, my father didn't want to tempt fate. I was also nicknamed 'Jay'. My father liked the Filipino tradition of nicknames, so not only did we all have one – Najib (Jib), Johari (Joe), Nizam (Jam), Nazim (Jim) and Nazir (Jay) – in sequence, the nicknames jived!

I didn't see much of my father growing up. While he had a strong public profile, my early memories of him are hazy. To be fair, he had a lot on his plate around the time I arrived. Malaya had become independent in 1957, emerging from the ravages of war, invasion, occupation and the collapse of the colonial order. He was the country's first deputy prime minister as the fledgling nation stumbled to its feet. The creation of Malaysia in 1963, which brought together Malaya and the territories of Singapore, Sabah and Sarawak, had proved unacceptable to some of our neighbours, especially the populist government of Indonesia. In the three-year *konfrontasi* which followed, President Soekarno made 'Crush Malaysia' his rallying cry. In the year before I was born my father led the team which negotiated Singapore's exit from Malaysia; and while my mother was pregnant with me my father was involved

4

in secret meetings in Bangkok with counterparts posing as staff of the Indonesian airline Garuda to bring the *konfrontasi* to an end. In the year of my birth the US president, Lyndon B. Johnson, visited Malaysia just as the Vietnam War gathered pace. My father helped to steer Malaysia and, through ASEAN, its neighbours away from the Cold War conflicts that would engulf much of the region in the decade that followed.

By the time I was three years old, he was busy engineering peace within Malaysia following the violent race riots that had erupted on 13 May 1969 after only the third general election. For about twenty-one months after the riots, my father was given absolute power to rule by decree. In that time, he recalibrated the country's political, economic and social system in order to return it to parliamentary democracy and mobilised the state to accelerate growth to eradicate poverty and eliminate the identification of race with economic func-tion. The political and economic system he put in place remains at the core of how the country works today.

It's never easy for a son to present a clear picture of his father. We have a natural tendency to idealise our fathers, to avoid weak-nesses and see only strengths. For me, understanding my father fully was even more complicated because his public persona looms so large across the nation he helped build. He is universally known in Malaysia as Bapa Pembangunan (the Father of Development) in recognition of his all-encompassing role in building the nation. So widely known is he by his public achievements, the institutions he created, the poli-cies he enacted and the treaties he signed that it's difficult to see the real, private person. Not only did I idolise him, much of the country did, and a great deal has been written about him. My efforts to get a clear sense of him, the principles he stood for, the way he conducted himself, were made harder by his untimely death at the height of his power and popularity when I had barely got to know him.

Devastated as I was, I nurtured memories of him as a man who put public service and nation building above all else; who was consultative and collaborative; who was kind and thoughtful; who was never pompous or self-important; who held himself to the highest standards of probity and honesty; who worked tirelessly, yet who always had time for other people and treated them with respect whatever their background. That belief in my father has been with me throughout my life; I have had a sense of him looking over my shoulder, reminding me to try harder, to achieve more, and always to do the right thing.

The portrait that follows of Abdul Razak and what it meant to grow up as his son is based on my memories, substantially filled out by insights from members of my family and people who knew my father well.[3] It is my attempt to understand the man my father was. I am enormously proud of what he did, his is a remarkable record of achievement, but I had never felt I got to the heart of who he was. After researching for this book, I have come to the conclusion that Abdul Razak deserves the pedestal that I kept him on all of my life. Of course, he wasn't perfect. He was a great human being, but all humans have frailties.

SERI TAMAN

The home I grew up in embodied the two sides of life with my father. Despite my father being preoccupied with affairs of state, my parents managed to create a real home for us in the extraordinary, magical setting of the prime minister's official residence at Seri Taman. We lived there because my dad's boss, the prime minister, the legendary Tunku Abdul Rahman, graciously decided that it was more sensible for his deputy, with his much larger family, to move into the new mansion when it was completed in 1962.

Seri Taman as seen from the perspective of a child was just a large playground. Its wide halls, high ceilings and huge garden were the backdrop to my games, adventures and exploits. Seri Taman was designed and built for its times: an elegant, light and airy work of Malaysian modernism, which spoke to the ambition to build a new nation, albeit one with a strong sense of tradition. Set on a hill above the National Mosque and Lake Gardens, a public park near the heart of KL, Seri Taman was designed before air conditioning became ubiquitous, to allow the breeze to rise up the hill and through the open ground floor. The house was built around a courtyard with an ornamental pool and fountain. At the front was a lobby and entrance hall with a double-height ceiling overlooked by a gallery. On one side was the dining room, large enough for state dinners and, on the other, the salons and living rooms in which to greet guests. At the back was a large open area where people could congregate for parties, 'open houses' to celebrate cultural festivities and, every four or five years, on election nights.

In one sense Seri Taman was like a shophouse. Our family only had privacy above the shop where my father often did his business of governing the country, engaging in diplomacy and dealing in politics.

Our bedrooms were upstairs, where much of the time I played with my brothers (Datuk) Nazim and (Dato') Nizam. By the time I came along, my elder brothers, (Dato') Johari and Najib, were already at boarding school and only occasional visitors. My parents had adopted two girls, Fathiyah and Rohaya, from families in rural Kedah unable to care for them, and they would also join in our games.

On this floor, at the back of the building was my father's study, with its desk and bookshelves, an old-fashioned wooden globe, his immaculate *Economist* desk diaries and a row of colour-coded telephones so he could speak speedily and safely to the Agong (the King), senior members of the cabinet and the heads of the security forces. This was also where we found the opportunity to snatch time with him on our own or to watch special events. I remember him being glued to the television one evening in 1974 in disbelief as his favourite football team, Holland, led by the great Johan Cruyff, lost to West Germany in the World Cup final.

My bedroom was bright and large, especially for someone so small, because the nanny would also sleep and do some chores in it. Before the age of one, clearly under-supervised, I managed to burn the back of my hand with a hot iron that she had carelessly left on after ironing some clothes. A scar on my left hand still takes me back to a time before I can remember. In between bedrooms and Dad's study there were many smaller spaces, on the verandah overlooking the courtyard, and on a balcony at the back overlooking the garden, where as a family we could sit, chat, read and play.

The prime spot was that gallery I mentioned earlier, at the front of the house, overlooking the entrance hall. From here, if you were small and insignificant, you could without being spotted watch the comings and goings below of generals and ministers, civil servants and ambassadors and also, from time to time, people even more glamorous. It was from this balcony that I saw Muhammad Ali and Joe Bugner come to dinner on the eve of their world heavyweight bout in 1975. This was my vantage point to watch Queen Elizabeth II and Prince Philip arrive, dressed in their finery, in 1972. The balcony could also be used in fights: my brother Nazim once launched a wet towel from it to destroy several rows of toy soldiers I had carefully constructed to do battle in the entrance hall below. I raced upstairs after him, outraged, as he sped away, bigger, faster, laughing. Below, politicians were jostling for power. Above, the warfare was sometimes more open.

The ground floor was a place of constant comings and goings, gatherings and meetings, of people waiting to see my father. They would assemble around a bamboo bar in the courtyard to chat as they waited. My father's long-time aide de camp and close friend (Tun) Hanif Omar recalls the alternative and more interesting gathering area, the large open-air car park, where gossips and rumours were shared.

If the main building was the shophouse, the rest of the compound was a village. There were a lot of other people living there too: guards, maids, nannies, cooks and cleaners to the side and below. Among the immediate family, only I, as the smallest, had reason to roam the village. I ate many of my meals perched on a stool at a large kitchen table among the domestic staff. It wasn't until I came of age at six or seven that I was invited to dine with the rest of the family. Along a path to the right, across the garden and away from the house, was the barracks where about twenty young policemen slept and hung out when they weren't on duty. I would cycle along that path on my shiny Raleigh bike knowing that along there would be a set of older playmates for my games.

Beyond the large kitchen, scullery and laundry on the side of the house next to the dining room lay a flight of steps cut into the side of the hill that led down to the servants' living quarters. These stairs were my portal to everyday life below stairs and a whole other set of play-mates who were more my age. At any one time there were four to five families with many young kids to play games often involving my large, precious collection of Action Man figures.

This is where I grew up until I was nine. At the heart of family life were my parents, although private family time was scarce and precious. We became inured to living in public, to sharing our lives with other people. My father saw Seri Taman as a national asset, so we were often open to *rombongans* (entourages) of the general public – although I was never sure how they signed up for the tour. My mother was busy with her own schedule as a leader's wife, as well as accompanying my father on official outings. Despite her best efforts, she found it hard to have as much time for us as she wanted; all the same, it was her steady hand, sense of fairness and good nature that set the tone for my upbringing. Her love was unconditional, but, of necessity, she had to delegate a lot to the nannies. Some nannies were superb, like my first, a Chinese *amah*, but I most recall one Malay *kakak* who often took to beating me; luckily the kind and motherly cook, Mak Rose, told on her before it could go on for too long.

My parents had a traditional yet loving relationship. He was eleven years her senior. Their marriage was arranged the old way, through family discussions over several months, yet there was no doubt that my father chose my mother. The family legend is that he was beaming from ear to ear after being taken by (Tan Sri) Taib Andak, his best friend from his days as a student in London, to see Rahah walking between classes at her school in Johor. She was just as Taib had described: a young beauty from a very good family. My father had gone there in search of a bride because his own late father had advised him to marry a girl from Johor, most likely because Johor was the centre of power and sophistication in Malay society of the time.

My parents met only three times before they married in September 1952, and never alone. Like most people she quickly fell for my father's quiet charm; their relationship blossomed after they wed. My mother left school at eighteen to get married; she had lived a sheltered life. When my father said he would be taking her to his home in Pekan her mother worried that my father's home state of Pahang was a strange and faraway place. My mother's father, (Tan Sri) Mohamed Noah Omar, was the astute and ambitious chairman of the United Malays National Organisation (UMNO) in Johor. He would have been well pleased that his new son-in-law was already both Pahang state secretary and UMNO deputy president.[4]

Not long after my parents were married, my father took his young bride to London. For a few weeks they shared a small flat in the city where he had been a student. She recalls it as the only time they were an ordinary couple, left to their own devices, with no entourage and no queue of people waiting to see Tun Abdul Razak. She kept house and cooked for him; their evenings and weekends were their own. It was, she recalls, a golden time, when she had him to herself. It would not last. She was already pregnant with their first child, Najib. My father meanwhile had his sights firmly set on a career in politics and the unfolding quest for Malayan independence.

At Seri Taman we lived with the trappings of power: the staff, the police guards, the chauffeur-driven cars. It cannot have been easy for my parents to try to bring us up without indulging us. But they did their best to establish the important principles in their own way.

Although I was growing up in highly unusual circumstances, I only really became aware of it once I started at St John's primary school in Bukit Nanas, the national school located in the heart of Kuala Lumpur. I noted that other children did not have bodyguards waiting for them at the end of the school day. I noticed that some teachers seemed to pay me extra attention, which also annoyingly involved keeping me in class during recess to get to know me. However, some didn't discriminate when I wished they did; I can't forget Cikgu Zaiton, who decided one day that the whole class had misbehaved while she was out at a teachers' meeting and spanked all fifty of us on our bottoms with a giant blackboard ruler.

It only really sank in that I was so privileged on those rare occasions when home and school met – as they did one day when I was six or seven years old. Mum forgot to ask the driver to pick me up, and I had no choice but to undertake the hour or so walk home. A friend named Ayub Majid, who came from a poor family living in Kampung Baru, the old Malay quarter in the middle of the city, decided to walk with me. He said he had nothing better to do. I can still remember the look on his face as we approached Seri Taman, the shock at the size and grandeur of it. That's when it sank in that, as much as I wanted to be normal, Seri Taman was a far from normal place to live.

Those early years in Seri Taman were sunny and bright, warm and full of fun. They did not last long.

THE PASSING

Abdul Razak passed away at the London Clinic, near Harley Street, on 14 January 1976 from complications brought on by the leukaemia he had been battling in private since it was diagnosed in 1969. Malaysia lost its prime minister. I lost my father. He was just fifty-three years old. Malaysia was nineteen; I was nine.

Even my mother did not know how ill he was until the last few weeks. He had discovered he was dying as he was charting the country back to peace and stability after the 13 May race riots. In those days not only was a diagnosis of leukaemia a virtual death sentence, but the remote chance of recovery required a horrible course of treatment. It was said that if the illness didn't kill you, the treatment would make you feel like killing yourself. He put his personal challenges to one side, without feeling sorry for himself, and got on with his job. The doctors gave him only two years to live; he told them he would live longer and got just over five years instead. If anything, the illness spurred him to act faster and go further. He was a restless blur of activity and he managed, somehow, to keep his condition a secret other than from his doctors and (Tun) Dr Ismail Abdul Rahman, his designated successor.

In early 1975, as the cancer's grip tightened, my father told people that the spots that had appeared on his arms came from getting too much sun while playing golf. Some were not fooled, though: the then minister of education, Mahathir, a medical doctor, became very suspicious. Hanif Omar noticed that my father's five-iron golf shots were only reaching the distance of a nine-iron. As the year went on, the illness became harder and harder to disguise; he lost a lot of weight, and his famous safari or bush jackets and batik shirts hung loosely on his angular frame. He was noticeably gaunt and frail; even in parliament MPs were calling on him to take a rest.

In late November he announced that he would go to Paris for a holiday, but soon after he got there his doctors advised that he should move to London for treatment, as blood tests showed that his cancer was back with a vengeance. A man who never took much rest tried to persuade people he was taking a long break. The truth was he was battling to save his life, away from the limelight. He intended to return home but was adamant that he would only do so when he looked fit and strong.

He said goodbye to me for the last time as he was leaving for that trip. I am not sure if he knew it could be the last time he saw me – probably not, because he had long defied his doctor's diagnosis. I sometimes regret that because my father gave so much to the country, so little was left over for the family. Even when he knew he was running out of time, he was a stickler for doing things the right way. He did not allow his wife to accompany him on the trip because it would be too expensive. Mum only joined him in London in mid-December, when his condition had deteriorated to such an extent that the cabinet insisted she go and had the government pay for her trip.

For those last weeks as he fought for his life in London, by his side were my mum; Najib, who was twenty-two and by that stage working for Petronas, the national oil company; and my other brothers, who were all studying in London. I carried on in Seri Taman without an inkling of what was afoot. Being so young and home alone in such a large house was an eerie, unsettling experience. I vividly remember consciously refusing to entertain any bad thoughts about what was really going on. I stopped worrying when, right after Christmas, Najib returned to get back to work. I was thrilled to see him and couldn't get enough of his company.

In London my brother Johari recalls eating turkey dinner around my father's hospital bed then playing games. The year before, my father had finally been called to the bar to practise law in Malaysia as part of his plan to retire before the next general election. Johari was reading Law, so they talked about how they could soon go into legal practice together: Razak & Razak. My brothers say that in those final days he talked wistfully about going back to his home in Pahang to fish and to farm. The *kampong* boy in him never left. Whenever he felt better, he would take visits from friends and government officials. And he did rally around the turn of the year and moved to the Sheraton Park Tower hotel by Hyde Park, but not for long.

One afternoon in January my brother Johari called Seri Taman; it was urgent. He told Najib that the end was coming, we should pack our bags and get on the next plane to London. Najib tried to shield the truth from me, telling me only that 'Daddy wants us to join him in London.' I was overwhelmed by the excitement of my first overseas trip, involving a long international flight. As soon as Johari put the phone down, he returned to the hospital room, only to find our father had passed away. It was 11 a.m. on 14 January in London – 7 p.m. for us in Kuala Lumpur. I recall standing alone with Najib, who was twice my size, in his bedroom at Seri Taman, looking up as he took the second call from Johari and seeing the distress fill his eyes.

I knew at once what had happened. I wasn't sure how to react. It wasn't something I had been taught or prepared for. My eyes filled with tears; they would not stop coming. Soon, extended family and close friends streamed into the residence, most of them in tears. Both TV channels, RTM 1 and 2, suddenly stopped scheduled programmes to feature readings of verses from the Quran. All I wanted was to be with Najib. I slept in his bed that night.

My father had gone, and a huge hole opened up. Previously there had been confidence and security; now it was very different. Judging by the public reaction, it was probably how most Malaysians felt. Abdul Razak had steadied us all with his quiet self-confidence. What would we do now?

Abdul Razak's death was announced officially on television by (Tun) Hussein Onn, his deputy and brother-in-law, who broke down in tears as he announced the news that shocked the nation.[5] His remains would arrive back from London the following evening. He would then lie in state at the parliament before being laid to rest at the national mosque on 16 January. Hundreds of thousands of people came to pay their respects as the coffin arrived back at Subang airport; while it spent the night at Seri Taman; as it lay in state at the parliament; along the route of the final march from parliament to the warriors' mausoleum at the national mosque; and finally, by his grave. They included ASEAN heads of state, and representatives from governments across the world. But most important for him would have been the throngs of fellow Malaysians from all walks of life, of every colour and creed.

Our family was not alone in our sorrow, but our private grief was lost in the tidal wave of public feeling. The fact that it was days before we had time to be alone as a family with our mother was indicative of how accustomed we were to being in public, to the public persona always coming first. It was only when Mum and I were finally alone, sitting on the balcony outside her bedroom, that I saw her real emotions break through. I was watching her read a tribute in the newspaper when I saw tears flow down her cheeks onto the paper. That's when it really sank in how sad Mum was. My Dad, her husband, was gone, forever.

What did he leave us with? Abdul Razak's legacy to his sons certainly wasn't financial. He left us enough to continue to live well by his own fairly modest standards. The government was kind to us. In addition to her pension, the government provided Mum with a capacious house on Jalan Eaton, close to the centre of KL, with household staff and a vast garden which in time, under my management, would double up as a highly social football pitch. Government scholarships were awarded to Nizam, Nazim and myself to complete our education in the UK.

How should Abdul Razak's legacy be measured, and what did it mean to live up to the memories he had left me and the standards he had impressed upon me? That question would remain with me for the rest of my life. What is in his name?

To understand the legacy we must go back to where he came from.

THE YOUNG
ABDUL RAZAK

My father liked to remind his children to *jaga nama baik*, a Malay saying that translates as 'look after your good name'. I always thought that was because he was a politician and didn't want us to do anything to tarnish his image. But I now think that it was a saying that he also grew up with. Abdul Razak inherited a good name, that of his father (Dato') Hussein Taib. Hussein's role is usually overshadowed in most of the writings on Abdul Razak's upbringing.

Abdul Razak's relationship with his father was not straightforward. In 1924, when Abdul Razak just two years old, Hussein left his home to become the district officer in Bentong, in the same state, Pahang, but more than 200 kilometres away. In Bentong he took a fifteen-year-old bride (not uncommon in those days) and had sixteen more children. Hussein left my father, with his sister and their mother in tiny Kampong Jambu Langgar, in Pekan, on the east coast of the Malay peninsula. Despite being the son of a high-ranking official, Abdul Razak would look after buffalo, bathe in the river and walk barefoot to school and Quran classes, covering more than seven kilometres a day, with a few sen in his pocket to buy some *nasi dagang* (a rice dish popular in the east coast of the Malay peninsula). That experience of seeing life from the vantage point of the hut and the riverbank never left him. He could see the quiet desperation of many rural folk, not just on account of their poverty but because of their sense of powerlessness to do anything about it. He never lost that sense of where he came from.

Hussein was a substantial figure in every sense. He was large in stature, larger than life in character and as district officer was akin to a local dignitary: about 10,000 people looked to him as the embodiment of public authority in the district. His pale complexion almost cost him his life during the Second World War when Japanese troops on patrol were convinced he was an Englishman in disguise. He was roped to a tree and had guns pointed at him. His life was saved only when some locals pointed out that he was in fact the Malay district officer.

The British clearly trusted Hussein. In the late 1920s he had a period as the governor's aide-de-camp in Kuala Lumpur. He was a fan of everything British, from Craven A cigarettes to Victorian values and starched shirts with ties. He even made the long journey to London to attend the coronation of King George VI in May 1936. He was a stickler for punctuality, tidiness and manners. He was very sociable, often seen having a drink and eating dinner with Chinese, British, Malay and Indian friends in a local club before coming home for a second meal. (No wonder he was so substantial.)

Hussein studied at Malay College Kuala Kangsar (MCKK), the so-called Eton of the East, established in 1905 to educate the Malay elite, royalty and future administrators. Among his classmates who went on to become lifelong friends was Onn Jaafar, who founded UMNO, and Tengku Ismail Ibrahim, who became the Sultan of Johor.

In 1928 Hussein was bestowed the title Orang Kaya Indera Shahbandar (OKIS) by the Sultan of Pahang, which made him one of the four highest-ranking nobles in the state. The title had been in our family since our royal Bugis ancestors from Sulawesi, Indonesia settled in the Pekan area in 1722, except on a couple of occasions when the Sultan decided otherwise, as was the case for Hussein's father. Hussein also became chair of the Persatuan Melayu Pahang (Pahang Malay Society), a precursor of UMNO in Pahang. Onn occupied a similar position in Johor, where he was a close advisor to the Sultan. This network of friendships would prove particularly significant as Malaya approached independence. Hussein attended the pivotal Malay Congress in 1946 to oppose the British proposal for a Malayan Union. That proposal would have created a very different Malaysia from the one we know today. The nine Malay states would have been consolidated under one colonial administrative structure; the Sultans would have been marginalised. More or less all non-Malays in the country would have been recognised as full citizens. The Congress voted to oppose the Malayan Union and instead it voted to form the UMNO under Onn's leadership.

My paternal grandfather was a political junction box connecting up the circuits of power in Malaya – from the Malay rulers to UMNO and the British. According to his son (my uncle) Latiff, Hussein was offered the post of chief minister and leadership positions in UMNO but he declined, citing the large young family he had to look after.[6] When my father rose to those positions he was in a sense continuing the family business, building on the legacy of public service at the highest levels that Hussein had left to him. Despite growing up apart in his early years, Abdul Razak looked up to his father who was determined his son would enrol at his alma mater, MCKK. Abdul Razak's ambition was to follow in his father's footsteps, and while still at MCKK he set off on the trail of a career in the civil service.

My father was one of a group of young, confident and outward-looking Malayans who dedicated themselves to creating a new nation. They started with imperfect materials. The country had been economically exploited by foreigners for generations. It was divided into mutually suspicious communities thrust together by the colonial ruler for its own economic ends: Chinese in the tin mines and Indians on the rubber plantations. Malays, Chinese and Indians lived in separate enclaves, meeting only at marketplaces. The Malays felt deeply insecure as immigration had eroded their share of the population dramatically. In 1911 Malays were already just 58.6% of the population of *Tanah Melayu*, or the 'Land of the Malays', as the peninsula states were referred to; by the 1930s they weren't even in the majority.[7] The non-Malays had their own insecurities; they were unsure who among them, and on what terms, would be included in the new nation state that was coming together. In the Second World War the Malay peninsula was invaded, occupied, plundered and then liberated in the space of a few years. After the war, the colony was on its knees economically, while fighting off a tenacious rural communist insurgency. Yet the period was also one of extraordinary ferment as aspirations for self-rule, democracy and freedom spread.

The first hints of Abdul Razak's nationalism, and the lengths he would go to in his commitment to it, came early. Aged eleven, while attending the coronation of the Sultan of Pahang in 1933, he was troubled by the sight of Malay chiefs standing while British residents were all seated comfortably. If he was troubled by the British presence, he outright resisted the Japanese occupation which followed. During the war Abdul Razak was sent to Singapore for indoctrination and language-training for six months, and then stationed in Temerloh as an interpreter. He opposed the Japanese occupation by joining the Wataniah, a Malay resistance movement, and used his role as an interpreter to source and pass onto the British information about Japanese troop activity. On 1 December 1945, at a ceremony to mark the disbanding of the umbrella resistance movement Force 136, he marched proudly in front of the Sultan of Pahang as Captain Abdul Razak.

Once the war was over the British returned gradually. Indeed, my father often debated with friends whether they should want the British back at all. In 1946 during the hiatus between the Japanese leaving and the British returning in full force, civil order hung by a thread. At the tender age of twenty-four, Abdul Razak was drafted as acting district officer of Raub, more than 100 kilometres from Bentong. He was pretty much on his own, and for two weeks in February the area seethed with violence. Many Chinese and Malays were killed and injured. To prevent further bloodshed my father toured every village and hamlet, accompanied by local leaders of all races, reasoning and commiserating with those who had lost relatives, getting them to air their grievances out in the open. He was on the go each day until midnight, slept in whatever accommodation the villagers provided and was off once more before dawn the next day. Gradually the enraged population of Raub calmed down.[8] The immediate trouble, my father thought, stemmed from the Malays fearing that the mainly Chinese communists were about to take over; but underlying that was a more fundamental problem: the economic imbalance between the races. As my father put it later: 'Whenever our village people went into a town, they could not help noticing that everything was owned by the people who they considered to be foreigners.'[9] This economic imbalance was a problem that he would return to over and over again in the years to come.

Abdul Razak became a member of the Persatuan Melayu Pahang and in March 1946 accompanied his father to the congress that called for the establishment of UMNO. However, at this stage his focus was on picking up his studies, which had been disrupted by the war. After Malay College he had gone to Raffles College in Singapore, the closest thing to a university in the region at the time, but his studies had been cut short in December 1941 as the Japanese Imperial Army invaded the Malay peninsula.

After the war Abdul Razak won a three-year colonial government scholarship to study Law at Lincoln's Inn in London. That journey and the years he spent in London studying, socialising and debating with his contemporaries were formative. In August 1947, on the way to London, his ship stopped in Bombay, where he was able to savour the sense of excitement of a newly independent India and abhor the tragic communal clashes it had unleashed. Independence was about far more than just evicting the colonial master, he realised. In London, Abdul Razak completed his Law degree in just eighteen months, leaving him with more than a year to wait for his graduation. During that time, he took up economics courses at Cambridge, attended summer school for colonial service cadets at Oxford (St John's College) and became an active student leader.

One of the first people he had met in London was Tunku Abdul Rahman, a prince from the northern state of Kedah and president of Kesatuan Melayu UK (KMUK), or the Malay Society of the UK. Tunku, nineteen years older than Abdul Razak, was an outgoing personality and the senior figure amongst the Malayan community in London. Abdul Razak became secretary and then in 1949 succeeded Tunku as president of KMUK. It was the start of a partnership that would shape the new nation.

My father threw himself into the political debates of the time, with a mix of people from Malaya and Singapore in an atmosphere that was more open and conducive to such discussions because they were away in London. Together with Singaporeans Goh Keng Swee (later finance minister) and Maurice Baker (later a top diplomat), he set up the Malayan Forum, a platform for Malays and non-Malays to discuss politics and especially the idea of independence. He often cajoled reluctant Malays to participate in the multiracial forum. He signed up as a member of the Fabian Society, the Labour Party affiliate credited with developing the intellectual basis for democratic socialism. His membership reflected his ideological leanings as well as a calculation that independence was more likely under a Labour government in Britain. He took every opportunity to meet with leaders of independence movements whenever they passed through London. He met up with Onn, of course, and through one of his closest friends, Des Alwi, he engaged with Indonesian freedom leaders Mohamed Hatta and Sutan Syarir, the first vice president and prime minister respectively. Inspired, he helped to organise fundraising events for the Indonesian independence movement. In April 1949, Abdul Razak addressed the World Youth Assembly in Brussels, cementing his reputation as a leader among the Malayans.

My father's time in London was cut short by the untimely death of his father in April 1950. He returned home to assume both the title of OKIS in the court of the Sultan of Pahang and his father's place in the federal legislature, representing Pahang in the national assembly appointed by the colonial administration. He joined the civil service as assistant state secretary of Pahang and would have an impressive if short-lived career as a high-flyer in the colonial administration. In January 1952, he was promoted to Pahang state secretary and then in 1955 was briefly chief minister, before he resigned to become a full-time politician.

The most fateful decision he made upon returning from London though was to accept his nomination to become head of UMNO's youth wing. Although he had his own student leadership record and excellent academic credentials, his family name would also have gone before him. His nomination was endorsed by party president Onn, my grandfather's old school friend.

While he had an easy entry into politics, my father would have to show his mettle very soon. Crisis struck the embryonic party in August 1951, before it had even contested an election, when Onn abruptly resigned because the members refused to back his proposal to open membership of UMNO to non-Malays. Onn was convinced that a 'united party of all communities' was necessary for self-rule and wanted UMNO renamed the United Malayan National Organisation. After resigning, Onn almost immediately set up the Independence of Malaya Party (IMP); the name itself oozed confidence that it would own the mantle to lead the nation to independence.

I imagine my father would have agonised about his position. He may have even sympathised with Onn's idea and it was no secret that Onn had the best rapport with the British. Onn was a towering personality. He had become synonymous with UMNO; he was a Malay hero for leading the successful opposition to the Malayan Union; and he had been chief minister of Johor. Yet even at this early stage my father showed the independence of thought and spirit that would run throughout his career. He took a risk. He stuck with UMNO even though it was far from clear it would prevail. We do not know for sure why he did that, but I believe it was because he would not put his own career ahead of his principles. He believed that while Malaya had to be multiracial, the downtrodden Malays needed their own political party to look after them.

My father then had no option but to step in to address the leadership vacuum left by Onn's resignation. He had a nose for power, where it lay and how it could be used. Yet that was matched by knowing his own limitations. He was never greedy for power for his own sake. Others might have been tempted to step into the leadership vacuum themselves, to see it as an opportunity to advance their own career. Yet my father resisted pressure from within the party to stand for president because he knew it needed a leader of stature and charisma, which he lacked. Instead, he helped to persuade his old student friend Tunku to stand for president. It will not have escaped him that Tunku's royal lineage made it easier for him to deal with the Sultans who would be party to the independence negotiations. When Tunku became UMNO president, Abdul Razak became deputy president and Tunku's right-hand man. He was just twenty-nine years of age and already, in the midst of so much upheaval, he had displayed a sense of poise amidst turmoil, a sureness of touch which led people to trust his leadership, and Tunku to rely on him as they navigated Malaya to independence.

Staying with UMNO and teaming up with Tunku to lead the party was a 'sliding doors' moment: a critical decision, that could have gone either way, which had a huge bearing on the future of the entire country. That began to become apparent in February 1952, when UMNO's electoral pact with the Malayan Chinese Association (MCA) won eight of the twelve seats in the Kuala Lumpur municipal elections. The successful partnership sowed the seeds for a national coalition of race-based parties, the Alliance that would go on to win a thumping victory at pre-independence Malaya's first and only general election in 1955. UMNO would remain the dominant component of the governing coalition for the next sixty-three years.

Over the next twenty-five years Abdul Razak would build a personal legacy that defined much of the political, economic and social contours of the nation even today. That legacy has two sides, an obvious and more public side, made up of the institutions, policies and programmes he enacted, and a less visible, more intangible and personal side, constituted by the values, principles and methods he applied, methods which I have drawn on heavily as I have navigated the relationship between public and private, business and politics in my own career. To understand what is in the Razak name one has to understand this dual legacy.

THE TANGIBLES

Abdul Razak's public legacy is everywhere to be seen in Malaysia. In Kuala Lumpur you can't drive for long without coming across a road or building named after him or an institution associated with him. That legacy is well known and widely revered. These are what I consider to be its most important elements. Though they might be familiar I set them out here for two reasons. First, I hope I will be forgiven for being enormously proud of what my father achieved, the difference he made to the lives of so many Malaysians, who lifted themselves from poverty by climbing the steps he provided them with: rural development, schools and universities, homegrown and Malay-run businesses. Those achievements I contend are all the more remarkable for one so young, with so little prior experience working under extraordinarily challenging circumstances. Second, because there is another side to all of this, one which I only became aware of later in my working life, as I contended with what became of much of this legacy when it was diverted from its original purpose. My father was a public problem solver; he used the power of government to solve the problems facing the new nation. Yet he knew that his solutions only worked in a certain context. As the context for Malaysia has changed, so has the relevance of the solutions he devised.

One cannot fully understand the choices and challenges Malaysia now faces unless one understands the political and economic system my father put in place to address the challenges of his time.

THE PATH TO INDEPENDENCE

Through his role in UMNO my father was a leading figure amongst the team that secured independence and significantly influenced the design of the Malayan nation at its inception.

There was nothing preordained about UMNO's role in leading the move to independence. Tunku found himself having to sell his personal assets to fund the party and often complained that its members were apathetic. Initially Onn seemed to have the edge on UMNO: he was popular with both the British and the network of chief ministers around the Sultans. Yet Onn was left reeling by IMP's defeat at the hands of the UMNO–MCA coalition in several municipal elections in the early 1950s. In February 1954 he dissolved the IMP and set up Parti Negara, a new Malay party, to compete head on with UMNO. It too failed.

In the run-up to the first general election in 1955 the Alliance strategically took the most aggressive stance on two critical issues: it pushed for more members of the new assembly to be elected rather than appointed by the colonial administration and for an earlier date for independence. The Alliance successfully identified itself with the rising fervour for independence.

When the Alliance won fifty-one of fifty-two seats at the pre-independence elections, it also won the right to form a government, negotiate independence and help formulate the constitution of Malaya. Abdul Razak chaired the Alliance Ad Hoc Political Committee that engaged the Reid Commission, comprising five top legal minds from Commonwealth countries, to arrive at the constitutional arrangements that all stakeholders could accept.[10] In his book *The Making of the Malayan Constitution* Joseph Fernando noted: 'The constitutional principles embodied in the document largely reflected the Alliance's political and constitutional aspirations embodied in their memorandum to the Reid Constitutional Commission.'[11]

The constitution set out the rules by which the new nation would be self-governing after in effect being run by foreigners for centuries.

The nine Malay Sultans would become constitutional monarchs of their states; they would elect an Agong, a King, every five years from among their number. There was and still is no monarchy quite like it. Independent Malaya's democracy and institutions were to be based on the Westminster model, including a first-past-the-post electoral system. Yet that system had to serve a multicultural nation. Citizens of Malaya would be identified by which ethnic group they came from: Chinese, Indian or Malay. So in the act of bringing everyone together as citizens of Malaya they were also more explicitly divided in ethnic groups. All citizens were equal, *yet* Article 153 of the constitution specified that Malays (and later natives of Sabah and Sarawak) had a special position which had to be protected. Malaya was a secular nation, *yet* Islam was the official religion and there are restrictions on propagation of other religious doctrine among Muslims. Malay was the national language, *yet* other languages were recognised and protected. The constitution was not drawn up in the idealised conditions of high-minded deliberation sometimes imagined by political philosophers. It was a way to make independent Malaya self-governing in the constraints of the time and so it contained compromises that were by turns ingenious, distinctive and yet fateful.

These tensions within Malayan nationhood were now written into the nation's politics and indeed its social psychology. In Abdul Razak's words the purpose of the Malays' special position was 'to give the Malays reasonable openings in the economic and commercial fields but, in doing so … not cause hardship to or diminish the rights or opportunities or interests of other races'.[12] This ideal was, of course, easier said than done, especially during unfavourable economic conditions. Managing the expectations and fears arising from this principle became embedded in the heart of the Malaysian political economy from then on.

My father went on to play a big role in the formation of Malaysia, helping to bring in Sarawak, Sabah and Singapore in 1963. In the process he was disappointed not to have succeeded in his negotiations to include Brunei as well. Then, in 1965, Abdul Razak was tasked by Tunku to negotiate Singapore's expulsion from Malaysia. Integrating the city state had precipitated communal tensions and political conflict between the Alliance and Lee Kwan Yew's People's Action Party (the PAP), which would go onto champion Singapore's independence and dominate its politics. Singapore proved a bridge too far. I would be fascinated to know what my father really thought of Singapore's amputation. There were groups within UMNO which advocated taking draconian action against PAP leaders rather than ceding the island entirely. Indeed, nations go to war over tiny real estate; Singapore was a huge island and strategic entrepot. Yet at the same time Abdul Razak was legally trained, a democrat and a realist. He would have known how difficult it would be to keep Singapore as part of the federation especially after the race riots in 1964 in which twenty-three people were killed and hundreds injured following inflammatory exchanges between UMNO and PAP politicians.

EDUCATING MALAYSIANS

After success in the 1955 elections, Abdul Razak, at the age of thirty-three, was given the education portfolio in the pre-independence government that was headed by Tunku. The colonial government had largely neglected education other than to provide the Malay branch of its empire with local administrators. There was no system as such, just a disparate collection of English, Malay, Chinese and Indian schools.

My father took education incredibly seriously. I can well remember standing anxiously before him as he went through my report card. We were expected to be in the top three of any class. He regarded education as the critical building block for the new nation. His approach to creating a national education system was indicative of how he would tackle even greater challenges later on. He was consultative and inclusive, bold and yet practical. He set up a fifteen-member committee to draw up the 'Razak Report', which became the Education Ordinance of 1957. Although the committee met only on eight occasions, it consulted widely, with teachers, educationists and parents, and studied the experience of other countries.

The Razak Report had to find a way to square the circle which had bedevilled earlier reform efforts to create a unified national system that would nevertheless respect cultural differences in schooling among different communities. Abdul Razak's vision for education was of 'a national system of education which will satisfy the needs of the people *and* promote their cultural, economic and political development as a nation'.[13]

The Razak Report created a national system with the Ministry of Education at its apex. It recommended that there should be government-funded national and national-type primary schools with a common system and syllabus. The national schools would teach the syllabus in Malay. National-type schools would teach in other languages, but Malay would be a compulsory subject. At secondary level, teaching would be in Malay, and two exams were set, Lower Certificate of Education (LCE) and Malayan Certificate of Education (MCE), to become the standard pre-qualification for tertiary education and jobs. A timeline of ten years was set for Malay to be the medium of instruction in English-medium schools too, during which both teachers and the language would be further developed.

The report paved the way for an extraordinary national investment in education which would pay enormous dividends in years to come. As a percentage of GDP, Malaysia outspent its ASEAN peers in education, and within a decade primary and secondary education enrolment was 85% and 34% respectively (by 1990: 93% and 55%, and by the turn of the millennium Malaysia was providing education for all).

My father's indelible imprint can still be seen in Malaysian education to this day. Debate will continue to rage about the impact of his policies, intended and unintended. The Razak Report sought to unite the nation through education and allowed millions to go to better schools; yet those policies also perpetuated segregation by persisting with vernacular schools in order to satisfy all communities.

The more controversial part of the legacy was the role affirmative action would come to play, especially in higher education after the introduction of the New Economic Policy (NEP) in 1971.

My father was always particularly concerned by the disadvantages faced by the Malays. Disparity in *bumiputra* (Malays and other indigenous people) access to tertiary education was identified as one of the Malays' major frustrations. Abdul Razak spoke of the 'widening gap between [Malays] and non-Malays particularly in economic and educational spheres'.[14] In the mid 1960s, Abdul Razak initiated Kolej Mara as a middle-level tertiary institution exclusively for *bumiputra*, which would in time evolve into Universiti Teknologi MARA, which today produces over 40,000 Malay graduates a year. He also spearheaded accessibility to boarding schools, encouraging the proliferation of MCKK-like establishments throughout the country. Following the introduction of the NEP, the government set aside pure meritocratic principles in favour of race-based quotas not just for universities but even for faculties within them, and to provide additional assistance for students from disadvantaged backgrounds. The new policies set in train the establishment of new universities like Universiti Kebangsaan Malaysia (1970) and Universiti Pertanian Malaysia (1971) and more scholarships, especially for *bumiputra* to study at home and abroad. Many thousands of Malaysians, who would not have had the opportunity otherwise, went on to become the first in their families ever to go onto higher education. However, all this came at a price of lower entry requirements and softer standards, which affected the quality and output of the system, which in time had unintended, corrosive and divisive consequences.

UP TO HIS KNEES IN MUD

In independent Malaya's first cabinet in 1957, my father was given responsibility for defence, working with the British, who were still providing Malaya's security. The country remained in a state of emergency to fight off the communist insurgency and was in the later stages of implementing the ruthless and unforgiving strategy laid out by British High Commissioner General Sir Gerald Templer. This was the only communist insurgency to be defeated in the whole of Southeast Asia. Doing so required a comprehensive mix of hard and soft power, methodically executed. On the hard side Templer saw fit even to defend the practice of decapitation. On the softer side, he developed well-defended New Villages for Chinese peasants to live in safely and to prosper. Of his strategy Templer said, 'The answer lies not in pouring troops into the jungle but in the hearts and minds of the people.'[15] Each time a village was pacified and put beyond the reach of the communists they would mark it on a map, replacing a tiny red flag with a tiny white one.

My father remained minister of defence until 1970, but two years after independence he also assumed the newly created post of minister of rural development, where he would remain for most of his time in government, until 1973. The photographs of him with farmers up to his knees in water in a rice paddy, crossing a rickety bamboo bridge over a river, looking at the construction of a new road, tell of a man in his element, doing what he most cared about. Lifting up the rural poor was his passion.

Abdul Razak brought to rural development his experience from battling the communist insurgency; he treated poverty as a war to be fought village by village. One of his most famous quotes echoes Templer: 'The greatest safeguard of our country's sovereignty is not only in defence but more so development.'[16] He set up a nationwide organisation with district, regional and state-level operations rooms reporting into the national operations room, over which he presided.

Each room was dominated by maps and charts with multicoloured drawing pins and, of course, tiny coloured flags to indicate project progress. He introduced the famous Red Books, which detailed the status of every rural development project and could be inspected at operations rooms at all levels of the system.

He loved to travel around the country to check on progress, comparing what he was being told by officials with what he could see with his own eyes. There are legendary stories of officials trembling at the news of his surprise visit and being traumatised by his questions, which were invariably very pointed, as he would review the relevant local Red Books himself.

Thanks to his childhood he understood the main challenges of rural life. Apart from the lack of infrastructure such as electricity and water in villages, raising up the villages was about providing land, increasing agricultural productivity and creating jobs and fair access to markets so farmers could sell their produce without going through exploitative middlemen.

Abdul Razak set up state agencies to help them. FELDA, in charge of resettlement and development schemes, which eventually relocated 120,000 families (roughly 1 million people) and became widely admired around the world, was just the most famous. The Federal Marketing Agency (FAMA), National Padi and Rice Board, FELDA Land Consolidation and Rehabilitation Authority (FELCRA), Fisheries Development Board (MAJUIKAN) and Rubber Industry Smallholders Development Authority (RISDA) as well as a slew of regional development agencies were set up to advise, provide input and equipment subsidies, help distribute and even stabilise prices for their produce. None of this was glamorous work, but my father knew that only through methodical attention to detail would life really change for the poor, and it would take time.

Despite those efforts, throughout the 1960s the Malays continued to be frustrated by the pace of their economic progress compared to non-Malays.

STEPPING INTO A CRISIS

By the time the 1969 elections came around, the wave of euphoria that greeted independence had begun to dissipate. The Alliance had found the experience of government tricky, to say the least. On one side the ardent Malay nationalists led by Parti Islam Se-Malaysia (PAS), the Islamic party, accused the government of compromising too much on Malay rights, while on the other Chinese opposition parties Gerakan and Democratic Action Party (DAP) were unrelenting in attacking the MCA for what they saw as selling out the Chinese community. That was the setting for only the third general election in the country's history. The previous two elections had been held in conditions of national fervour and unity. The first, in 1959, was a celebration of national independence achieved two years earlier (before the federation of Malaysia had been formed). That was followed by what was the first *Malaysian* general election in 1964, held in the shadow of the confrontation with Indonesia. The 1969 election, then, was the first real test of the democratic system in what might be regarded as normal conditions. The system fell at the first hurdle.

At the end of voting day, on 10 May, the Alliance had won only 44% of the Peninsula Malaysia vote, compared to 58% in 1964, and lost the coveted two-thirds majority in parliament needed to effect changes to the constitution (Sabah and Sarawak had not yet voted). The Alliance lost the state of Penang, while in Selangor and Perak the state assemblies were too close to call, and both sides jostled to win the support of the one or two MPs who would decide which party would form government. The MCA, stung by its bad showing, quickly announced that it would not be joining the national cabinet, while the DAP celebrated like winners. Not only were the Malays economically disadvantaged; it now seemed the main Malay party was losing its grip on political power. The Chinese community also found itself in an odd position: while Chinese parties made great strides electorally, the Chinese community was no longer represented in government.

In the days following the vote, marches and counter-marches were organised in Kuala Lumpur. Inflammatory insults were thrown, tempers frayed, rumours spread, and the city descended into violence. Disturbances spread to other parts of the country. According to the official count, 196 people were killed, 439 injured, many of them badly; hundreds of business and shops were torched. Over 9,000 people were arrested. Many people believe the official report into the race riots seriously underestimated the number of lost lives.

In the wake of the riots my father's partnership with Tunku unravelled as the latter's authority drained away. We will never know for sure what kind of power struggle went on following the riots. Tunku initially contemplated declaring martial law but was advised that the military might never give power back. Instead, a state of emergency was called. With parliament suspended, power was handed to the director of the National Operations Council (NOC), Abdul Razak, to rule by decree: my father's word effectively became law.

In UMNO, recriminations started quickly. A group of 'Young Turks' in the party, most prominent among them Mahathir and (Tun) Musa Hitam, criticised Tunku, alleging that the Alliance's dismal performance in the elections was due to the ineffective laissez-faire economic policies pursued by the aristocratic and Western-leaning Tunku, who was said to be too close to the Chinese and unpopular with core Malay voters. The Young Turks called for more concerted, ambitious state action on behalf of the Malays and mobilised student protests against Tunku. Mahathir was expelled from the party; Musa was dispatched on study leave to the UK. Yet that did not calm things down; the NOC had to take the extraordinary step of banning demonstrations calling for the PM's resignation. Tunku's authority was irretrievably weakened. He remained prime minister in name but Abdul Razak was in charge.

Towards the end of his life, Tunku grew somewhat bitter about the circumstances in which he had relinquished office. He sympathised with those who believed that the declaration of a state of emergency was in effect a coup and that the riots were premeditated by Abdul Razak or his supporters. After fifty years, no evidence has ever been produced to support this thesis.

The most recent repetition of these rumours came from the former attorney general (Tan Sri) Tommy Thomas. In his lengthy memoir *My Story: Justice in the Wilderness*, Tommy claims 'the evidence' points to the 13 May riots being conceived as a coup to depose Tunku. He then produces no evidence at all to substantiate this wild claim beyond my father being the 'main beneficiary' of the tragic events and that he was in a hurry to take over from Tunku because he had just been given a few years to live having just been diagnosed with cancer. Neither of these would pass as 'evidence' in any setting. And Tommy even got his facts wrong: Abdul Razak was only diagnosed with cancer in November 1969, and doctors at the time suggested that the stress of dealing with the riots may have brought on the cancer. Tommy also expressed surprise that Tunku chose Abdul Razak as director of NOC when he did so by his own volition; Tunku also endorsed Dr Ismail's appointment as Abdul Razak's deputy. Indeed according to Dr Ismail's son Tawfik, himself a former MP and now a social activist: 'If my father, who was loyal to Tunku, had any suspicion at all of such a conspiracy he certainly would not have joined Abdul Razak's cabinet and would have mentioned it in his secrets memoirs. He did neither.'[17]

That view is endorsed by Musa, who himself would become DPM in 1981: while Abdul Razak aspired to be PM, he remained a loyal deputy and steadfast in resisting all the Young Turks' moves to undermine Tunku. My father protected his boss from growing criticism within the party. There was, of course, an ideological difference between the left-leaning Abdul Razak and more liberal Tunku which cascaded to the circle of people around them. Yet these quite predictable political disputes risk clouding the bigger picture we should always bear in mind. The partnership between Tunku and my father lasted longer and achieved far more than most political partnerships. My father could not have achieved what he did without the cover of the Tunku's more charismatic leadership. Together they charted the country to independence and through its first troubled and difficult decade. Those who worked closely with them on a daily basis say they were like brothers, and it would have been agonising for him to contend with the clamour for Tunku to step aside in his favour.

It was perhaps hardly surprising that there would be racial strife at the end of a long and bitter election campaign in which racial issues had been front and centre. There had been warning signs already. In 1967, reflecting on the race riots in Singapore three years ealier and in Penang that year, Tunku himself had acknowledged the underlying risk of communal violence: 'We are sitting on a keg of gunpowder, and if we are not careful this could explode any time,' he told parliament.[18] In 1969, the keg did explode; the system was inherently unstable.

The following twenty-one months was pivotal for Malaysia and for my father. He had to reconcile competing priorities: stabilise the country and secure peace; address the economic imbalances that were at the root of Malay frustration; chart the country back to democracy. I feel it was in many respects his finest hour. He was calm and methodical, consultative and yet bold.

BACK FROM THE BRINK

My father's first task was to quell the riots with the support of the police and the army. For several days, Kuala Lumpur was on a knife-edge; curfews were imposed across the country. By the end of the first week about 15,000 refugees were camped at stadiums and auditoriums around the city. Once the situation was brought under control, Abdul Razak knew nothing short of a recalibration of the entire political, economic and social system was required. That system was structurally unsound: returning to business as usual was not an option. A new, more solid foundation had to be put in place for Malaysia to grow and develop.

To help lay those foundations, in January 1970, Abdul Razak set up a National Consultative Council (NCC), to start the dialogue on systemic failures and possible reforms.

The NCC's sixty-seven members were drawn from across the country's communities and faiths, representing different parts of Malaysian society. Reconstructing its discussions is not easy, as the meetings were on purpose not recorded to allow people to speak freely; very few of those who took part are still alive. We only have brief snippets of press reports and a few speeches to work with.[19] While a lot of the spade work would have been done by government officials, namely at the Economic Planning Unit aided by advisors from the Harvard Studies Group, the Department of National Unity and the NOC, the Council's deliberations were critical to chart a new way forward for the country.

The NCC met every two or three months for two or three days at a time. These meetings weren't for show: Abdul Razak and Dr Ismail were usually in attendance and they urged participants to engage in free and frank debate, to challenge and question government proposals. The NCC enabled them to listen to the whole range of dissenting views and provided a degree of legitimacy to systemic reforms that would be needed.

The Council paved the way for three really significant innovations which together created a new system for Malaysian development.

The first recognised that the highly diverse Malaysian population needed a common core of beliefs, a North Star for a renewed Malaysia. The Rukun Negara, or 'National Principles', were established to foster integration, de-escalate racial tensions and encourage a sense of nationhood.

The Rukun Negara came in two parts. First, the ambitions for Malaysia, which are: achieving unity; creating a just society; guaranteeing a liberal approach to culture and tradition; preserving the democratic way of life; and building a progressive society through science and technology. The second part consists of the principles Malaysians pledge to be guided by. It is this portion that is arguably the most commonly remembered by citizens:

- Belief in God
- Loyalty to King and Country
- Supremacy of the Constitution
- Rule of Law
- Courtesy and Morality

The dissemination of these core beliefs was widespread. It was made mandatory in schools and government agencies and encouraged in public spaces. School children were to recite the Rukun Negara every day during assembly, and it would be printed in workbooks. The text would hang in prominent positions in workplaces and offices.

In 1971, the Rukun Negara provided the guiding light for the Second Malaysia Plan, which said: 'the Rukun Negara, which declares the national objectives and the fundamental principles to guide the citizens and the nation ... and represents a national consensus and commitment to the task of creating a united, socially just, economically equitable and progressive Malaysian nation'.[20]

Yet as the prescient Abdul Razak aptly put it: 'The secret of the perfection of Rukun Negara is in its practice. Without practising it, the Rukun Negara will be a piece of paper that has no meaning.'[21] I will come back to this point later.

ROOT CAUSES, FUNDAMENTAL SOLUTIONS

The second innovation was the most ambitious. The final consensus about the root cause of the 13 May riots was that the country was built on unequal and unbalanced economic foundations that systematically disadvantaged the Malays. These fundamentals needed to change before the communities could unite under a Malaysian identity. Malays needed a fair share of the economy to become 'full partners in all aspects of the economic life of the nation', in Abdul Razak's words.[22]

The NEP was announced as part of the Second Malaysian Plan (1971–5) as a twenty-year programme with the twin aim of eradicating poverty and eliminating the identification of race and economic function. The state would be deployed unapologetically to shift the economy to achieve these aims. Of course, at the time I had little or no idea what my dad did all day. Looking back now, one cannot but be full of admiration for how bold he was prepared to be by daring to tackle what he saw as structural inequalities written into the very make-up of the nation.

Policies to protect Malay interests had been in place since the early twentieth century, with immigration controls and reserved lands. Article 153 of the constitution enshrined the special position of the *bumiputra* and goes on to mention quotas for entry into the civil service, scholarships and public education. The NEP took state support for Malay development to a new level. Dr Ismail used an analogy from golf to explain the strategy: the NEP would give Malays a one-off, twenty-year handicap, by the end of which they could play an equal role in the economy.[23]

My father declared the government's intention to create a Malay commercial and industrial community that would be capable of directing, managing and working in enterprises at all levels of complexity on a par with the commercial classes of other races. That in turn meant enhancing the way Malays were educated, trained and employed so that Malays could do higher-level jobs. The ownership of business would also have to be shared more equally. In 1970, Malays owned 2.4% of the shares of commercial companies. Most of the economy was still owned by British conglomerates and Chinese families. The NEP set a target that, within twenty years, 30% of corporate Malaysia would be owned by *bumiputra*. It was one of the most radical and far-reaching attempts to restructure the ownership of a democratic market economy in modern times.

As (Tun) Michael Chen, the former MCA deputy president, told me: 'Without the NEP there would be no Malaysia, for it would have been consumed by the growing anger of the disaffected Malays.'[24] The idea was that every group in Malaysia could gain under the accelerated growth driven by a proactive state, but the Malays would gain more. The NEP sought to correct injustice without being unjust, over a twenty-year period.

Abdul Razak was steadfast in his faith in the government and its agencies to carry out this task. Under the guise of the NEP, government agencies and state-owned enterprises proliferated. The government also embarked on a far-sighted strategy to take control of valuable, foreign-owned Malaysian assets. The Malaysian corporate landscape was reshaped. For instance, Pernas, set up in 1969 as an investment holding company for the interest of the *bumiputra*, took over the controlling stake of foreign-owned Sime Darby. Today Sime Darby is the largest listed palm oil plantation company in the world. In the spirit of state activism Petronas was set up under the Petroleum Development Act (1974) to own and develop all Malaysia's hydrocarbon resources. Today Petronas is a Fortune 500 company. There were, of course, many agencies and state enterprises that didn't do so well.

The enhanced role of government in the economy also meant its presence became ubiquitous, with new rules and regulations, and affirmative action for *bumiputra* becoming deeply ingrained in the

42

economy. The policy was ahead of its time, an early demonstration that emphasising equity did not necessarily mean compromising on growth. Between 1970 and 1984 the economy grew on average at about 8% while the incidence of poverty dropped from 49% to 20.7% while the Malay share of corporate equity rose from 2.4% to 19.1% and foreign ownership fell from 63% to 26%. In time, however, as we will see, the NEP generated negative, unintended side effects, including corruption and a dependency culture among *bumiputra*. I was to come across much of the backwash created by the NEP when I started work. Yet in the early days it seemed the NEP had squared the circle: stimulating growth and reducing inequality at the same time.

I strongly believe that, had later politicians respected the pledges made by Abdul Razak and Dr Ismail that the NEP should last for no more than twenty years, it would have been regarded as a shining success. Sadly, their successors were unable or unwilling to keep that promise. The NEP lives on fifty years after its creation, a distorted, twisted and often counter-productive version of the original creation. According to the leading economist Jomo Sundaram in his assessment of the NEP: 'It is unlikely that (Abdul Razak) would have approved of how the NEP has been invoked to justify all kinds of self-serving abuses by those in power as well as the pursuit of various policies undermining efforts to improve national unity.'[25] Later I will have a lot more to say, based in part on my own experience, about what went wrong with the NEP.

POLITICAL BALLAST

The final piece of the jigsaw altered the dynamics of Malaysian democracy in profound ways. Abdul Razak was a democrat but he was also aware that intense political competition in a plural society could be counter-productive because it so easily inflames racial grievances and threatens to heighten communal tensions. Public criticism and questioning of sensitive issues – the status of the Malay language, Malay special privileges, the role of Malay rulers, citizenship rights of non-Malays, the role of Islam as the official religion – were deemed seditious. Free speech was curtailed. As a committed democrat it must have pained him, but as a pragmatist he would have judged that the country needed stability above all else.

That would not be enough on its own. To secure the new order required political innovation to provide Malaysian democracy with the ballast it needed to remain stable. The deliberative and cooperative discussions on the NCC paved the way for talks to put together a grand coalition of political parties. The Alliance – which had almost fallen apart in 1969 – was superseded in 1973 by the Barisan Nasional, the National Front, with UMNO at its core. All major political parties except the DAP agreed to join the coalition. The BN would provide the stability and predictability that a fragile democracy in a plural society needed. Although PAS would leave in 1977 and new opposition parties would be created, BN became a mighty election-fighting machine and remained in power until 2018.

An initiative with more controversial long-term effects was how Abdul Razak addressed UMNO's own financial sustainability. His aide Hanif recounts a conversation between Abdul Razak and Dr Ismail in the early 1970s, where they lamented UMNO's financial dependency on the MCA and Chinese businessmen.[26] There were barely any wealthy Malays at the time. Without its own funding sources UMNO would always have to do deals with Chinese political and commercial interests. They turned to the leading Malay corporate high-flyer of the time, the young (Tan Sri) Tengku Razaleigh Hamzah, to develop a more systematic way to raise funds for UMNO, including the party investing in businesses whose profits could then support the party. Razaleigh set up Fleet Group as UMNO's investment vehicle, and as the party's needs grew, so did its activities. In good hands, managed by people with integrity, such a system might have avoided corruption and conflicts of interest. It was not to be. Not surprisingly the power and responsibility that came with being in government and the interests of the party would come into conflict, time and again.

My father had a key role in setting in train the new mode of political funding. Political funding remains a bane of Malaysian democracy, and politics in many other countries for that matter. Was there – is there – a better way? Could he have set in place a more robust oversight framework? Perhaps, but I am certain that he would not have condoned what became of the funding model he set up. Later, I will have much more to say about the damage that funding model has done both politically and economically.

A DICTATOR VOTES FOR DEMOCRACY

The thing I am perhaps proudest of is that my father did not succumb to the attractions of remaining a dictator. He stood by his values and returned the country to democracy. The NCC provided the deliberative forum in which a new architecture for Malaysia's political, economic and social system was thrashed out. Once it was in place, Abdul Razak was ready to restore democracy. My father became Malaysia's second prime minister on 22 September 1970, when Tunku formally stood down. Five months later, on 20 February 1971, Abdul Razak addressed the restored Dewan Rakyat (House of Representatives) for the first time as prime minister.

It is worth quoting his explanation of his decision to restore parliamentary rule because it defines what it means to exercise power for the public good: 'If you want to serve the people, too much power is no good,'[27] he said. Too much power, concentrated in too few hands, tends to compound, corrupt and self-justify itself. He went on:

'Even if you do not intend to misuse it, you may do so inadvertently … especially through delegation. You cannot check everything yourself. You may be sincere, but can you be sure that all your officers who act in your name are sincere? Now with a democratic system you've first of all got parliament and the state assemblies to put a brake on you; then you've got the opposition parties, who will make a public outcry if things start to go wrong; but most important of all you know that every few years you've got to face the electorate, who will hold you accountable for all that has been done.'

My father was one of a very rare breed: a politician given the powers to become a dictator he renounced them in favour of democracy because he could see it was a better system for public governance.

MAKE FRIENDS, NOT ENEMIES

My father achieved all this while guiding the country through turbulent times internationally. He quickly realised that the stability so needed at home would depend on Malaysia making the international context work in its favour. For Abdul Razak that meant not just depending on old relationships with the US and the UK but forging new alliances, especially within the region. He was an instinctive internationalist without that ever compromising his commitment to Malaysia.

Abdul Razak was defence minister when Indonesia objected to the formation of Malaysia to include Sabah, Sarawak and Singapore in 1963. The *konfrontasi* involved serious military skirmishes on the border between the two countries in Borneo. The closest it came to Peninsula Malaysia was on the evening of 2 September 1964, when the rumble of two Hercules C-130 aircraft was heard over the town of Labis, in north Johor. Almost 100 Indonesian paratroopers dropped from the sky right into a tropical storm, which dispersed them over a large area. It took a month for the entire force to be killed or mopped up. The operation was a military disaster for Indonesia and a turning point in the confrontation. Subsequently Abdul Razak worked with his old friend from London, Des Alwi, to organise behind-the-scenes negotiations and he eventually signed the declaration of peace on 11 August 1966 with Adam Malik, the Indonesian foreign minister. The definitive change in Indonesia's stance, though, followed the downfall of President Soekarno in a military coup led by General Suharto in October 1965.

The negotiations to end *konfrontasi,* which involved Thailand as a mediator and the Philippines, which was also critical of the formation of Malaysia, was the genesis of Southeast Asian regionalism. Abdul Razak was a founder signatory of the ASEAN Charter in 1967, which has been a cornerstone for peace in the region for the last fifty years. As host of the ASEAN summit in 1971, he is credited with originating ZOPFAN – the concept of ASEAN as a Zone of Peace, Freedom and Neutrality based on two principles: the agreement of the Great Powers not to use the region as a zone for competition through proxies; and a commitment among regional states to refrain from interfering in one another's internal affairs. My father focused on making Malaysia more secure through peaceful collaboration with its neighbours. This strategy still pays dividends today. Since 1971, ASEAN economies have lifted many millions out of poverty only because they have enjoyed continuous peace and stability. As we will see later, ASEAN would become the stage on which my own career played out.

Biographies often paint Abdul Razak as a cautious technocrat. Nothing could be further from the truth: he was methodical, but that did not stop him taking big risks. The most obvious example of that in action was the other striking achievement of his foreign policy. It all began on an official visit to Canada in 1971, when he started a conversation on the sidelines of an event in Ottawa with the Chinese ambassador. That kicked off three years of intense bridge-building including trade missions as well as so-called ping-pong diplomacy involving the Malaysian Table Tennis Association. Our association arrived in Beijing with an unusually large roster of senior foreign office officials to accompany them. The officials went off for clandestine meetings while play went on at the tables. Malaysia backed China's application to become a member of the United Nations, and, eventually, the diplomacy led to my father becoming the first ASEAN leader to visit the communist regime. He visited Beijing in May 1974. It was still only two years after Nixon's visit, in 'the week that changed the world'. The Vietnam War was not long over, and there were still fears of its domino effect across Southeast Asia.

Abdul Razak met Chairman Mao and Premier Zhou En Lai in one of the latter's last official engagements before his death. These are towering, legendary figures in a country which is set to become the largest economy in the world, with a population today of 1.4 billion, almost 20% of the world's population. They clearly regarded this politician from little Malaysia, the boy from a *kampong* in Pekan, as someone worth bothering with. For his part my father knew which way the wind was blowing and how important it would be to have China as a friend.

The talks were not window dressing. My father won important assurances regarding China's attitude to Malaysia. Mao made it clear that the Chinese Communist Party did not have expansive military ambitions; the Communist Party of Malaysia's insurgency was an internal matter for Malaysia; China did not regard people in Malaysia of Chinese origin as Chinese citizens whom they had a duty to defend. In exchange for its official recognition, Malaysia had won from the Chinese leadership a promise not to destabilise its smaller neighbour.

I can remember the cheering crowds greeting him upon his return. He declared a national holiday. When you are seven it is pretty cool that your dad can give literally everyone a day off.

In summary, I take huge pride in my father's many achievements. Millions of Malaysians benefitted from the independence of the enlarged nation and the developments he set in train with the Razak Report and rural development programmes. He worked in partner-ship with many people and was a good deputy: loyal, hardworking and honest. As Musa recounts, Abdul Razak never once sought to belittle or minimise Tunku's enormous contributions to Malaysia.[28]

As prime minister he brought the country back from the brink of the disaster it faced in 1969. The national recalibration he orchestrated ensured that since 1970 Malaysia has enjoyed continuous peace and stability, with only minor episodes of heightened communal tensions. Plenty of other newly democratic and plural societies suffered lengthy civil wars, insurgencies and communal violence. Or they fell into the hands of dictators. That Malaysia never suffered these fates is arguably my father's greatest achievement. The choices he made, drawing on the sage advice of many others, in those critical months after the 1969 riots were critical for Malaysia.

Given the scale of these achievements it might seem odd for me to suggest that this, however, is only part of his legacy and not even the most important part of it.

Later I will come back to consider in more detail why many of the policies, programmes and institutions my father helped to set up are in need of a fundamental overhaul. Modern Malaysia needs a national recalibration as far-reaching as the one he led in 1970. With the benefit of ample hindsight, not all of his decisions were right. Some initiatives simply didn't succeed. Some that were right for the time are probably not fit for purpose now and the challenges we face coming over the horizon. One of the lessons of his career is that you can only make decisions in the imperfect context you find yourself in. There is no such thing as a blank slate. Nor are there solutions which last for all time. Some of the good policies he enacted have been distorted by vested interests, others were at odds with one another or diverted from their true purpose by the way they were implemented.

With his regard for evidence, analysis and argument, my father would have been one of the first to acknowledge the need for a periodic, honest and thorough review of his legacy. He was never a defender of the status quo for its own sake. He would perhaps only want to remind us that his actions and decisions should always be understood in the context and the light of the imperatives of the time.

Abdul Razak left us a dual legacy. The other part of that legacy was a less visible set of values and beliefs, principles and methods which guided the way he exercised his power. To understand that legacy we have to look not at *what* he did but at *how* and *why* he wielded power for the public good. These two legacies need to be seen together, both how they have supported and reinforced one another but also how they have become so at odds.

THE INTANGIBLES

When we were all still young my brothers and I once trooped into my father's office with a request to make: we asked him to build a swimming pool in the grounds of Seri Taman (pools were by this time becoming a feature of homes owned by wealthy and powerful families). My eldest brother Najib was the ringleader, corralling the rest of us to make the case, standing in front of my father's desk in his study. My father listened to our proposal carefully and then calmly dismissed it. 'How would it look,' he asked, eyebrow raised, 'if the prime minister spent public money on building a swimming pool for his family?' I didn't mind: I was still small enough to splash around in the ornamental pool in the courtyard, alongside the constantly replenished population of tadpoles. All the same, the parable of the swimming pool loomed large in my sense of what my father stood for. We had to be conscious of other people's perceptions of how we lived. We had no right to fritter away money that belonged to the public.

The swimming pool story is what social psychologists would call a 'reference narrative': a story we use to sum up a person and a situation, to remind us how we should see the world and to act. That was one of our family reference narratives to explain what my father stood for.

My father has been an enormous presence in my life in part because of his absence, the fact he was taken from us when I was still so young.

Perhaps it was due to that absence that I have strongly felt the need to honour his memory and understand his legacy. He has not been there to explain it to us; we've had to fill in the story ourselves. As Steve Jobs used to say: 'You join the dots up backwards.'[29] You can only make sense of who you are and where you find yourself by looking back, by understanding where you have come from. As I have got older I have grown to see more clearly how my father's values and methods have influenced my own. He never taught us any of this explicitly. He did not sit us down and give us a lecture. He often delivered his judgements with no more than a raised eyebrow. Yet I now feel, despite our many differences, he imparted an enormous amount to me, through his conduct rather than his words. It is here that we find his lasting legacy, one that does not show signs of ageing.

My recollection of times with my dad almost seem like stolen moments – sitting on his lap showing him my report card; perched next to him in his study while he watched the news; burying my head in his waistband at the end of a tiring official function; watching my parents come to my room hand-in-hand to check on me while I pretended to be asleep. My father wasn't at home much and when he was at home he worked most of the time. But when he could get the time for the family he was warm and playful, kind and gentle. He was never pompous or self-important. During brief holidays he loved to go on boat trips, swim, water-ski and fish. He was a keen golfer and he loved watching sport, especially the sports he used to play: hockey and football. He had a serious look but a dry, understated sense of humour. He was never the life of the party but he loved socialising. He could seem reticent, but he wasn't introverted: he was 'clubby' with his close friends. He had, everyone says, impeccable manners.

The accounts of my father provided by my family, his friends and those who worked closely with him invariably tell the same story. Stories abound about his frugality. On one trip to Switzerland he moved his entire entourage from one hotel to another because he thought the first was too expensive. It is said that he would not even accept toothpaste bought for him from government petty cash. He preferred substance to small talk but he treated everyone he met with respect regardless of whether he was dealing with a pauper or a prince, a gardener or a general.

My father was not bad-tempered by any measure, but he would display his annoyance when he felt people had let him, and themselves, down. But in general he was calm and good-natured. There was never any inkling of the pressure he must have been under, of the difficult dilemmas that must have weighed upon him. Throughout his entire time as PM he kept his terminal illness a secret. Most politicians love the limelight, yet he did not feel the need to attract attention to himself.

That self-assured poise, I think, was the source of his power. He could remain calm while everyone else around him was feeling the pressure. That meant people trusted him, which in turn allowed him to make better decisions, which people respected.

Robert Kuok, who was a fellow student at Raffles College, provides a clue to what made my father so special. Robert says my father had the ability to be kind and stern at the same time.[30] He imparted high expectations and exercised strict discipline with warmth and generosity. That ability to combine what seem to be irreconcilable qualities is at the heart of the person he was and the leadership he provided. Most people are good at one thing, which requires one skill and one kind of knowledge. I have come to understand my father better by seeing that he could combine different qualities, skills and insight at the same time.

I have come to see that my father was a 'both/and' person; he liked adding things together, even when they appeared contradictory rather than an 'either/or' person setting them apart. He preferred bringing people together rather than polarising them. He was proudly a Malay nationalist but not a divisive one. Let's take each of these combinations in turn.

CONSULTATIVE YET BOLD

Abdul Razak was trained as a lawyer; he listened to advice and evidence before deliberating and weighing the arguments. He was a skilled, attentive and thoughtful listener. People say that when you were talking to him you would believe that he was entirely focused on you. He didn't have to prove he was the leader by talking unnecessarily; he learned more by listening adroitly.

Abdul Razak recognised the need to listen not just to people who agreed with him. He searched out people who would challenge the way he thought because he knew debate and feedback would lead to better decisions. (Tan Sri) Rafidah Aziz, Malaysia's longest-serving female member of parliament, was appointed a senator at the age of thirty-one, thanks to her earlier interactions with Abdul Razak: 'I had shown a willingness to speak out and out of turn when necessary. He never minded my lack of deference, my challenging him in front of others at times.'[31] His first deputy prime minister was Dr Ismail, who could not help himself but to always speak his mind firmly, even to his boss. Indeed Dr Ismail was more decisive than Abdul Razak, but he was so feared that people tended to prefer to engage Abdul Razak.

Politicians who are consultative are often seen as indecisive. Or they end up making expedient compromises, which settle arguments by avoiding the issue and suppressing division. What was unusual about Abdul Razak was that he applied his calm, consultative approach to the most difficult issues, made tough decisions and then made sure they were acted upon. It was a quality remembered vividly by his nephew (Dato Sri) Hishammuddin Hussein, himself a senior figure in UMNO, who said that when Abdul Razak became PM 'the challenges were unprecedented. There was no model to learn from, and handling them required courage, exceptional wisdom and leadership. It was a time when the nation desperately needed a leader who had the political will to do what was right. Something needed to be done, urgently. The business-as-usual model was no longer viable, which is what persuaded Abdul Razak to embark on a mission to create a better Malaysia.'[32]

He could be consultative *and* decisive, considered and bold; he built agreement across Malaysian society to tackle the biggest shared issues society faced. There is no better example of this approach in action than the workings of the NCC, which charted the country's return to democracy at a pivotal moment when Malaysia could have taken many wrong turns. Had he done too little to address Malay concerns about economic inequality, there could have been further ethnic violence. It would have been all too easy for him to have given in to those around him who were advising him not to restore democracy and to keep hold of his autocratic powers, to establish a dictatorship. Malaysia avoided these outcomes because of the way he governed in those critical months; and the heart of that were the deliberations of the NCC. For me the NCC is where his leadership, values and methods all came together. In the final section of the book I will come back to the lessons the NCC has for us today in Malaysia as we grapple with our own, difficult issues.

SMALL STEPS AND BIG LEAPS

My father was methodical and analytical. His early experience of working with the British to defeat the communist insurgency village by village stayed with him throughout his career. When he was minister in charge of rural development, he knew the importance of planning out what was going to happen right down to the level of each village. The methods to make big change real at the grassroots was laid out in his famous Red Books. He had an eye for detail but he accepted that as leader he couldn't monitor everything so he had a system of surprise spot checks, to find out what was happening. It was once said of him that he was commander in chief of the civil service: he believed the job of government was to get things done for the good of citizens. He was a methodical, some say dour, doer.

Yet it would be quite wrong to conclude that as a result he did not grasp the big picture. He knew how to spot important details rather than getting lost in minutiae. He didn't flinch from thinking big. He knew the message of the 13 May riots was that the entire system, how democracy, government, economy and society worked, needed recalibration, and he dared to do it. He did not fiddle around in the margins.

Those who are careful and considered are often too cautious to take big risks that require a leap of faith. Not so my father. Time and again, both through necessity and choice he made big leaps and stepped into the unknown. It is easy with hindsight to see the logic of having a close relationship with China, the rising world power. It was less obvious in 1974 when communist China, led by Mao, emerging from the disaster of the Cultural Revolution and tacitly supporting an insurgency inside Malaysia, was still regarded with fear and suspicion in much of the world. When Abdul Razak went to Beijing on the first official visit of a head of state from an Asian democracy, he was breaking the mould. I remember that, for years after, new Chinese ambassadors to Malaysia would always pay a courtesy call to my mother. One of them reminded me of the Chinese saying: 'He who drinks water must never forget who dug the well.' In the parlance of modern-day entrepreneurship Abdul Razak was hoping to gain first-mover advantage: Malaysia has been reaping the rewards ever since. First movers are usually not cautious, considered people. Yet my father managed to combine the two qualities; he was a methodical risk taker who knew that real change requires both many small steps and some big leaps.

THE SELF-ASSURED TEAM PLAYER

Despite lacking charisma (every account of him agrees on that point) my father was a compelling political leader because he was always himself. He was at one with himself. In contemporary terms he was authentic: what you saw was what you got. He never pretended to be something he wasn't. His old friend Michael Chen said of him: 'It is generally held that a man has three characters: the one he exhibits; the one he thinks he is; and the one he really is. With Abdul Razak there was just one: he was always himself.'[33]

When his aides tried to make his speeches more exciting by injecting some poetry into his dogged prose he would always reject their suggestions, on the grounds that the flowery language didn't sound like him: he shouldn't have to pretend to be someone he was not, he would tell them. He was not a performer – more like an engineer. His prodigious work ethic required enormous self-discipline. He could only demand so much from the people around him because he applied such high standards to himself. There was no 'one rule for them, another for me' with my father.

Just as he asked a lot of the people who worked for him, so he cared for them. (Dato') Shafie Yahya, who served as his private secretary, recounts how emotional he felt when a couple of weeks after my father passed away he was handed a gift of an Austin Reed shirt that my father had bought for him just before he died. A number of his closest aides received similar presents. Just before he died he had the consideration and generosity to think of them. No wonder he engendered tremendous loyalty and commitment from others.

His self-confidence in his own abilities did not make him arrogant; on the contrary it allowed him to see when he needed the help of others. One of his most important early decisions as director of NOC was to find a partner to work with him as it was not a job he could do alone. He chose the highly respected Dr Ismail as home minister and his deputy. Dr Ismail had once been Abdul Razak's rival for the UMNO deputy presidency and had a strong personality. By all accounts Ismail was an effective check and balance to Abdul Razak's absolute authority. Ismail was there to challenge him. My father knew that he could achieve nothing significant alone. Not only did he need a check to his absolute power, he needed different points of view to make good decisions. Some leaders try to disguise their insecurity by surrounding themselves with mediocre people who will never challenge them. That was not my father. He welcomed capable, challenging people who would add to the quality of decision making, And he knew he would need a capable successor.

My father excelled at spotting talent: he wasn't threatened by people with new ideas, energy and ambition; he was keen on people with the self-confidence to challenge him. As you will see, I flatter myself to think this is a quality he passed on to me. He nurtured an entire generation of political leaders, including Mahathir (who credits my father with resurrecting his political career and being appointed DPM in 1976), (Tun) Abdullah Ahmad Badawi, Musa Hitam and (Tun) Ghafar Baba – to name but a few who became UMNO presidents and deputy presidents. He expected his officers to challenge him when they thought it necessary, stating their opinions honestly and clearly. My father knew his own intelligence would be multiplied by his willingness to listen to others, to take in different points of view.

ROOTED COSMOPOLITAN

Abdul Razak was a rooted cosmopolitan, confident in venturing into the wider world because he had such a strong sense of where he came from. He was an aristocrat who grew up in the *kampong* and walked to school barefoot for the first few years of his life before going off to the Malay College with the sons of the elite. He was at ease mixing in and moving around all tiers of Malay society.

As minister of rural development, he was always impatient to get out of Kuala Lumpur at the end of the week to travel by road, river and air, visiting some of the forty-five regional operations centres and 118 district operational rooms directing rural development efforts across the country. He welcomed being among people, engaging in conversation with them, listening to their views, seeing things from their point of view. This sense of rootedness anchored him, personally and politically. He was genuinely at ease amongst the people.

When he was PM, he decided to build a house in Pekan for us. He modelled it after the *kampong* house where he grew up, instead of a brick house with modern amenities. To be honest, I used to loathe staying there and being deprived of my usual comforts of Seri Taman. He, on the other hand, was obviously more at home there than at Seri Taman.

Yet while he was a *kampong* boy, and a Malay nationalist, he was anything but parochial. He drew inspiration from international sources and ideas; he was at ease in the office of the US president or speaking to the United Nations. Much of the groundwork for independence was laid in London. He was inspired by the independence movements in India and Indonesia, by economic development in Taiwan and by ideas about social and economic development from Europe, including from the Fabians and his advisor Just Faaland, the Norwegian development economist who helped draw up the NEP. My father recognised the need to engage with the wider world, including ASEAN and the Non-Aligned Movement. He was emotionally, morally and politically rooted in the *kampong*, yet intellectually he was curious, cosmopolitan and open-minded. He saw no reason why the two could not go together.

Plato said the main job of a statesman was to 'weave the future', and it was what Abdul Razak did.[34] He was not in power to defend the past but rather to find a path to a future in which Malaysia could come into its own. He was visionary yet practical; he was concerned about the here and now but he always looked to the future. He understood the value of tradition and respected the role the Sultans played in national life. Yet he was also a democrat, a nationalist, an egalitarian and a radical moderniser who brought in new ideas. He had an innate sense of Malaysia's enduring spirit of optimism; he wanted us to live up to our enormous potential.

Those four combinations – consultative yet bold, small steps and big leaps, self-assured and a team player, rooted and cosmopolitan – were at the heart of his leadership, the way he went about his work. I think this is where we find his lasting legacy because through this he created a recipe for how power can be used for the public good.

THE DUAL LEGACY

I grew up the son of Abdul Razak, the master builder of modern Malaysia, the structural engineer who put in place the foundations which have largely sustained the country till this day. My father left us a legacy with two sides.

While my father was alive, as Malaysia was taking shape and in much of the twenty years after the NEP was launched, I like to think that the two sides of his legacy worked in tandem. At least they were not at odds with one another. His values and methods supported the institutions and policies which in turn provided the benefits in terms of growth, stability and equity which justified the values and methods. Abdul Razak left Malaysia with a strong platform of public power, which was designed to work for the greater good, setting the country on a path to economic and social development that benefitted millions of Malaysians in succeeding decades. Malaysians became better-educated and lived longer; they had modern houses with air conditioning, fridges and televisions; they earned, spent and saved more. Abject poverty was virtually eliminated; life expectancy was extended. In the process the country urbanised, developing a modern economy based on manufacturing and services rather than commodities and agriculture.

However, as my adult life unfolded, I became aware of the growing tension between the two sides of the legacy. By the end they had become like Dr Jekyll and Mr Hyde. My career was made at the intersection of those two legacies. Too many of the institutions, programmes, policies and agencies were diverted from their true purpose. Misused and misled, they began to serve not the people but those in political power. Eventually I came to see that in the name of the values my father had left us with, I needed to advocate the overhaul of the system he had created. For the sake of my father I had to disavow some of what he put in place. And for the sake of my father I risked my relationship with the older brother I so admired and who had looked after me on the night of his death. But all that comes later.

After Abdul Razak's passing, the responsibility for leading the nation fell to a succession of 'Razak boys'; Hussein Onn (1976–81), (Tun) Dr Mahathir (1981–2003) and Badawi (2003–8). Ironically the first PM who was not a Razak political protégé would be his son, Najib.

After leaving Seri Taman, my mother created a new home for us at Jalan Eaton, just around the corner from where the Petronas Twin Towers would be built. Najib quickly took on the mantle of my father's parliamentary seat in Pekan. I was shepherded off to school at Oundle in the UK to become the only Asian in my boarding house and had to quickly learn to fend for myself. From there I went to Bristol University as an undergraduate and on to Cambridge University, as a postgraduate. When I returned from my studies in the UK, I had little or no idea what I wanted to do. But I knew I would have to earn a living, and that I would have to make a name for myself on my own terms.

After spending the whole of the 1980s in the UK, where the name Razak only meant anything at meetings of the Malaysian and Singapore Association, when I returned I had to quickly adjust to an environment where that name resonated with everyone. It was then that I realised that my father had given me perhaps the greatest start of all: a good name, a reputation for public service to build upon. He left me a legacy but also a deep sense of obligation. The name gave me advantages, for sure, but it also meant I had a lot to live up to; not least because I felt my father would be with me, looking over my shoulder, urging me to be my better self. This opening section has been an attempt to understand the name that I inherited from my father and the dual legacy he left behind, not just for me but for all Malaysians. The next section is about what I did with that inheritance, how I tried to make a name for myself and how I witnessed the two sides of that legacy come into conflict.

SECTION TWO

INVESTMENT BANKER

EMPLOYEE SIXTY NINE

It was a hefty, spiral-bound book and it was heading straight for my nose. I threw my hands up and ducked out of the way just in time. The man who'd thrown the book was sitting behind his desk, knuckles clenched, face red, furious. He was shouting so violently the words were barely comprehensible. I beat a speedy retreat to my desk. Sweat had broken out on my forehead. I was shaking.

That was my first boss, Steve Wong, a workaholic, hard-driving chartered accountant turned corporate financier. He wasn't everyone's cup of tea, but even those who didn't like him had to acknowledge how persuasive, charming and highly effective he could be when he wanted. Steve had a growing reputation as *the* deal maker in town. I had wanted to work for him and felt lucky to have the job. I could live with the odd hurled book. I was determined to prove to both of us that I could succeed.

The book in question was my first attempt to draft a submission to the Capital Issues Committee (CIC), the forerunner of the Securities Commission, on behalf of Nam Fatt Berhad, a construction company we were advising. The CIC required mountains of paperwork to prove that a company deserved to qualify to raise funds from the public and have its shares traded on the stock exchange. Putting that thick book together was the hardest work I had ever done. It meant starting early, finishing late most nights and working through the weekends. Steve told me I had produced one of the worst drafts he had ever seen, and I had better buck up.

It was not an auspicious start to my career as a banker. No human resources manual would ever recommend throwing your employee's work at them, and these days it would doubtless get you into trouble. But it was a different time, and Steve's passion, aggression and high expectations were all part and parcel of the culture of the Corporate Finance department at Commerce International Merchant Bankers, CIMB for short. In no time at all, I had fallen in love with the raw, upstart culture of the place. All I could think about as I dodged the book was doing better. And something must have worked because, for the next twenty-nine years, CIMB would be my second home.

I had become a banker almost by accident. The deal my brothers and I had with our parents was that after a good British education at public school and then an undergraduate degree, we would return to Malaysia to work and support ourselves. This was the Razak family standard operating procedure; because my father didn't want us to be spoilt by our exceptional home comforts or given special treatment because of our name. My return was especially significant for my mother: she regarded educating her five children as one of her life's principal missions.

I spent the requisite three undergraduate years at Bristol University reading Economics and Politics, but as the end approached, I didn't feel ready to go home. I wanted to improve my academic credentials, sensing that a Bristol undergraduate degree wouldn't be enough to differentiate myself in the jobs market. I got Mum's permission to stay on for an extra year and won a place at Cambridge. In September 1988, I entered Pembroke College to study for an MPhil in the Economics and Politics of Development. At that time its curriculum and academics were still largely left-wing: we learned that everything that was good tended to be done by the state. I left Cambridge thinking my next move was a career working for the government, the Malaysian diplomatic service perhaps. After all, my father had once said that he would like at least one of his sons to join the civil service and my brothers were already pursuing other careers.

What kind of Malaysia was I returning to? Things had changed a lot while I had been away. Let me briefly set the scene to which I was coming home.

My father's legacy had been built on, but also in the process it had begun to change, quite fundamentally. Mahathir had become president of UMNO and prime minister in 1981, succeeding my uncle Hussein whose short tenure was largely a continuum of my father's in terms of policies and priorities. In Mahathir's first few years, power was dispersed amongst several Abdul Razak protégés but still his rise marked a change of gear, at first rhetorically and then in action. Mahathir had a talent for bold and inspirational plans.

In my father's time the state had become an active enabler of development, to eradicate poverty and create a fairer economic balance between ethnic groups. Soon after he came into power, Mahathir launched the idea of 'Malaysia Inc.' to signal that the private sector would now become an equal partner with government in economic development. It signalled a more collaborative relationship between an ambitious state and private enterprise.

The Malaysia Inc. slogan consciously echoed the idea of Japan Inc., the close coordination between the Japanese government and leading companies, which commentators had invoked to explain why Japan was the rising force in so many industries, from cars to electronics. It complemented Mahathir's 'Look East' policy, itself a corrective to the assumed dominance of Western ideas, companies and investors which had continued since independence. Yet the Malaysian version would need significant mobilisation of state capital because the private sector was predominantly Chinese controlled. The original, 1.0 version of Malaysia Inc. was characterised by massive investment in heavy industries spearheaded by state-owned enterprises (SOEs), most notably

Heavy Industries Corporation of Malaysia (HICOM), Perwaja Steel and the car company Proton as well as various incentives for the onshore development of complete eco-systems around those companies.

A combination of high government indebtedness, poor project execution by SOEs and a weak external sector brought about a sudden recession in the mid-1980s which in turn added fuel to intense infighting within UMNO between three Abdul Razak protégés: Razaleigh, Musa and Mahathir. Each was convinced that they were the rightful heir. First, Razaleigh and Musa twice competed to be Mahathir's deputy president of UMNO (and therefore DPM). Then, in 1986, Musa resigned as deputy prime minister and at the next year's party elections, joined forces with Razaleigh in a bid to depose Mahathir as UMNO president. The party split down the middle: Mahathir won by just forty-three of the 1,479 votes of UMNO delegates. Razaleigh then launched a legal challenge against the results which ended with the Supreme Court declaring that UMNO was an illegal organisation. UMNO splintered into two competing parties – Mahathir's UMNO Baru (New UMNO) and Razaleigh's Samangat 46 (Spirit of 1946, the year in which UMNO was founded).

It did not take long for Mahathir to use the power of incumbency to take over UMNO's assets and consolidate and secure his power. In the party he marginalised everyone who had sided with Razaleigh and Musa and made it much more difficult for anyone to challenge the president by setting high hurdles for any aspiring contestant. In government senior civil servants became disgruntled that their advice was often disregarded; heads of government agencies who didn't toe Mahathir's line were pushed aside. As for constitutional checks and balances, the Sultans had their powers curbed, while the lord president of the judiciary was removed, and several Supreme Court judges were suspended. Mahathir also presided over the largest crackdown on political dissent modern Malaysia had ever seen. In 1987, under 'Operation Lalang' 119 people were arrested and detained without charge under the Internal Security Act. Three newspapers sympathetic to the opposition were shut down.

My father had relinquished the dictatorial powers vested in him as director of NOC in favour of a return to democracy; now one of his favoured successors embarked on almost two decades of what became more and more like one-man rule. A new circle of power emerged around Mahathir comprising the likes of Anwar Ibrahim, (Tun) Daim Zainuddin and Rafidah Aziz. Daim, a former businessman, was the new economic czar. I have often wondered who among his protégés Abdul Razak would have endorsed had he lived and what he would have made of Mahathir's methods. His untimely death meant he did not have to make fateful choices between those who followed in his footsteps.

A new version of Malaysia Inc. (or 2.0) came out of the recession: state-owned entities would be privatised, swathes of activity such as power plants and telecoms were transferred to the private sector and ownership rules were liberalised to attract foreign investors. While privatisation is associated with the free-market policies of Ronald Reagan and Margaret Thatcher, Malaysia's approach was a peculiar hybrid; it went with enhanced concentration of power around the prime minister and also as a tool to fulfil the ambitions of the NEP, to build a strong *bumiputra* business class, which in turn supported the centralisation of power around the prime minister.

This was the dynamic, ambitious Malaysia to which I was returning as a fresh-faced graduate interested in following in my father's footsteps as a public servant.

When, finally, I arrived home in July 1989, I consulted my career advisors, my brothers Johari and Nizam, about my options. They advised me to join the corporate sector rather than the government, saying that the civil service wasn't what it used to be in Dad's time. My brothers pointed out that, as power now lay with politicians and the private sector, I would get bored and frustrated as a civil servant. One alternative was to work for a multinational, which would pay me a very good salary. So I applied to work for oil majors with operations in Malaysia, Shell and Esso and one homegrown multinational, Sime Darby. The international firms promptly called me for interviews, and Shell offered the best package. The Shell interviewer was intrigued that I had applied 'normally'. 'Why didn't you get someone to just call the boss?' he asked. It had never occurred to me not to go about applying in the regular way. I remember noting the irony that surprising with humility could actually get me further than pulling strings. Sime Darby only responded to my application after I had started work, a fact that stayed with me until our paths would cross again many years later.

The other option suggested by my brothers was to work for a merchant bank, where I would learn about companies from many different sectors, although it wouldn't pay as well. It would be the perfect way, Johari and Nizam explained, to survey the corporate scene and explore what I wanted to do in the long term. Banking would be a stepping-stone to a real career. A two-to-three-year stint at a merchant bank seemed a more enticing option, despite the lower salary, than a long-term career at a multinational. And after studying Politics, Philosophy and Economics (PPE) at Oxford, Nizam had first worked at a merchant bank and was doing very well for himself.

I had only the vaguest idea of what a merchant bank did so I had to look it up (in books, there was no Google Search then). Merchant banks started life financing trade: merchants would commission fleets of ships to sail long distances to acquire spices, fine clothes or precious materials to sell at a handsome profit when they returned. To raise money to fund the ships, to provision them and pay the crew, the merchants turned to banks to share in the risks and rewards of the venture. There were plenty of risks: the ships might get lost at sea or plundered by pirates. The industry I was now planning to go into was the modern incarnation of this inherently riskier version of banking. In Malaysia, though, it wasn't so risky or exciting. There were only twelve merchant banks, mostly joint ventures set up in the 1970s between

local and foreign banks, and they specialised in serving large companies, lending to them, taking their deposits and advising them on how
to raise share (or equity) capital typically by an Initial Public Offering (IPO) of shares and a new listing on the Kuala Lumpur Stock
Exchange (KLSE, later renamed Bursa Malaysia) or through a rights
issue of shares for a company that was already listed. Merchant banks
also advised companies on mergers and acquisitions and how to comply
with the NEP condition that *bumiputra* should own at least 30% of a
company; without which the company would face limitations in getting
government licences or contracts and raising funds from the public.

Every aspiring banker wanted to work for Arab-Malaysian
Merchant Bank (Arab) in those days: it was the largest of the merchant
banks and had a certain swagger. It was owned and led by (Tan Sri)
Azman Hashim, the iconic *bumiputra* banker and entrepreneur. Nizam
deftly steered me in another direction though: he told me about a small
merchant bank called CIMB that, although ranking only seventh in
asset size at that time, was aggressive and interesting. It was a bit like
suggesting a promising footballer play for QPR rather than Chelsea, on
the grounds he would get more playing time. Nizam said I should pitch
to work for the top corporate finance manager there, who would 'train
me up'. His name was Steve Wong; he would become the book thrower.

To hedge my bets, I applied to both merchant banks. I interviewed
officially with Arab's human resources department and only met casu-
ally with Steve. The Arab application involved lots of paperwork, and the
HR manager made me feel I had to impress her to get a job. Steve, on
the other hand, oozed self-confidence and got straight down to the kind
of work I would do. I sensed a contrast in organisational cultures: Arab,
the best and the biggest, had a sense of entitlement; CIMB had a challenger's street-fighting mentality. That was what principally appealed to
me. I had never been afraid to challenge conventional wisdom: as the
youngest of five boys, you were never going to win from business as
usual. At Oundle School I had co-written a paper for the headmaster

that persuaded the school to do away with hundreds of years of tradition and allow football to become a mainstream sport, as opposed to a game played purely for fun on a Sunday. That disruption saw the virtual end of hockey as a competitive sport at the school (until it became co-ed years later). I loved being the little Asian boy who had made a big difference to the sporting life of a very old British institution.

Steve arranged for me to meet (Dato') Robert Cheim, head of the Corporate Finance Department. Shell, Esso and Arab all wanted me, so I was confident I would be offered a job. I thought the interview was going well until Robert closed it off by saying that CIMB did not hire fresh graduates and, besides, I had no accounting background. He would disclose years later that he also doubted whether someone with my privileged background could put in the hard work expected at CIMB Corporate Finance. He thanked me for my interest in the firm and showed me the door. I trudged home, head bowed, called Steve and told him I was resigned to accepting the offer from Arab. A few days later, Steve called back to say he had appealed to Robert and the then CEO of CIMB, (Tan Sri) Dr Munir Majid. Thanks to Steve they agreed to give me a chance. I was going to be CIMB's first ever fresh graduate. I was ecstatic. I would now do anything for Steve. Perhaps he knew it.

My first day was 11 September 1989. I was employee number sixty-nine, and the entire staff was on the top floor of the Pernas International Building on Jalan Sultan Ismail in the heart of downtown Kuala Lumpur. I was *so* keen.

The bank I was joining had its own quite complex family tree.[35] CIMB was a cultural hybrid, with quite old and grand parentage, founded in 1974 as Pertanian Baring Sanwa Multinational; its official opening was marked by a speech by Prime Minister Abdul Razak. After the first few months Multinational Bank of the UK withdrew, and the bank became Pertanian Baring Sanwa (PBS). The government agriculture bank, Bank Pertanian, owned 68% and thus control, even though PBS had nothing to do with agriculture. The other 32% was split between Baring Brothers, the oldest merchant bank in the City of London, set up in 1762, and Sanwa Bank, the Japanese bank, which traced its roots back even further, to 1656. PBS, though, was very small. In 1983 it had share capital of RM12.5m (the market leader, Arab had RM76m). From the outset it operated like a colonial outpost of Barings. Staff were often sent to Barings' HQ in the City to be trained; the bank rode on Barings' international prestige and corporate finance expertise. PBS specialised in advising mainly multinational companies on raising capital, mergers and acquisitions and compliance with NEP. It did very little lending and deposit taking.

PBS became Commerce International Merchant Bankers after Bank of Commerce (BOC) acquired a 51% stake from Bank Pertanian in 1985. BOC started life as a commercial bank in 1924 in Kuching, Sarawak named Bian Chiang Bank. In 1979, it was taken over by the Fleet Group, the investment vehicle of UMNO and JP Morgan, the legendary Wall Street bank founded in the early nineteenth century, which came in with a 30% stake. For the first six years, management was led by staff from the Wall Street bank and then, in 1985, a young New Zealand-trained accountant, (Tan Sri) Md Nor Yusof, took over as chief executive. Md Nor continued with the tone of professionalism and meritocracy, and the strategy of focusing BOC on corporate clients set by JP Morgan. Meanwhile, in the late 1980s, Fleet Group was taken over by the Renong Group and BOC became the banking arm of the vast UMNO-linked conglomerate.

With the staid government agriculture bank taking a back seat, CIMB signalled its intention to embark on a new era with the appointment of Dr Munir as CEO the following year. Munir, who has a PhD from the London School of Economics, had been group editor at the *New Straits Times*, the main English daily, where he fell foul of Mahathir. He was retained 'in the system' as it were, probably because he was a rare Malay talent: smart, articulate and urbane. If you just heard his voice you would think he was an Englishman.

So it was that the bank I joined in 1989 was a small upstart desperate to punch above its weight, and the corporate finance team I became a part of (one of five teams in the department) most epitomised it. I was thrown in the deep end with no water wings. Steve's philosophy was that you don't learn to swim standing on the side of the pool. Everyone got thrown in, regardless of their experience or qualifications. I learned to swim but only by almost drowning on several occasions.

I learned an awful lot that first hard year. It felt as though I was climbing a mountain every day. It was exhausting, punishing and rewarding. I often had to ring (Dato') Azlina, my soon-to-be-wife, who helpfully was working at an accounting firm in London, to ask her about troubling concepts like 'debit' and 'credit'. Tan Choon Thye, an engineer with an MBA and Steve's number two, and my peers Ng Kok Teong, and Ng Pin How, both qualified accountants, helped me a lot. They never said it, but I suspect they were shocked by how little I knew about finance. Mainly what I learned, though, was what it was like to work really hard. In those days quite a lot of banking was actually a form of manual labour. More brawn than brain was needed in corporate finance then. There were a lot of reports, proposals and prospectuses to be written. The authorities demanded lots of documentation to support any application, and doing anything seemed to require regulatory approval. We had secretaries to do the typing, but we hand-wrote the first draft and then had to check and re-check their work. Steve did not tolerate any mistakes; punctuation and even the alignment of margins had to be perfect.

Steve had a 'work-first' mindset which he instilled in the team. It never left me and proved important throughout my career. As CEO, I would always tell new CIMB recruits, to get ahead you have to be prepared to put in the hours; if you don't, someone else will. And when you're the boss you have to work hard to set an example.

We worked late most nights. Steve seemed to be in meetings most of the day. To get hold of him, to ask his advice, we usually had to wait around until 10 or 11 p.m. If I went home for dinner at 7 p.m. I would return to the office. My colleagues gave me no special favours. I don't think I ever quite matched Kok Teong and Pin How in terms of hours, but I earned their respect by putting in a lot more than they expected me to and bringing new dimensions to the team. If they were most at home poring over numbers and spreadsheets, I was at ease with talking and selling. After my first client meeting Choon Thye asked me: 'Do you always talk so much?' I wasn't sure whether he was telling me off or encouraging me.

To maintain some balance to my work life, on Wednesday afternoons a group of fifteen to twenty KL 'yuppies' – the cool term for young professionals then – including Johari and Nizam and some of our Malaysian friends from our student days in London would gather on the large lawn of my mother's Jalan Eaton house, where I was still living, to play football. We called ourselves Eaton Wanderers. After the game, others would go off for drinks and something to eat; I would usually go back to work.

Weekends often turned into workdays; vacations were few and far between. In those days CIMB allowed staff to carry over leave they had not taken and eventually the company would 'buy out' the unused holiday. That policy ended when management discovered that Choon Thye had accumulated about eight months' worth of holidays! Management was concerned about the unrecorded contingent liability. The rest of us saw it as a badge of honour for Choon Thye. For someone who had been born with a silver spoon in his mouth, CIMB's work ethic was an invaluable awakening. My natural competitive instincts, and the desire of a youngest child to show that he could do it, made me want to persevere. But that was nothing compared to the way that the commitment to my colleagues spurred me on.

All my colleagues in Steve's original team were of Chinese descent. Several came from less well-off families, where they were the only ones in professional jobs; the entire family depended on their success.

They taught me to see past which school people had gone to, or which community they came from, and instead to judge people by the quality of the work they did and the kind of person they were. They quickly started calling me NBL, which I found out meant Natural Born Leader. They also joked that I could sell ice to Eskimos. It is a mark of the bond we made in that team that all these years later we have a WhatsApp group (without Steve, the boss) and meet up regularly – the executives, the secretaries and typists too.

As the only Malay in Steve's team, I was the diversity, the odd one out: the only Malay, Muslim and Western-educated one. Sometimes, it was like being at Oundle again, where I was the only foreigner in a house of sixty boys. Most of the time, though, I felt we were a team of Malaysians. Race was just a fact, never a cause for separation. We not only respected our different cultures, each person's dos and don'ts, but instinctively leveraged our differences: I would tend to handle the Malay and more Westernised clients and copy edit the marketing documents. The result was that from the very start of my career I was strongly aware of the power of diversity to strengthen rather than divide.

Early on I also learned what it was like to be an underdog in a competitive market, looked down upon by those who were bigger and more established. Clayton Christensen's classic work *The Innovator's Dilemma*, which made the idea of disruptive innovation fashionable, was still almost a decade off.[36] Nevertheless, at the CIMB corporate finance department we saw ourselves as disruptors. It was the only way we could get noticed in an industry dominated by much larger competitors. We had no option but to challenge the status quo. As the cheeky youngest child in a large family, I knew what that meant: you had to punch above your weight, to be nimble. When riling an older brother, speed of thought, quick words and fast feet were all important if you didn't want to get bashed.

That year, my first at CIMB, we managed to stun the competition by advising on all four of the largest of the twelve IPOs in the year, topping the IPO league table for the first time. Arab and Bumiputra Merchant Bankers had always kept the top spots for themselves, and CIMB was part of the chasing pack, in the second tier, along with the similar-sounding MIMB and D & C Sakura. That year, however, driven by Steve's little corporate finance team, we broke through, making a profit before tax of RM4.9m. As a bank we were still tiny: Arab's profit before tax was RM40m. All the same, the year that I came to CIMB was the year that the company first made its mark as a force to be reckoned with. In the hotly contested inter-bank sports competition I represented the firm in bowling, athletics, soccer, squash and, believe it or not, basketball (everything bar netball basically), because we had so few staff. The following year, we noted that suddenly it was import-ant for the big merchant banks to beat us on the sports field, because we were providing such unexpectedly stiff competition in the field of business. Beating us mattered – and it felt great even when we lost (which was most of the time).

The culture to which I was introduced in my corporate finance team in those early months had a huge bearing on the culture we developed across CIMB subsequently. In the years to come, CIMB would grow and change, developing many different businesses and strategies, products and services, yet the core culture remained strong: work hard as a team, think originally, challenge conventional wisdom, value people according to the work they do and never forget to have fun sometimes.

The way we worked in those days taught me a lot about why people work well together and where success comes from. My view is that first and foremost people work hard because they share a sense of mission. Creating such a shared mission is the main task of good leaders, who need to bind people together in a shared cause, as teammates. Yet individuals also have to see how it satisfies their own self-interest and ambitions. It all has to fit together: mission, leadership, teammates and self-interest.

Business books refer to 'mission' as the organisation's *raison d'être*, its purpose and goals. They advise that mission statements should encompass what a company does, how it does it, for whom and what value it creates. Yet those mission statements can often be vague and bland. I found that it was vital for the mission to set an agenda that everyone in the company could understand. At the start of my career the team's mission was being Malaysia's top corporate finance outfit; after I became chief executive, CIMB's mission became to become the top investment bank in Malaysia; once that was achieved, CIMB became about building a leading universal bank across ASEAN. There was always a simple overriding mission, and it was up to the leaders across the organisation to create the sub-missions for their teams. When missions are not compelling to staff because they are unclear or too convoluted, a great deal of drive and energy is lost.

Good leadership doesn't mean telling people in detail what to do; that can be demeaning. Good leaders make people want to work hard by praising them and building them up in order to demand more of them, like a coach. People are more likely to work hard if they have leaders who are by turns encouraging, inspiring and demanding, whom they want to please because they want their respect and praise. Steve certainly could be inspiring and demanding, but his approach wasn't sustainable; it took too much out of people – and, in fact, Kok Teong and Pin How ended up retiring in their late thirties, way too soon. Even though I was grateful for all that he taught me, I would not have worked for him for much longer than I did.

My first year also taught me how hard people are prepared to work for the sake of their teammates. What I found most compelling about work at CIMB was the camaraderie. We were all in it together. A good organisation is like a community or an extended family. I learned the motivational power of being on a mission in a team that must sink or swim together. I would try to create that spirit over and over at different levels of the organisation and at different scales as CIMB grew.

Finally, we must never forget there is always a degree of self-interest which is clearly motivating; people want something for themselves. Money was an important factor for me; I needed to sustain my life-style. But it was only one factor; I had more lucrative offers from larger companies. What tied me to CIMB was the possibility of work that would be challenging and demanding. The sense of achievement that comes from that kind of work is also a personal reward. I felt good about myself at the end of my first year because of the sense that I had achieved things. I hadn't just pushed paper around. The relatively flat hierarchy and the can-do environment meant greater opportunity and sense of ownership for everyone, even relative newbies like me.

By the end of 1990, thanks to my brother's advice, my colleagues' forbearance and Steve's incessant demands, my career at CIMB had started in earnest. I didn't know it at the time, but it was an extraordi-nary time to be entering the finance industry. It was as if the industry had just been put on steroids; there would be plenty of twists and turns, thrills and spills, and highs and lows. It wasn't my stepping-stone after all, it was my calling.

THE TENAGA BOOST

It's all very well winning the league, but can you keep it up? Especially when you are small? At CIMB, we were determined to show that our performance in 1989 was not a flash in the pan. Steve thrived on the pressure, hated losing and would commit to all sorts of crazy deadlines, which of course then became his team's responsibility to meet. The work was so demanding and draining that I did momentarily flirt with moving for a moment following an unsolicited offer from Arab. That came after Steve ruined my Christmas and New Year in 1990. I had been looking forward to some time off and some fun at last. But towards the end of the year, the Minister of Finance (MoF) set a year-end cut-off point for applications by stockbroking companies for a listing on the stock exchange, after which it might never be possible. Steve saw this as a huge opportunity and decided to offer to advise any stockbroking company which wanted to list, guaranteeing that his team would meet the deadline come what may. I was woken up at 8 a.m. on the last Sunday of the year by a phone call from Steve. 'I need you here, now,' was all he said. When I arrived at the office, I found the entire team had been called in to work on the submissions. We worked non-stop until late on Monday night: thirty-six hours of paperwork and maybe an hour of sleep on the office sofa. I spent New Year's Eve catching up, not with friends but with sleep.

Our efforts paid off, though. In 1990–91 we managed to take a fifth of all corporate advisory fees earned by the twelve Malaysian merchant banks. The larger merchant banks made much more money overall as they had big lending books, whereas we continued to focus on corporate finance. As a small merchant bank CIMB's strategy was to stand out by excelling in one area. Corporate finance was glamorous and high-profile yet didn't require much capital. Steve got promoted to head of the whole Corporate Finance Department and imposed his style on all five teams, not just ours. And Corporate Finance soon defined how corporate customers saw CIMB – small, smart, hard-working; the outfit that always delivered.

I was lucky that I joined CIMB as the Malaysian economy and financial sector was taking off. In 1988, GDP grew at 9.9%, bouncing back strongly after the mid-1980s recession (1987: 5.2%, 1986: 1.2%). And for the ten years to 1997, GDP growth averaged about 8%, one of the best records in the world.[37]

The Malaysian economy had always been highly international. Prior to independence, most of the capital to develop the economy had come from Britain, raised on the London Stock Exchange. Most of the products went to international markets: Malaysian commodities like tin and palm oil went into manufacturing industries all over the world, while Malaysian rubber played an important role in the rise of the US car industry in Detroit. In the late 1980s, thanks to the liberalisation and globalisation of finance, and the search for lower production costs by companies in developed countries, emerging markets came into fashion. The British heritage of many of our institutions, and the fact that English was widely spoken, made us a relatively easy place to do business. China and India were not yet even on the map of investable markets. The Latin American debt crisis of the early 1980s was still fresh in the minds of investors.

Malaysia was strategically positioned to benefit from the globalisation of capital flows. Through its Malaysia Inc. 2.0 reforms, the government placed greater emphasis on the private sector. Government-owned companies were being privatised in deals similar to successful IPOs in the UK. On 1 January 1990, the government delisted all Malaysian-incorporated companies from the Singapore stock exchange, signalling its intent to make Kuala Lumpur a regional financial centre. To promote trading on the KLSE the government made it easier for foreign funds to invest in stocks listed on the exchange; rules governing the foreign ownership of stockbroking and fund management companies were relaxed.

When international fund managers in London, Tokyo and New York were choosing which countries to invest in, Malaysia always came close to the top of their list. At the start of 1990, the Malaysian stock market's capitalisation was only 108% of Malaysian GDP. In 1991, it rose strongly but still modestly to 115%. By the end of 1993, that percentage would triple. The main asset allocation benchmark for international funds was the MSCI Emerging Markets Index, and in 1994, at a time before China and India were investable markets, it gave Malaysia a 19.9% weighting, compared with only 1.7% in 2020.[38] Without any of us realising it, our KLSE was on the launch pad and about to take off.

That was the context in which a huge potential prize presented itself – the proposed listing of Tenaga Nasional, the national electric utility, which had recently been converted from a statutory body to a company. All the major merchant banks received the 'Request for Proposal' (RFP) in early 1991; there was little doubt that Tenaga would be raising the largest amount ever by a Malaysian company. The significance of the deal could not be overstated. By its very size it would push the boundaries of what was possible. The largest IPO until then had been Telekom Malaysia, handled by Arab in November 1990, which raised RM2.4bn and valued the company at RM9.6bn.[39] The trading volume on Telekom's first day was so large the stock had to be suspended for ten minutes to allow everyone to calm down.

The Tenaga listing was going to be too large to be digested entirely by domestic investors. For the first time, international investors would need to be attracted to a Malaysian IPO. That meant there had to be exemptions from the existing rules for IPOs set by the CIC. Whoever advised on the flotation would gain valuable international exposure *and* play a role in remaking how the IPO market worked. As challengers, we were desperate for the part.

Until the Tenaga IPO came along the CIC provided very limited room for manoeuvre. The CIC 'Guidelines', updated from time to time, was the capital markets bible, setting out not only the application process and approval criteria but also the pricing range. For instance, construction companies might find that they could apply for a listing only after achieving certain profit levels for five consecutive years, and if their application was successful, they could only raise money at an IPO price of say between five and eight times their expected profits per share. The CIC would decide on the actual IPO price within that range based on its assessment of the company's track record and future prospects. IPO prices were set below fair market value, so primary investors in the offer were almost certain to make a profit. Merchant banks and stockbroking companies could therefore underwrite the share offerings without much risk, as IPOs were almost never undersubscribed.

Demand to buy shares in an IPO was typically overwhelming; retail investors could only get an allocation by being chosen in a ballot. Some people would make multiple applications in the names of cousins, uncles, aunts, secretaries – basically anyone they could reasonably trust. If the CIC ever checked it would have found that some homes had hundreds of occupants to ensure that return application cheques would get to the mastermind first. If shares were offered to *bumiputra* investors – to meet the ownership requirements of the New Economic Policy – the allocation was decided by the Ministry of International Trade and Industry (MITI); if the company was in financial services or being privatised by the government, by the Ministry of Finance (MOF). Getting your hands on *bumiputra* shares became a sure way of making money.

The task of designing and running an IPO, which was the job of corporate finance departments like ours, was largely an exercise of complying with all these regulations and processes. Most of the decisions were taken by the CIC, including the fees merchant banks could earn from sponsoring IPOs. It was a 'nanny knows best' capital market but it would in time mature – and deals like Tenaga would bring about the change.

As the Tenaga offering would need foreign institutional investors in the primary market the price for them had to be set by demand and supply. So we designed a proposal for Tenaga's IPO which involved dual pricing: the price of the tranche of shares sold to foreign investors would be set by market forces, and the local price would be fixed at a discount to the price of the foreign tranche. Local institutions could also bid for the foreign tranche (to get more shares) if they wished.

Our proposal to become advisor to Tenaga was full of innovative ideas. At least it seemed so in our market; in reality, we adapted what had already worked in developed markets and tweaked them to our understanding of what the authorities in Malaysia would tolerate. Apart from dual pricing, we proposed an extensive pre-IPO roadshow for investors in major global financial centres, the first of its kind for a Malaysian IPO. We knew that at Tenaga the decision on which advisors to appoint would be made by committees comprising senior staff so we pushed the envelope in terms of the amounts of shares staff could get; and we went beyond CIC limits on employee ownership by including a loyalty scheme through which staff stood to be allocated more shares if they held onto their initial allocation for a few years. That was an 'innovation' adapted from one of the UK privatisations. It was not rocket science but it required initiative and drive, traits which Steve made sure were abundant in anyone working for him.

Despite our recent success in leading the league tables for corporate finance work, the conventional wisdom was that the deal would have to go to one of the big merchant banks. We were the pretenders;

the general view was that our fifteen minutes of fame were up. A friend at Arab even thumbed her nose at me: CIMB was only making up the numbers; CIMB couldn't win as it hadn't done any government privatisations; CIMB's balance sheet was too small – on she went. But we had on our side the best recent track record, some very clever ideas in our pitch and Dr Munir, who made sure that anyone who could influence the decision had heard the case for CIMB.

When the news came that CIMB had won the role as lead advisor, managing underwriter and global coordinator for the Tenaga IPO, our competitors were incredulous, and we were ecstatic. We jumped for joy around the office. But the celebrations did not last long. It was our humungous break, it would make or break our franchise; we wanted every second to make sure it would be the former.

Working on the Tenaga deal was an early turning point in my career. Although only twenty-six years of age, I was the most senior Malay in the CIMB team and connected more easily with many of the Tenaga staff involved. And yes, Abdul Razak's son was sometimes treated like a celebrity at the former government agency. Steve's team had expanded; I was promoted to assistant manager and got some rookies to boss around. I loved the unprecedented scope for creativity this project offered. And, I learned that by working with regulators you could persuade them to back innovation; show proof from other markets that they work and help draft the rules and regulations to make them feel in control.

I also became the go-to guy for the international bankers, probably because I was more at ease in facing up to self-professed 'masters of the universe', as global investment bankers saw themselves. One of my tasks was to advise Tenaga on which banks to appoint as international placement agents. Once it became apparent to the foreign bankers how much sway I had, they courted me relentlessly. We ended up working with the who's who of international banking: Barings in Europe, Daiwa in North Asia, and Salomon Brothers in the US.

I took full advantage of my popularity to learn as much as I could about global investment banking, visiting their offices and asking whatever I wanted to know. It was eye-opening to see the investment bankers in action in London, New York and Hong Kong. It made me aware of how much more CIMB could do as a business. They were what we wanted to be when we grew up.

At times the contrast was almost comical; we were so small we didn't have any specialist teams and were multi-tasking and making things up as we went along. I remember being on the phone to travel agents booking flights and hotel rooms for Tenaga management – and their spouses where necessary – to go on the roadshow, then immediately taking a call from Salomon Brothers to discuss the alternative methods for valuing the company. Straight after that, I went to the Sungei Wang Plaza shopping centre, where we were distributing retail application forms for Tenaga shares. The rule was that the broker or bank that had its stamp on the successful forms would get paid 1%. This was easy money. There was convention but not rules on how many forms the advising bank could stamp for themselves against other banks and brokers, so we not only printed more forms with CIMB stamps but also handed them out ourselves to increase the likelihood of our forms being used. No one had ever seen an operation like it: I must have been quite a sight in my fancy suit (replete with tie and braces) pleading with shoppers to take and use our IPO application forms. But it paid off quite handsomely for the firm.

The underwriting ceremony for the Tenaga IPO on 10 February 1992 is still the biggest ever in Malaysian corporate history.[40] A total of 63 companies were involved including: all 12 merchant banks and 48 of the 50 stockbroking companies in the country. All sat at a long table that spanned the length of the Tun Dr Ismail Hall at the Putra World Trade Centre, which is owned and mainly occupied by UMNO. The symbolism was hard to escape: everyone that mattered in the Malaysian capital market was there under a roof provided by the owner of political power.

The Tenaga IPO was a resounding success. We had share applications from twenty-seven countries, worth a combined total of RM9.3bn: the RM3.2bn issue was about three times subscribed. And everyone made money. The shares rose to RM8 on the company's debut on 29 February 1992 (I will always remember the extra day of the leap year), 70% above the price paid by retail investors and 20% higher than the price paid by institutional investors. The share price peaked in July that year at RM10.20, a cool 127% above the price of the retail offer.

The only fly in the ointment for CIMB was that though we had led the listing as Tenaga's main advisor we didn't make as much money from the deal as many others did. We couldn't change the CIC regulated formula of fee payments for IPOs and we didn't have the set-up to earn much in other ways. We earned a fee for underwriting shares; unfortunately our capital base was small so we couldn't underwrite much. There was also the commission on the successful retail application forms which we maximised, but still, large merchant banks like Arab profited a lot more by being able to underwrite so much more. The real winners were the foreign placement agents who were paid a high commission for placing the shares to institutional investors and afterwards made even more trading shares daily in the secondary market. Barings, Daiwa and Salomon got the lion's share based on the convention that institutional investors would buy more and sell through the agents that placed the shares to them in the first place.

We had done the heavy lifting; we designed and executed the entire process, yet most of the money was made by people who distributed shares to institutional investors and/or had bigger balance sheets. Even among Malaysian brokers, it was our competitors, the likes of Rashid Hussain Securities and Arab Malaysian Securities, that enjoyed the brokerage fees generated by our creativity. We did have a securities business – CIMB Securities – but it mainly dealt with retail rather than institutional clients.

I wouldn't say it made us look like mugs, but Steve felt like one when we showed him the breakdown of who earned what, including estimates based on secondary trading volumes on Tenaga shares. What really upset him was the thought of what other individuals had earned from his and our hard work. Bank Negara regulations stipulated that bonuses for people working in banks were capped to a maximum of six months' salary. Yet we all knew that at stockbroking companies individuals were paid commissions on income, including income from corporate finance work, which made them vastly more money than us. At CIMB the management went to considerable lengths to get around the cash bonus cap, buying staff reward-holidays and subsidising their cars. We even had staff lotteries in which everyone won a big prize – another CIMB innovation – to circumvent bonus restrictions. But there was only so much management could do before they risked Bank Negara's ire.

The Tenaga listing catapulted CIMB into becoming a major force in corporate finance. Between 1991 and 1994 alone CIMB was responsible for 42% of the gross proceeds raised via IPOs. In 1989 its share of the advisory fees earned by Malaysian merchant banks was about 15%; in 1994 it was 38%. We were on our way.

Unfortunately, we would have to go on without many of the people who got us here. The deal marked the end of an era in the small world that I operated in. Steve decided he needed to make big bucks so he gave management an implied ultimatum about compensation he knew they couldn't meet. He then set up a new unit combining broking and corporate finance at TA Securities, Malaysia's largest retail brokerage, and took Kok Teong, Pin How, and a few others with him. Dr Munir's reputation was much enhanced by Tenaga's success and he was appointed the first chairman of the newly formed Securities Commission in April 1993. Robert Cheim took over as CEO, Choon Thye took Steve's position as head of Corporate Finance, and I was rewarded with a promotion to manager and head of the Privatisation Unit in the Corporate Finance Department. Not bad for someone three years out of university, I flattered myself.

Yet I was also hungry for a fresh challenge. I had done three years in corporate finance and my sense of self-interest and (probably inflated) sense of self-worth kicked in. I also wondered why I was working so hard and not earning as much as people elsewhere in finance who seemed to be no brighter nor harder working. It didn't help that suitors started calling to tempt me: I had mouth-watering offers from Lehman Brothers and Merrill Lynch, both of which had glitzy offices in Hong Kong. Both banks had seen me at work: Lehman when we collaborated to raise a $600m Yankee Bond for Tenaga, just after the listing, and Merrill when we collaborated to issue Malaysia's first ever call warrants (on Maybank shares). At the time, both were cutting-edge and lucrative (for the investment banks!) capital market products. They offered me more than ten times my then-salary and a variable bonus each year *plus* a signing-on fee: I felt like a top footballer. My head was turned.

Before this flirtation with Wall Street outposts in Hong Kong could go any further I spoke to Robert Cheim, with whom I had developed a good rapport as he overcame his initial scepticism about whether I would make the grade and I increasingly found Steve's idiosyncrasies hard to stomach. He suggested I take on a new challenge to build an institutional stockbroking business of the kind we so sorely lacked: 'You keep complaining that we don't have this kind of business and we're losing out so why don't you build one?' We spoke at length about how much the old British merchant bank model had lost out to US investment banks. Robert assured me he would support my idea that CIMB should operate more like a US investment bank by developing CIMB Securities' institutional broking business and integrating it with the merchant bank. At the same time Gary Loong, a senior dealer whom I personally liked, invited me in to be a part of his team, to show me the ropes and share his clients.

I went home and drew up a list of positives and negatives: becoming a Hong Kong-based global investment banker was on one side; on the other, helping to build the institutional business at CIMB Securities.

Staying in Malaysia mattered enormously to me, not just because it was my home. It was an optimistic, even heady, time in the country. Mahathir had only just launched his ambitious Vision 2020, to turn Malaysia into a fully developed economy within less than thirty years. The vision was not just economic. It looked forward to a self-confident Malaysia that would be mature, liberated from the psychological shackles of colonialism, ethical, tolerant, democratic, scientific, prosperous and progressive. That Malaysia would be defined by a sense of ambitious and proud patriotism rather than the divisions created by ethnicity and genealogy, history and religion. Mahathir wanted the Malays to grasp the future, to assert themselves confidently rather than being trapped in a sense of victimhood. At the end of the book I will have more to say about why Malaysia needs a renewed national vision of this kind.

I did not take the decision entirely on my own.

The year 1992 marked an even more important turning point for me personally. Azlina and I got married in early January 1992 before the Tenaga flotation was launched. We had met at a family function in KL and became friends when she enrolled in Bristol at the start of my second year but only started dating when I was at Cambridge in 1988. Azlina would often visit her sister Afizah, who was an undergraduate at Cambridge, and on hearing of one of Azlina's impending trips I orchestrated an elaborate plan for her to be invited to an exclusive Dining Club dinner and have her seated next to me. We finally hit it off that evening and never looked back. Azlina has a strong moral compass not dissimilar to that of her father, (Tan Sri) Aziz Taha, a strict and highly principled former governor of Bank Negara, who famously resigned as governor in 1985 on a matter of principle and in conflict with the two most powerful men in the country, Mahathir and

Daim. Azlina is one of the most determined people I know. A graduate of economics and accounting who went on to work at KPMG and then at Barings Securities, she totally changed tack after our children were born, studying English Literature part-time at Exeter University, while juggling the demands of young twins (and a busy and often absent husband.) She would go on to achieve the remarkable feat of completing two Masters and a Doctorate, all from Oxford University. Back in 1992, the timing of our wedding wasn't ideal, but it wasn't something that was in our control. In traditional Malay families it is the parents that decide everything. Festivities were spread over three nights – the *akad nikah* – and his and her family hosted celebrations at the Kuala Lumpur Shangri-La and Hilton hotels respectively. At my family's dinner reception, I remember walking down the aisle hand in hand with my beautiful new wife, in front of about 1,500 people, including five Sultans, the PM and his entire cabinet, and from the corner of my eye I could see CIMB colleagues entertaining Tenaga management at their tables and feeling guilty for not being with the team and our clients. If Azlina knew of my thoughts she might have changed her mind; instead she would learn about my obsession with work and CIMB the hard way over many years!

I discussed my potential move to a Wall Street bank with Azlina and we decided that I was too invested in CIMB to leave. I wanted to see how far I could take it. With Robert's support I thought I would be able to make more of an impact on the whole organisation than if I were just another banker at Merrill Lynch or Lehman Brothers. I knew that at CIMB Securities I should also be able to make a bit more money, to make up for turning down the mouth-watering offers from the US banks. As it turned out, I timed my entry into stockbroking so perfectly that I was even able to redefine the whole notion of what mouth-watering income meant to me.

RIDING THE BULL

In April 1993 I was given a shiny new title: senior vice-president (SVP) of CIMB Securities. Perhaps there is a lesson here: Beware of jobs that come with fancy titles.

When I arrived for work at the seventh floor of the Promet Building on Jalan Sultan Ismail, across the road from the merchant bank, I found something that resembled a civil war more than an institutional securities trading floor. It turned out I was only one of seven SVPs, most of whom ran their own self-contained team as if it were their own brokerage business. CIMB Securities was the playing field on which they competed, not only with other firms but with one another too. They were meant to deal for institutions – fund managers, pension funds and corporations. Yet they each had retail clients too, friends and no doubt their own accounts as well. There was no coordination, which led to a lot of duplication, friction and wastage. What I saw was alarming, financially (we weren't making as much money as we should); organisationally (it was open warfare); and ethically (I discovered some very dubious practices, such as staff recommending clients to buy shares they were selling personally). But then the industry as a whole could be called the Wild East: rules, regulations and infrastructure were basic. The stock exchange was controlled by brokers themselves. It was a club for self-preservation. Insider trading was rampant because there was simply no effective policing. The Securities Commission was still finding its feet as the new capital markets regulator.

I spent the first few months dealing in shares for some of Gary's clients but mainly learning and thinking about the best way forward for a business that was quite new to me. There was definitely a better way, but exactly what was that, and how do we get there?

Eventually I reached the conclusion that what the institutional business at CIMB Securities needed first and foremost was a leader, someone to lay out a strategy, operating rules, coordinate actions and ensure conformance. This was an obvious opportunity for me, I just needed to convince everyone that I should be the leader. I started by assuring the team heads that we would all make more money by working together to beat the competition rather than trying to beat one another. I then showed how we could organise the business – research, distribution, sales and dealing – and allocate and demarcate clients fairly. As the overall boss, I said I would be their link with the merchant bank to bring them referrals, and represent their interest versus management.

They were all tired of the infighting and quickly welcomed my idea. We got organised, and I got a fancier title – executive director of CIMB Securities – and a seat on the board of the company. It was a timely move; not only were the equities indices climbing everywhere but so were trading volumes and equity deals. Our stock market's capitalisation was worth 150% of Malaysian GDP in 1992; a year later it was 320% and, after dipping down to 240% in 1994 and 1995, it rose again in 1996 to more than 300%. To put that in context, in 2020, the Malaysian stock market was worth about 108% of GDP. In the mid-1990s we were on a crazy, dizzying ride. CIMB Securities' pre-tax profit would rise tenfold from RM5.3m in 1992 to RM55.9m in 1993, and then RM60.1m in 1994. In contrast, the parent merchant bank only made RM17.3m in 1992, RM19.7m in 1993 and RM32.1m in 1994. The tail was wagging the dog, and I was now conducting the tail.

I was working long hours in a heady atmosphere. After a noisy day in the trading room, there were often raucous nights in restaurants and clubs entertaining clients or just celebrating amongst ourselves. Years later I would joke that it was like being in *The Wolf of Semantan*, a riff on *The Wolf of Wall Street* (KLSE was located in Semantan, and CIMB was relocated to the area in 1995). An irony, but we will come to that later.

It was easy to get carried away. I thought I was a brilliant equity salesman because every stock I recommended went up, and usually quite quickly. My international clients seemed to love me. The truth, though, was that every other stock went up as well and they loved anyone helping them make returns they could only dream about in developed markets at that time. It was like shooting fish in a barrel. Everyone seemed to be at it. I overheard a lady outside our retail trading floor who was boasting about making money from investing in a company called Omega. When asked what line of business the company was in, she said, 'Obviously sell watches, lah': Omega was a listed stockbroking company. I visited my optician, and during the entire time he was testing my eyesight he was pleading to be hired as a *remisier* (commissioned retail broker).

Brokerage fees were high (1% for retail and institutional sales; 0.5% for dealing with foreign brokers). On top of that dealers would often be found adjusting the average prices they disclosed to clients to make a spread for the company and personally earn their share of it. The whole commission framework was based on historical volumes, and never in anyone's dreams would volumes go up so much; in 1992, 19bn units were traded on the KL stock exchange for a value of RM51bn. In 1993, there were 107bn trades worth RM387bn.[41] Assuming everything else being the same, there was 6.6 times more commissions to be shared amongst KL's community of dealers. I had arrived just in time for a gold rush.

My last monthly pay-cheque in corporate finance had been RM7,000; my first quarterly commission as an equity salesman was

RM90,000 (on top of my monthly salary). And that was the least I made in a quarter throughout my three years at CIMB Securities. When I was at Oundle, the parents of a friend once took me out to Sunday lunch in their Jaguar. I always remembered settling into the leather seats telling myself that I must own one one day. Now, at the age of twenty-eight, I was going to and from work in the back of a chauffeur-driven Jaguar. I appeared on the December 1994 cover of the *Men's Review* magazine with the headline 'Young, free and bullish' under a picture of me wearing a Gucci suit and braces. If I saw my son doing the same today I would feel *menyampah*, a Malay word that doesn't have an equivalent in the English language: 'like throwing up' would probably be the closest translation. I was quite obnoxiously self-confident. It was a market full of bull, and I was lapping it all up.

I was enjoying the Wild East, but soon it started to wear a bit thin. I discovered that while I enjoyed making money, it wasn't fulfilling enough. Building the business and the team gave me more satisfaction. Three years in, I was making money hand over fist, but I felt I was getting the balance wrong. Not only did I grow increasingly uncomfortable with the lifestyle – what would my serious and frugal father think? – I knew I wasn't intellectually engaged. One of the lessons I learned at CIMB Securities was that money can be a trap as well as a means to gain freedom. If you only follow the money you become dependent on it: it drives you rather than the other way around, and you may reach a dead end, because you stop thinking about the world around you.

I also started wondering about the sustainability of what was happening in the stock market and the stockbroking model. It really was too good to be true – surely it couldn't be long before the music stopped.

One day in January 1996, Robert asked me how I was doing, and I shared my doubts. He surprised me: Robert asked me to return to the merchant bank to become deputy CEO. Together we would manage the merchant bank and the securities firm as if it were a fully integrated investment banking business. Robert is quiet and thoughtful;

we nicknamed him 'Uncle Bob' because he reminded us of the uncle who would proffer only sincere advice. You never need to second-guess him. The years of putting in long hours, of weekend work and constant stress, were getting to him. Even though he was only in his forties, he was preparing to step aside in two to three years' time, he said, and I would be in position to become Group CEO in his place. In the meantime, while he was still running the show, I could learn about other parts of the business, such as lending, treasury and bonds, in preparation for the top job.

I became deputy chief executive of CIMB in April 1996, after successfully building a competitive institutional securities franchise at CIMB Securities that put us among the top local institutional brokers, maybe just a peg behind RHB Securities and one or two others. When the securities business was combined with corporate finance, though, we were the strongest across what was technically known as the origination and distribution of equity capital market products. I was not yet thirty, but I did not harbour any doubt that I deserved my new role even if almost the entire management team at the merchant bank had been more senior than me when I left three years earlier. I was so sure of myself and eager to get to the top.

I was determined, though, to be a diligent, helpful deputy to Robert. Being a good deputy is not easy (something my father knew well). Try to do too much and you are accused of getting in the way and being impatient to take your boss's job; do too little and you are dismissed as a lightweight. It turned out that I didn't have to worry: In June 1996, Dr Munir, as chairman of the SC, decided that the industry should set up a new stock exchange for high growth and technology companies; named MESDAQ, it would be Malaysia's answer to NASDAQ. Without any notice Dr Munir called a group of industry CEOs and announced (without warning me) that I would chair the 'Industry Action Committee' to set it up. That gave me a lot to chew on, so it was easy for me not to get in Robert's way.

It was 1996, and everything seemed to be going in the right direction. My career seemed aligned with the financial markets and the state of the world. Communism had been defeated; the Iron Curtain had come down; liberal democracy and free markets were spreading around the world: everything was going up, up, up. There were bad days, of course, but they quickly passed.

Success generally inclines you to carry on, to do more of what you're already doing. One of the key skills in business is to spot the approach of changes in sentiment and direction. And to do that, you have to spy out signals, things that run counter to the conventional wisdom. Looking back on the heady boom of the 1990s, I noticed several warning signs but didn't join the dots or take them seriously enough for that matter.

One such warning sign arrived early one morning in February 1995. Johari Muid, a senior dealer at CIMB Securities, arrived unannounced and somewhat flustered at my home shouting and waving what turned out to be a printed copy of a Reuters article. I couldn't believe his words 'Barings has collapsed.' *The* Barings? *The* Barings which founded and owned CIMB until 1993? *The* Barings where Azlina was a director at their KL research office? And the purported reason for it was even more incredible: the hidden transactions of one derivatives trader in a Singapore subsidiary company. The episode said a lot about the fragility of financial institutions, the limitations of regulatory oversight and new risks emanating from the culture of overly incentivised staff and management in financial institutions.

There were also signs of things going awry at home. I could not help but ask myself about the incestuous links between politics and business being created by the way the NEP was being used to justify all sorts of nefarious purpose. There was already ample evidence that the first of my father's legacies – the institutions and programmes he created to lift up the Malays – was now being used to line the pockets of the few rather than the many. The abuse of the system my father initiated nagged away at me.

Under the NEP, a public company needed to be at least 30% owned by *bumiputra*. As shares became more valuable and IPO shares became even more attractive, sure things, the politics of share allocations, deciding who would get shares, became intense. It wasn't just IPOs: after being listed, a company would need to issue new shares (at a discount to the market price) if the *bumiputra* shareholding fell below the 30% threshold. The rules were always kept ambiguous enough that ministers and their officials needed to make the final decisions about who would get the shares. For instance, a *bumiputra* director could be allocated a large portion of shares but only if he had been on the board for a minimum number of years. But there could also be exemptions, making the approvers very powerful indeed; they could decide who would be a millionaire literally overnight, or at least after listing day.

I learned in my first year in corporate finance that the process for allocating *bumiputra* shares was far from transparent. On one IPO, as soon as we received CIC's approval to proceed, the file disappeared from my desk without explanation. Try as I might I could not find it. A couple of days later my boss returned it, without explanation but with one crucial change: the name of the *bumiputra* shareholder, the person getting most of the 30% allocation of shares in the company, had been inserted. At the listing ceremony a wizened and slightly confused Malay chap turned up as a new member of the board of directors. It was, to say the least, extremely opaque, if not shady. What I did know was that this was being done in the name of the NEP. How does making this one individual Malay wealthy overnight help to progress the Malay race? Perhaps they weren't really his shares; perhaps he was holding them in trust for someone else, a politician, maybe, a political party even.

When I was handling the Tenaga IPO, I was taken by surprise by the long list of individuals who had been allocated *bumiputra* shares, not least because it meant a lot of laborious work for me to contact so many recipients to send them forms to fill and so on. The usual practice was to allocate most of the shares to federal and state government funds and agencies, such as Permodalan Nasional Berhad (PNB), to benefit large numbers of unit holders or help fund programmes for the people. Only later did I find a plausible explanation for the allocation of shares to so many individuals. In the UMNO party elections of 1993, Deputy President Ghafar Baba was heavily defeated by Anwar Ibrahim. It was an inside joke that Ghafar was 'electrocuted' because Anwar as minister of finance had been able to distribute Tenaga shares to many UMNO delegates and their associates. The NEP started life as a scheme to redistribute wealth to reduce inequality; I was seeing it being used as a tool for political funding and for individual politicians to gain and hold on to power.

I also noticed all sorts of corporate governance malpractices, some bordering on corruption. When I asked why CIMB Securities never got much business from local investment institutions, I was told that to do so we would have to be willing to kick-back commissions to those giving us the business. I refused to believe it only worked that way and personally went to see all the main local institutions. We made some headway, but then at the end of one trading day the head of investment at a government fund called to request that from the large quantity of shares that I bought for the fund I should book a few that were at the lowest prices into his personal account. I declined, and he noticeably gave me less business after that. I am not claiming to be a saint: I didn't report him to his superiors, nor to the authorities for that matter. I played safe; I did not want to rock the boat. I too was enjoying the ride. However, I stayed within my own legal and ethical boundaries.

Too often rules were being flouted, by the very people who should have been upholding them, for the sake of making a quick buck or winning political favours. At the end of his life my father had worried that corruption was beginning to seep into the system. He was right to have worried: it would become deeply entrenched as political influence and government power overrode competitive, market forces.

It wasn't just money politics, governance and corruption, though; it was also hubris and wastefulness. MESDAQ was an example. By mid-1997, MESDAQ was ready with its rules and regulations and a trading system, and I handed over the project to a full-time management team. As the project evolved, though, it became clear to me that MESDAQ should have been set up by the KLSE, which had the infrastructure and experience, but the Securities Commission wanted a new exchange because it felt that the KLSE was being too independent-minded. MESDAQ cost so much more and had difficulties getting brokers to come on board because it was not set up by the KLSE. And it was also clear that we were putting the cart before the horse; we had an exchange before we had the entrepreneurial companies or venture capitalists to support them. In time, MESDAQ would find its logical place – in March 2002 it was placed under the KLSE (renamed BURSA by then), but still not many companies to list on it.

Money politics, corruption, poor governance and hubris of the go-go 1990s would inevitably meet its comeuppance. Spectacularly so.

THE RECKONING: THE AFC AND ITS AFTERMATH

In July 1997, everything still seemed rosy. Occasional warning signs could be written off as mere blips: Asian emerging economies were booming, as were the stock market valuations of their companies. The average prediction by research houses was for the Kuala Lumpur Composite Index (the KLCI) to rise from 1,209 points at the start of the year to 1,400 points at its end. It was as if we had found the secret recipe for economic dynamism, leaving the rest of the world to look on with envy. Huge amounts of wealth were being created in a short space of time; stock price rises were making heroes of CEOs and businessmen. A little more than three decades earlier Malaysia had been a fairly simple economy dependent on commodities, agriculture and fishing dominated by firms with their roots in the colonial era. Now, along with others in the region, it was touted as a powerhouse, driven by a young, educated population with an amazing working ethic, unrecognisable as the economy my father had presided over. High economic growth year after year all seemed to be a vindication of the Malaysia Inc. 2.0 strategy pursued by Mahathir's government, based on close linkages between government, favoured businessmen and banks. It seemed that nothing could stop us from realising the ambitious goals of Vision 2020. No wonder it all went to people's heads.

There was a kernel of truth to that optimistic story. It was just that it overlooked something quite fundamental; we were living in a bubble created by financial flows rather than the real economy. Capital was flowing into the region, causing shares and other asset prices to rise far beyond what was economically justifiable. In their eagerness to get a piece of the action, international investors were happy to believe all sorts of stories – a new government contract or licence, a merger or an acquisition, investment in new production capacity – you name it. As share and asset prices rose, so the balance sheets of these companies looked stronger, enabling them to take on more debt to make further investments and acquisitions, which in turn led to further asset price rises. It looked like a virtuous economic cycle but in reality it was a spiral of inflated valuations underpinned by an influx of foreign money desperate for investments that would yield a high return. While the markets were going up, investors were only interested in good news and turned a blind eye to any concerns or question marks they might have. Once the bubble burst, markets plunged and people panicked, and only bad news seemed to travel.

What happened in Thailand in the second half of 1997 came as a rude shock. The Thai economy had seemed in robust health, growing strongly with its currency stable by being pegged to the dollar. Its government finances seemed sound and sensibly managed. Yet in July, a speculative run on the baht that had started in May picked up pace and turned into a fully fledged currency crisis, which was dubbed the Tom Yum Kung crisis after the soup. Financial markets had turned hot and sour at the same time.

The Thai baht was pegged at a rate of 25 to the US dollar, which was fine as long as people wanted to buy Thai baht to invest in the country. That summer, however, money suddenly started to flow out of the country. No one seems to know what started the run, but to maintain the baht's rate against the dollar, the country's central bank stepped in to buy up baht that was being offloaded. That quickly used up its scarce foreign reserves. Interest rates were raised to attract investors into baht assets, but many Thai companies had taken on too much debt in the previous few years, and higher interest bills hurt them. The larger companies that borrowed in foreign currencies were hit by a double whammy of higher rates and a weaker baht. As the baht continued to be sold down, national reserves ran thin, and the government had to stop defending the fixed exchange rate with the dollar. It was a painful defeat for the government at the hands of the financial markets. By January 1998 the baht had slumped to 50% of its pre-crisis levels, and the Thai stock market index was down a whopping 75%.[42]

The Tom Yum Kung crisis set off a chain reaction of panic across the region.[43] Every major economy in East Asia was affected as investors who had wantonly pumped money into the region in the previous years now were rushing to take it out. Indonesia and South Korea were badly affected, but so too were the Philippines and Malaysia. Other markets such as Hong Kong and Singapore, Taiwan and Japan were also affected but buffered somewhat by their stronger economic fundamentals, large reserves and lower reliance on debt.

In the second half of 1997 and during 1998, these economies suffered the same trauma to different degrees: a run on the currency; investors pulling out their money; stock markets in freefall; foreign reserves depleted; interest rate rises to protect the currency that made life more difficult for households, companies and government which had gone further into debt. It was a vicious vortex, the flip side of the dizzying bull run that had preceded it. It was to have political consequences too. In Thailand, PM Chavalit Yongchaiyudh felt compelled to step down in November 1997. In Indonesia, people took to the streets in May 1998, forcing the end of the thirty-year rule of President Suharto, who had come to power at the end of *konfrontasi* in 1967. Indonesia would go through many years of unstable politics and several attempts to recalibrate its entire system. Dynasties were crumbling in business and politics.

The crisis took a heavy toll on Malaysia. In the five years before the crisis you needed between 2.36 and 2.50 ringgit to buy one US dollar. In 1997, the ringgit followed the baht and almost virtually halved in value to reach a low of 4.88 on 7 January 1998. The KLSE dropped by 50% by the end of 1997. The ratings agencies downgraded Malaysian government debt to junk status. Despite the financial turmoil the Malaysian economy still managed to grow by 6.8% in the year the crisis hit. The following year, however, what had begun as a financial and currency crisis enveloped the real economy, affecting millions of people and their families. The economy contracted by 6.7%. Daim Zainuddin remarked that a few weeks of currency speculation had undone fifty years of painstaking economic development. As the ringgit halved in value the average Malaysian saw his per capita income fall from the equivalent of $5,000 a year to close to $2,500. People who had only just clawed their way out of poverty were being plunged back into it. The path to Vision 2020's promised land suddenly looked incredibly steep.

In Malaysia, the causes of the Asian Financial Crisis (AFC) are disputed to this day. Mahathir was not alone in blaming foreign speculators for plotting to bring down successful developing countries. While speculation certainly played a role in the crisis itself, to find its underlying causes you have to look at why the preceding boom was unsustainable. In the mid-1990s, when I was patting myself on the back for being a brilliant equity salesman, a nasty cocktail of factors was coming together.

In the aftermath it was easy to see that the signs of economic vulnerability were there in the numbers. The total amount of mobile capital (short-term borrowings plus portfolio flows) jumped from $6bn in 1990 to $50bn in 1997. Yet foreign reserves stagnated at 1993 levels of $30bn, driven by high imports and Malaysians investing overseas, leaving insufficient funds to counter a rush of outflows. There was a massive credit boom, outstanding loans to GDP averaged

86% in the 1980s jumped to 120% in 1994 and 160% in mid-1996, driven by loans to the property sector and shares. Although Bank Negara and the Ministry of Finance officials did express concerns, they came across as party poopers, not least to a leadership that was determined Malaysia would be a developed country by 2020, and there was just so much that still needed to be done to reach that goal. Of course, research houses and bankers were not going to spoil the party; they were experts at finding reasons why the market would keep rising.

I hold my hands up: I never saw it coming. I assumed that if sophisticated international investors and investment banks wanted to put their money into Malaysia, they knew what they were doing. I never seriously contemplated the other side of the equation; the risk that investors would rush to the exit and the carnage they would leave in their wake. As is now clear, the Asian Financial Crisis was a moment of reckoning, the coming together of two toxic cultures.

On the one side was the rampant greed of developed market investors and their financial advisors. That was matched by money politics, corruption, poor governance and hubris in the investee countries to different degrees. The flood of easy money into the Malaysian economy enabled those in power, be that in government or business, to entertain all sorts of unrealistic ambitions. Systemic weaknesses, a lack of proper checks and balances, governance and regulation, in markets as well as in government, allowed these ambitions to be pursued because the right questions were never asked. Add to all that the influence of unregulated money politics and it is not surprising it all became combustible. The boom created many business empires, built on political favours and preferential loans, rather than on serving customers and creating value. These hollow empires were exposed by the crisis.

One project was emblematic of the flaws in Malaysian business practices at the time: the huge, very expensive and deeply troubled

Bakun hydroelectric dam project in Sarawak. Bakun was to be one of the largest rock-filled, concrete-covered dams in the world; as large as Singapore.[44] It was controversial on both economic and environmental grounds. There was insufficient demand in Sarawak and neighbouring Sabah for the electricity it would generate, and supplying peninsular Malaysia would require 648 kilometres of submarine cables. The building of the dam across the Balui river threatened to be an environmental disaster. Yet Dr Mahathir was determined to revive a scheme that had been shelved twice, in the 1960s and again in the1980s; it was the kind of mega-project that was all the rage at the time. To question it would have been to invite accusations that you lacked the scale of ambition to back bold projects that would modernise Malaysia.

In January 1994, the contract to build the dam was awarded to a local company, Ekran, a timber company which had never built a dam before. At the time it was best known for building hotels in Langkawi at record speed at Mahathir's behest. Its principal shareholder was a rather brash, politically connected Sarawakian Chinese named (Tan Sri) Ting Phek Khiing. Ekran estimated it would cost close to $5.7bn to build the dam. It would be the prime contractor, awarding sub-contracts to the likes of ABB, the Swedish-Swiss engineering group, which would provide the turbines. A project company, Bakun Hydroelectric Company (BHC), would be set up with Ekran as its dominant shareholder at 32% while the balance was to be shared amongst various federal and Sarawak government entities. What was disturbing was how Ekran was anointed as the project lead: there was no tender or indeed attempt to justify its selection, and government agencies were being assigned to provide financial support to the project. The natural suspicion was that Ekran would be able to profit handsomely from contracts awarded to friendly parties and thereafter be relatively unconcerned about the future well-being of the project company it shared with government agencies.

Long Live The King.
My grandfather, Hussein, in London on May 1937 during the coronation of King George VI.

Seated on the front from left to right are HRH Tuanku Abdul Rahman of Negeri Sembilan and also Malaysia's first King, HRH Sultan Sir Abu Bakar (Sultan Pahang).

Standing on the back row from left to right are Ungku Mohamad (Tengku Muda Pahang), Tengku Muhammad (Tengku Panglima Perang Pahang) and Hussein.

The translator. In 1943, 21-year-old Abdul Razak (seated second from right) served as a translator for the Japanese Army while also being part of Force 136, the resistance movement.

The world is their oyster. Abdul Razak and his fellow law students in London in 1948. On Abdul Razak's left is his best friend Taib Andak.

Leaders at tea. Abdul Razak sharing tea with Hussein on his right and Hussein's father, Onn on Abdul Razak's far left. Probably sometime in 1950 when Hussein handed over the position of UMNO Youth Chief to Abdul Razak. Hussein would go on to leave UMNO with Onn, rejoin after Abdul Razak became President and then succeed Abdul Razak as PM. Hussein was married to Rahah's sister Suhaila.

Young bride. In 1952, 30-year old Abdul Razak weds 18 year old Rahah

First Cabinet. Malaya's first cabinet meeting on 10 September 1957. Abdul Razak was appointed as Deputy Prime Minister and Minister of Defence

Father of Development. Abdul Razak was most passionate about rural development and would travel all over the country to monitor progress and meet the people. Here he is pictured in Jeli, Kelantan in August 1961.

A keris for JFK. Abdul Razak presenting President John Kennedy a gift in the Oval Office on April 1963. Years later I could show this photo to Caroline Kennedy who remembers playing with the keris (dagger) together with her brother, John Kennedy Jr.

Negotiating Malaysia. Tunku and Abdul Razak met with British Prime Minister Harold Macmillan in London on November 1963 to discuss the merger of Malaya with Sarawak, North Borneo and Singapore

Sous Chef. Watching my mother cook for Hari Raya festivities in the kitchen at Seri Taman circa 1971.

Farewell. Abdul Razak saying goodbye to an awkward 7 year-old me in July 1973 as he was watched by his deputy, Dr Ismail. Abdul Razak was leaving to attend the CHOGM in Canada. This would be the last time he saw Dr Ismail who passed away on 2 August 1973.

Towering father. Trying out Dad's new camera on him, in the garden of Seri Taman. Circa 1974.

Annual family photo. Abdul Razak insisted we a took a formal family portrait once every year. This was the 1974 edition, taken in the courtyard of Seri Taman.

Great diplomatic foresight. Tun Razak met Chairman Mao Zedong in Beijing on 29 May 1974. His was the first official visit by an ASEAN leader.

Last photo. A gaunt looking Abdul Razak in London's Hyde Park with (seated on his right) High Commissioner Datuk Abdullah Ali, Taib Andak, (standing right to left) Johari, Nazim, Nizam and an unidentified security officer.

Seri Taman was a village. A final photo with many of the staff that looked after us at Seri Taman. Taken in July 1976, a few days before we moved out. I am seated far left.

To further help finance the project, BHC would be allowed to undertake an IPO under new rules for infrastructure companies, which meant that the project company did not even need a profit record. But first, to fund its stake in BHC, Ekran called a rights issue of RM1.5bn in May 1997. Ekran was a longstanding BOC and CIMB client so we had been appointed as advisors for the rights issue. Soon after, though, we became increasingly nervous about what our client was taking on and agonised about whether the issue should proceed. We concluded that we were in too deep and unless we dared to tell Mahathir that the project had to be abandoned, we had to support our client as no one else would. The only mitigation we could think of was to insert a clause that required Ekran to return the rights money to shareholders if the project was cancelled, which we felt was quite likely by then, given the scale of funds required by BHC and the deteriorating economic environment.

The rights issue was an abject failure; 63% of the shares were not taken up.[45] As the major underwriter, CIMB had to take up the bulk of the unsubscribed shares. Ting had committed to buy them back from us but we knew it was unlikely he would have the money to do so. We prayed for the project to be called off, because that would trigger the clause that compelled him and Ekran to return the money to shareholders. We would have to sit and wait.

We didn't need to wait for long; almost as soon as the AFC hit, the project became untenable. In September 1997, Mahathir announced that the Bakun project would be shelved once again. We immediately demanded that Ekran repay the unused money from the rights issue, only to find most of it had already been used up.[46] We complained to the Securities Commission that Ekran had broken the terms of the rights issue, but nothing was done about it. CIMB had to write down the value of the shares, a sum that exceeded the total operating profit of the rest of our operations. As a result, we made a loss of RM87.6m in 1998: it was the only year we didn't make money in the course of my career at CIMB. It was only a small consolation that the legal process took its course and Ting was declared bankrupt, although that took some thirteen years.

The ill-fated Bakun dam project was a wake-up call for many of us. It was staggering that the client could, in broad daylight, walk away with most of the proceeds of a public rights issue without anyone being willing to do anything about it. Perhaps Ting felt protected by his close relationship to those in power, and everyone around seemed to play to that tune accordingly. The potential for this kind of incestuous relationship between business and politics was implicit in the model which combines an activist state and unregulated money politics; in the 1990s the potential became a well-honed system of patronage and clientelism which thrived on centralised and unchecked power and massive inflows of funds into the growing economy. The AFC marked the unravelling of the economic and financial aspects of that system.

The consequences of the AFC were deeply personal as well; people's livelihoods and careers got caught up in the crisis. Many stories left a lasting impression on me, but none more so than the sorry tale of Tommy Ng, one of our equities dealers.

At the height of the crisis Mahathir chose to point the finger of blame at foreign 'short-sellers', in other words those traders who sold shares they did not possess pushing prices down and buying them back at much lower prices than they had sold them. It was a legitimate way to make money, but when markets are falling in panic short-sellers amplify the fall in share prices. Mahathir called out hedge funds and even named one, George Soros, as the main protagonist. The hunt for the evil 'short-sellers' was on and the Securities Commission duly obliged.

Maybe it was because our office was located next door to the Commission; maybe it was because I issued an instruction to staff that we should be as helpful as possible as the body was run by our ex-CEO, Dr Munir, but the only short-selling case the investigators pursued involved CIMB, our dealer Tommy Ng, and our client Crédit Lyonnais Securities Asia (CLSA). The accusation was that we were guilty of short-selling 22,000 Amcorp, 76,500 Public Finance (foreign) and 141,000 Proton shares – quite paltry amounts in a market which trades billions of shares a day. The reality was that Mercury Asset Management, a major fund management company in London, sold the shares in question via CLSA but failed to deliver the share certificates in the requisite time, as was not uncommon. Such a failure is rectified by a process called 'buy-in' by the stock exchange: millions of shares are bought-in each day. To execute the trade, CLSA passed the orders to CIMB Securities, as CLSA was not a member of the KLSE. We would not even know the ultimate client's identity unless the client or CLSA chose to tell us.

At first, only CIMB Securities and CLSA were charged. When our company was summoned to court at the historic Sultan Abdul Samad building, on Dataran Merdeka (Independence Square), to hear the charges of short-selling read against it, I decided to attend the proceedings with our dealer Tommy and others. Tommy was sitting next to me when suddenly officers from the Securities Commission came in and marched him out onto the kerb of the main road outside the court room. They handcuffed him with press photographers in attendance. I protested to the officer in charge at the way Tommy was being treated only to be literally shoved away.

Throughout what followed we stood by Tommy completely. The idea that the trades were short sales was ludicrous. Furthermore, I knew Tommy had only taken the CLSA order on behalf of its regular CIMB dealer who just happened to be away from his desk those few fateful minutes. All he did was write down the order for the usual dealer to execute. I remember consulting my brother Johari, who was then a worldly-wise lawyer at Shearn Delamore, about the injustice of it all, and his prescient words to me were: 'Jay, in Malaysia today, just because you are innocent doesn't mean you won't be found guilty.'

The judge in charge of the case, I am sure, didn't understand the workings of financial markets. Tommy was found guilty, fined and had his licence withdrawn. The judge died before he could write his ruling, so to appeal would have meant a retrial, which would have taken years. Tommy didn't want to appeal – the five years he had been through were traumatic enough. CIMB paid Tommy's fine and proceeded with our appeal, which we eventually won.

The personal cost to Tommy was immense, although he and his family bore it stoically. We continued to employ him, but his licence had been withdrawn, so he couldn't deal in shares. His wife took his young sons to live with her family in Los Angeles. The boys were old enough to know that something was wrong and can recall their pain and confusion about what had happened to their father. Tommy was turned into a notorious figure in Malaysia, and the family lived in the shadow of shame. With a conviction on his record, Tommy found it difficult to move to the US to be with them and find work. It was years before he succeeded. Now he is fit-as-a-fiddle and proudly promoting the Malaysian takeaway food business his sons have set up in Canada.

At the time, I felt so powerless. I wrote Dr Munir a letter bluntly telling him he was wrong and sent a copy to every single CIMB member of staff. The injustice of Tommy's case was one reason I became so committed to doing my bit to evolve a better corporate Malaysia.

It is perhaps true of all crises that they expose underlying weaknesses in systems that could be ignored during the good times. That was certainly true of the AFC: it was a moment of reckoning for the system created in the name of Malaysia Inc. 2.0, one based on dense linkages between preferred business leaders and politicians, in which banks were often willing accomplices. This incestuous system of patronage and clientelism was a case study in bad governance – the very opposite of checks and balances. It was unsustainable economically and financially. Too much of it depended on financial engineering and stock prices as opposed to value creation, innovation and productivity growth. Malaysia did too little in this period to move into the new growth areas driven by entrepreneurship and technology that other Asian economies were developing. Nor did this system achieve the social goals of the NEP, to lift up the Malays as a group. The system was failing on its social and economic missions while encouraging an epidemic of bad business practices.

It was clear after the AFC that Malaysia would need far-reaching reforms. Despite Mahathir's rhetoric on the causes of the AFC his actions showed he agreed. I was encouraged by the fact that substantial reforms were launched, especially in the economy and the corporate sector. But as we will see later the failure to reform fundamentally the system as a whole, especially the political component and the NEP meant that it wasn't long before many of the much maligned bad practices would come to dominate corporate Malaysia once more.

The AFC had profound lessons for Malaysia but also for me personally. Two legs of my father's legacy were now in direct conflict. Too many of the institutions he created were being abused through poor governance and shady back-hand deals. From this point on, I became increasingly aware how difficult it would be for me to pretend I could remain loyal to both those legacies. At some point I would need to make a choice between what had become of Abdul Razak's system and his enduring values.

I learned something else by going through the AFC: The power of anticipation. In January 1997, Md Nor phoned me out of the blue to instruct me to raise a rights issue for the Commerce Group. 'Get me at least 1bn ringgit,' he commanded.

Md Nor sat right at the top of the organisation. He was the de facto leader of the Commerce Group as a whole, which comprised Bank of Commerce, the commercial bank where he was chief executive, and CIMB, the merchant bank. The holding company, Commerce Asset-Holdings Berhad (Commerce), was set up in 1991, when Bank of Commerce merged with United Asian Bank. UAB itself had an interesting mixed parentage: it had been set up in 1972 following the merger of the Malaysian branches of three Indian banks, which became a casualty of the mid-1980s recession, when it had to be taken over by Bank Negara.

Normally, when a company calls on its shareholders for funds in this way, there is a justification such as a shortage of capital, to pay down debt or to make an investment. None of these applied here. When I questioned why Commerce needed a rights issue, Md Nor told me he simply felt uneasy about the environment, and it was my job to persuade the Securities Commission to consent to it and our shareholders to support it. Convincing the regulators turned out to be the easy part. The Tom Yum crisis erupted as the rights issue was just about to close. The Commerce share price fell below the rights issue price of RM6.50 per share, investors who wanted our shares could buy them more cheaply on the stock exchange – so, logically, the rights issue would be well undersubscribed. This would have been embarrassing for us, so I personally pleaded with several major institutional shareholders not only to take up their rights but also to bid for shares not taken up by others. The deal was, thankfully, a success for us, although less so for investors: not long afterwards the stock would fall all the way to RM2.40, way below the rights issue price.

I still marvel at Md Nor's foresight. The money we raised would be critical to our survival: we went into the AFC with substantial fresh capital, whereas most other banking groups would not have enough capital to cover their loan losses. We were in a strong position. In a strange, very Malaysian, twist, instead of that making us a predator, looking for banks to combine with, we became prey, a target for take-over by a politically connected bank with a strained balance sheet. What followed was another tale of the nexus between politics and business in Malaysia.

UNINVITED
VISITORS

As signs of distress began to spread in 1998 from institutions to companies, from banks to individuals, you could sense the desperation. And witness unusual behaviour. One of our clients saw his paper net worth of RM600m turn into a deficit of RM150m in weeks. No one could contact him for months. I sent (Datuk) Iswaraan Suppiah, who oversaw credit collection at CIMB Securities, to see a client to demand repayment for a large share-trading loss. The client answered by showing him the pistol he wore around his ankle. Iswaraan legged it back to the office and asked me for a pay rise!

In contrast to the rest of the industry, Commerce Group was sitting pretty. Other banks were seeing rapidly rising bad loans and gasping for capital; Bank of Commerce had asset quality issues but also a large chunk of available capital from Commerce's rights issue. In January 1998, we received an unwelcome advance for a merger from our competitor, RHB Bank, built up by its eponymous founder (Tan Sri) Rashid Hussain and his partner (Tan Sri) Chua MaYu (who would play a critical role in a later chapter in the CIMB story). Both were larger-than-life characters, ahead of their time. They got into the institutional stockbroking business long before CIMB and made even more money than we did from the stock market boom of the 1990s. With the profits they went into banking and, through a string of mergers and acquisitions, made RHB in short order the third-largest banking group in Malaysia. I was in awe of what Rashid had achieved by going from broking to universal banking, even buying a minority stake in an Indonesian bank in the process (PT Bank Niaga, which would also later become part of the CIMB story). Robert Cheim recalls one morning in the mid-1990s getting a call from Rashid praising a deal CIMB had structured in a clever way. It was like getting praise from Alex Ferguson, is how Robert recalls it. Now Rashid's people had come calling at CIMB's door. There would be no room for deference: Rashid was the invader.

The KL rumour mill was on overdrive about the deal so it wasn't a complete surprise when RHB asked to meet at our office and sent a merger proposal in advance for us to study. The RHB team, led by their Thai-born in-house deal maker Chartchai Pusavat and (Datuk) George Ratilal, CEO of RHB Investment Bank, arrived at Commerce Group's HQ located together with CIMB on Jalan Seman-tan. They immediately placed a presentation deck on the table. On the surface it looked like a merger to be consummated by a share swap. Yet the valuations given to the shares of the two companies meant it was a takeover: RHB shares were valued much more highly than Commerce shares. Dr Rozali, executive director of Commerce led our team, but the details of the deal were my responsibility. I politely told them that while we were open to a discussion about a possible merger it would have to be on the basis of a fairer deal that I had prepared, and not theirs. I put an alternative presentation deck on the table. 'You do not understand what the minister of finance and Bank Negara want. They have already agreed to our proposal,' Chartchai bluntly told us. I didn't think he was making it up, Rashid was known to be part of Minister of Finance Anwar Ibrahim's inner circle, but it was simply too arrogant and rude for me to accept. I retorted: 'If that is your position, then we have nothing to discuss.' Rozali and I stood up. The meeting ended almost as soon as it started and marked the opening of hostilities, with proposals and counter-proposals flying back and forth, many of them leaked to journalists, who were loving this clash of mega banks, which resembled a political proxy war – Commerce was part of Renong's stable and linked to Daim and Mahathir at a time when the relationship between Mahathir and Anwar was becoming increasingly tense.

Eventually a message was relayed to both Md Nor and me separately, by another businessman in Anwar's inner circle – (Datuk) Tong Kooi Ong of PhileoAllied, another banking group. He said that it would be foolhardy for us to continue to resist a merger that both the Minister of Finance and Bank Negara wanted to see happen. If we did, we would find our directorships revoked by the central bank. I considered Tong a friend, so I was surprised by the message. Years later we would revisit the conversation, and he recalls that his motive was to warn me of the potential consequences because he was worried for me. I remember it as being a threat. Regardless, the outlook for us was dim.

We were being strong-armed into a deal that made no financial sense for us. We were financially strong, whereas RHB had been growing its corporate lending book very fast in the years preceding the crisis; and that could only mean one thing given the evolving scale of loan defaults across the economy. But we had every reason to believe the threats about Bank Negara, or at least someone powerful in the central bank, being on their side. At one stage, after we issued a press release refusing another 'offer' from RHB, the response that arrived by fax to all the media outlets a couple of hours later was on a RHB letterhead, but there was also an identity marker of the sending fax machine which showed it belonged to Bank Negara. I still wonder if that was carelessness or intentional, to let us know what we were up against.

We tried everything to stall the deal. Flat-out opposition risked alienating Bank Negara and being painted as refusing to cooperate with their push to create stronger, bigger banks in the wake of the crisis. We had to be seen to be engaging constructively, even if we could not see Rashid agreeing to a fair deal. First, we proposed that RHB should merge with Bank of Commerce, the commercial banking subsidiary, rather than the Commerce Group as a whole. RHB rejected that because they wouldn't get their hands on the rights issue money, which sat with the holding company. Then we proposed an even larger merger, involving several banks, but that deal wouldn't allow RHB or RHB's shareholders to take control. Eventually we ran out of options: we couldn't stall any longer.

Md Nor and I sat alone in our large boardroom to discuss our next move. For some reason the lights had been dimmed, and that suited the mood. We were both quite emotional about the impending end, one way or another, of our Commerce careers: if we accepted the RHB takeover, neither of us would survive under Rashid; while if we stood out against the offer we would be removed by Bank Negara. Perhaps it is only in a crisis, when you face difficult choices, that you find out what really matters. For me the values of my father's second legacy kicked in, and we agreed then that come what may we must do the right thing, and Md Nor would get the board's endorsement for our stance. We then called a press conference and unilaterally announced that the merger talks were off. There was uproar. The journalists were firing questions at us, challenging us to explain why, and what was our alternative, given that the central bank wanted consolidation? They assumed we must have had a replacement deal. 'Which is it: Bank Bumiputra? Hong Leong Bank? Sime Bank?' they asked. Dr Rozali improvised one of the best lines I have heard at a press conference: 'We will consider every deal, even if there is none.' It was worthy of Eric Cantona at his philosophical best. The journalists were left in bemused silence, and we just got up and left the room. We were sure, though, that our time was up. The forces ranged against us were too great. But at least we were going to go with our heads held high.

We waited for the *coup de grâce* to be delivered with uneasy feelings, contemplating what we would do next. It never came, and after a while we dared to allow ourselves to realise we might have seen off the predators. Two things transpired to save us.

The first was that Sime Bank had just declared massive losses, and its severe capital impairment meant that Bank Negara took charge. This diverted RHB towards an easier target: presumably if they got concessionary terms, Sime could also be attractive. The other factor was that in the course of 1998, as we played for time, Anwar Ibrahim's political influence started to wane, and that had everything to do with the political fallout from Malaysia's response to the Asian Financial Crisis.

As the debate about the government's response to the AFC heated up in 1998 the dominant view, derived from the so-called Washington Consensus, was that countries in trouble should get International Monetary Fund (IMF) assistance. But only if they took its harsh medicines: significantly raise interest rates; close down loss-making businesses; cut public spending; open up markets to international competition. Textbook stuff.

Malaysia did not accept IMF support and was able not to do so because, unlike their counterparts in Thailand, Indonesia and South Korea, Bank Negara had been very restrictive with foreign currency debt. The Malaysian government and corporates were rarely permitted to borrow in foreign currency. Malaysia's main problem was with outflows of short-term money. In December 1997, Anwar announced a set of policy responses which were dubbed 'IMF without IMF' – higher interest rates, spending cuts and even shortening the time given to banks to recognise a loan as non-performing, from six to three months. At the same time as putting in the economic squeeze, Anwar weighed in against what he called 'crony capitalism', bailouts for politically connected companies and politically inspired megaprojects. He alleged that loans to politically favoured businessmen were worth at least RM70bn. Renong, the group that ultimately controlled CIMB, had accumulated debts of RM28bn, almost a third of all commercial loans in Malaysia.[47] All this seemed like a thinly veiled attack on business interests aligned with Mahathir and Daim. It was a dangerous tack to take.

On 7 January 1998, the day the ringgit plunged to its lowest, Mahathir announced setting up the National Economic Action Council (NEAC) to oversee the recovery, brought Daim back as NEAC director and chaired it himself on almost a daily basis. Power over economic matters shifted to the PM and the NEAC, which then began reversing Anwar's measures, reducing interest rates and providing a stimulus package instead of austerity. In May 1998, the institutions and framework to clean up the financial mess left by the crisis were created – a body called Danaharta would buy up non-performing loans from banks, while another called Danamodal would recapitalise banks and the Corporate Debt Restructuring Committee (CDRC) was set up to help companies to restructure debt.

Over the summer of 1998, working with a group of key advisors, Dr Mahathir fashioned a plan to respond to the crisis in a different way. What followed over the next month was nothing short of remarkable. On the first day of September 1998 the government announced the introduction of capital controls. Rather than try to attract capital with higher interest rates, Dr Mahathir proposed simply to control its movement. I remember standing on the equities dealing room floor that morning, along with our chief trader. We were blown away by Dr Mahathir's audacity. I said that if he pulled this off – flying in the face of Western institutions, the economics establishment and the financial markets – I would never bet against him in future. I looked on both in awe at his bravery and in fear of what would happen next.

Mahathir's capital controls came in two parts: first was the selective foreign capital control measures. The aim of the government was to discourage speculative and short-term trading, and capital flight from locals. Hence, movement of capital by and to foreign institutions and persons was restricted. Some of the measures included stopping ringgit loans to non-resident banks, restricting the transfers of the ringgit held in external funds by non-residents and prohibiting locals from taking money out of the country. Foreign investors who had invested in Malaysian shares and bonds could sell their investments, but the proceeds would be locked in Malaysia for a period of twelve months.

During the crisis, Malaysia faced massive depreciation of the currency driven by capital flight, which led to the second part of pegging the ringgit to the US dollar. Countries cannot control both interest rates and currency exchange rates while allowing unrestricted capital flow. By having a fixed currency rate at RM3.80 to USD and restricting capital flows, Malaysia was able to lower interest rates without triggering capital outflows.

Having insulated the economy, Mahathir was still not done yet. The financial crisis, which had already turned into a full-blown economic recession, was now turning into a political crisis.

Anwar had challenged Mahathir by refusing to sanction bailouts for what he deemed politically linked businesses. Yet it is far from clear how genuine or far-reaching Anwar's reforms would have been. He himself seemed to be building up an alternative business base, which included RHB, with its ambitions to acquire CIMB. Anwar had also been fomenting dissent against Mahathir within UMNO. One of his allies, the leader of the UMNO youth wing, had openly attacked Mahathir in his closing speech at the youth party congress, accusing the party's president of creating 'crony capitalism' and of supporting bailouts for politically favoured businesses. The stage for a leadership challenge was set, but Anwar did not go ahead with a planned no-confidence motion against the president at the June 1998 UMNO General Assembly. Perhaps he was shaken by the Mahathir's team's pre-emptive strike: a book and some articles that accused Anwar of all sorts of personal misdemeanours. Anwar blinked and lost.

The day after capital controls were announced, Anwar was sacked as deputy PM and minister of finance. Three days later, he was suspended as deputy leader of UMNO and expelled from the party. Before the month was out, he had been arrested in a high-profile raid by a special forces police squad who broke down his front door. He was then arraigned on charges of sodomy and corruption. One day he emerged from custody with a black eye after being beaten up while in prison. It was a brutal show of power, and a spectacular fall from grace.

The immediate impact on Commerce was positive. Anwar's fall meant that the threat of an RHB takeover was lifted. At one point in 1998, it had looked as if my career at CIMB was about to come to a very sudden end. By sticking to our guns, we had found a way through. We had refused to endorse a deal that had been foisted upon us, despite being certain it would cost us our jobs. Md Nor would go on to engineer BOC's merger with Bank Bumiputra Malaysia Berhad in 1999 to become the country's second-largest bank, branded Bumiputra-Commerce Bank Berhad (BCB). I will come back to the BCB story in due course.

The impact on Malaysia of the crisis and the responses to it were far-reaching and arguably still unfolding. In Malaysia the crisis had been caused by a toxic cocktail of rampant financial speculation and hot money flows combined with hubris, poor governance, money politics and corruption. By imposing capital controls and other measures, Mahathir kept Malaysia's economy afloat and contained the extent of bankruptcies, redundancies and unemployment which led to severe social and political turmoil in other countries. Debate still rages, though, among academics and economists over the necessity and long-term impact of capital controls. They certainly angered foreign investors; many had funds trapped in the country and vowed never to invest in Malaysia again. For a still young nation, only forty years old, it was a critical moment: as we were spared the extreme hardships of the crisis, there was as a result less pressure for system-wide reforms. There were reforms on the economic front: a 3.0 version of Malaysia Inc. would emerge, spearheaded by (Tan Sri) Nor Yakcop, who replaced Daim as the de facto national economic czar in 2001. But on the socio-political front the system remained intact. For a while, politics and politicians kept their distance from business, deterred by new governance rules and better practices among the GLCs. But the toxic links between politics and business were suppressed rather than exorcised, and would one day re-emerge with a vengeance.

BABIES AND BONDS

The AFC resembled a motorway crash involving a large number of cars moving at high speed, bumper to bumper in dense fog. The lesson I took from all this was that you didn't have to go with the herd. It's important to be independent, critical, to think for yourself. Crises are sapping, but they also often create conditions for innovation and change. They instil a sense of urgency. Business-as-usual no longer works: unconventional thinking may be needed, involving people putting aside their differences and working together. Resilience and stamina are vital. It is important to keep reserves, some spare capacity, because you can never know when a crisis might hit you. I also learned the importance of my father's second legacy. In a crisis, when chaos creates uncertainty and confusion, it matters more than ever to have clear values, a clear sense of direction to guide you through. Otherwise you become prey to and at the mercy of events.

The year 1998 was a turning point for me personally as well as professionally. At the height of the AFC, Azlina became pregnant with our twins. It was not an easy pregnancy. In October I warned Robert that I thought we would need to decamp to London for a few months so she could be near the best possible medical support. I was prepared to quit to be with her; nothing could matter more than the safety of Azlina and our children. That threw a spanner in the works of Robert's carefully planned transition; but he persuaded me to take a sabbatical instead. As it turned out, that time in London proved to be vital for me to reflect, learn and plan. Over those five months I developed some of the core ideas that would shape CIMB over the next five years. If I hadn't gotten some space to think before taking the top job, I may have been much more conventional in my approach.

The most important move was to build up our capacity to intermediate the nascent ringgit bond market, connecting investors who wanted to put their money in bonds which offered a reliable long-term return with corporates who wanted to borrow for longer durations than banks tended to offer. Our business until then was primarily in equities; corporate finance advised issuers, and CIMB Securities placed shares and bought and sold them for investors. Yet we saw that in developed economies bonds were a much bigger component of capital markets and so also the business of successful investment banks. Large corporates were bypassing banks and borrowing straight from investors by issuing bonds on the capital markets. Equity issuances were actually relatively rare, and investment bankers were making much more money helping companies to issue bonds and then trading in them. This was a big shift for the business, because making markets in bonds involved using much more of our own capital and balance sheet than when dealing in shares, where there is a lot of liquidity. You can't make much money advising clients to issue or invest in bonds; you have to be a market maker, offering to buy and sell bonds. To do that, to be a player in the game, you have to put some of your own money into it because you have to carry an inventory of bonds on your own books.

At the height of the equities bull run in the early 1990s, when broking companies were making money hand over fist and ploughing it all back into the securities business, CIMB decided to invest profits from our broking unit in a new line of business. We set up a 'Capital Markets Unit' to advise companies how to raise funds with bonds. Only a handful of corporate bonds were issued in our first few years, but that small sample underscored the huge potential of the new business for us. But the business needed someone with the necessary experience to take it to the next level, and for that we had to look beyond Malaysia.

One of my first acts as deputy CEO in 1996 was to interview (Dato') Lee Kok Kwan, a Malaysian who had been working at a leading Canadian financial institution and who for family reasons needed to return home. Kwan was a quant – a mathematician – who understood the complex numbers involved in a bank's treasury functions, bonds and related products. He had a plan to build a modern treasury business at CIMB. Its counterpart, he pointed out, was that we needed an enterprise-wide risk-management framework to handle the increased complexity and risks involved in taking positions where our own money would be at risk. I didn't fully understand what he was talking about at the time, but he was convincing, and I sensed he was someone I could trust. I promised to lend him my support, first to design the risk framework and then to head up the treasury team and build the business. Once Kwan was done with the design work he became treasurer and head of a newly created Debt Markets and Derivatives Division. I convinced (Dato') Dr Gan Wee Beng, a former IMF economist and now chief economist at CIMB Securities, to become the head of Group Risk Management, since he was probably the only other person in the group able to understand new financial technologies, and Kwan, for that matter.

The AFC was the catalyst for the exponential growth of the ringgit bond market. The concentration of funding in bank loans had compounded the crisis across Asian economies as many banks got into trouble and stopped lending, choking business activity. Moreover, as bank lending was relatively short-term, for longer-term borrowing corporates turned to international markets and bonds denominated in foreign currencies, which then exposed them to foreign exchange risks. During the AFC some companies went bust just because of the sharp jump in the value of their foreign currency debt. Yet in principle there was no reason why local companies needed to turn to foreign borrowings. The high savings rates in countries like Malaysia meant that local institutions actually had lots of capacity to lend and invest in local currency for the long term. If Malaysia and other economies had developed local currency bond markets the AFC would have taken much less of a toll on our economies. Developing the ringgit bond market became a government imperative.

So in early 1998, one of the early post-AFC reforms initiated by the Malaysian government was to set up the National Bond Market Committee (NBMC) comprising the Ministry of Finance, Bank Negara and the Securities Commission to address the infrastructure and regulatory changes required to accelerate the development of the bond market. Then the various government agencies set up to clear up the aftermath of the crisis – Danaharta and Danamodal – tapped the bond market for funds. Similarly, the CDRC's typical approach to restructuring troubled bank loans was to convert them into longer tenured bonds to give borrowers more time. As the key intermediary, CIMB provided a lot of input to the NBMC, so much so we felt that we were one of the founders of the market.

With Kwan and Dr Gan in place, we leveraged our client base to make CIMB the 'go-to' bond house. No other bank was as well prepared for the shift to bonds as the value of outstanding ringitt corporate bonds issued went from about 9.5% of GDP in 1996 to 41% of GDP in 1998 to 63% in 2006. The beauty of the business was that it could scale almost exponentially without requiring many more people or additional infrastructure. The same tools, rules and people could structure a 50m, 500m or 5bn deal. Compare that with the corporate finance business which I joined back in 1989, where if you got more work you needed more people; or with the dwindling commissions earned in the securities business. The success of our bond business was the primary reason CIMB went into the AFC as one of the top merchant banks in the country and came out of it as number one by some distance.

Over the few months I was in London with Azlina, Kwan and Gan supplied me with lots of reading material on bonds, interest rates, hedging and derivatives, as well as on risk management, to prepare me to oversee a much more complex CIMB.

At the same time I read a lot about investment banking and capital markets; my favourite book was *The Death of Gentlemanly Capitalism* by Philip Augar,[48] in which he recounts the collapse of British stockbrokers and merchant banks following Margaret Thatcher's 'Big Bang' and the invasion of the City by US investment banks. It was strange to go from high-octane deal making and noisy trading floors to a tranquil, small, rented apartment on Queensgate opposite the Natural History Museum. As Azlina rested, I drew charts plotting the future of CIMB. In addition to growing the bond business I planned for us to operate as if we were an integrated investment bank on a US model. We would create an 'Investment Banking' unit, which would market bonds, equity, advisory and loans to clients. Until then each department had looked after its own products and clients. If the Corporate Finance team was visiting a client, they would be offered an equity product; the Corporate Banking team would offer them a loan. The initial Investment Banking unit, which had only three people, was a start-up within the bank and a trailblazer in the industry; not long afterwards practically every competitor followed suit.

Building up our bonds business as well as an investment banking unit were crucial moves. One of the biggest mistakes in business is to keep on doing only what has already made you successful. Good companies often falter when they become trapped doing what has worked in the past, only to find that the world shifts around them. They become conservative, defensive, complacent and short-sighted. Success never lasts long. We had made money in the equities business because we were paid handsome fixed commissions as the markets boomed, and there was little pressure to drive down the fees. But we knew it wasn't going to last; we just had to look at what had happened in the City to see what was coming. Liberalisation was opening up the market to more competitors and technology was starting to change the business. The handsome 1% commission we earned from institutional investors in the securities business in the mid-1990s would over time shrink to just 0.1– 0.15%, while much of retail trading would move online for negligible commissions. Meanwhile, our corporate finance business was so strong that there was little room for growth. CIMB would get stronger only by developing a wider base to its business.

When I reflected in London on what kind of business I wanted CIMB to become, I knew I wanted it to be strong in a dual sense. I knew that CIMB had to be strong financially. That meant we had to become a bigger, better, more soundly capitalised bank, with less reliance on particular lines of business.

I was also determined that CIMB would be a strong institution in a second sense: it would have a strong character, morally and ethically, an expression of my commitment to my father's second legacy. That sounds like a high-minded, abstract idea, easily said. Actually, it felt very personal. I didn't want to do anything I felt uncomfortable about and I didn't want to force anyone else to do so on my behalf. We had to make money in the right way. Although obvious and a little clichéd, I was having to say it to myself and the team because it wasn't par for the course in the days of Malaysia Inc. 2.0. I wanted CIMB to be part of the making of a new Malaysia Inc. We didn't always get it right – old habits die hard – yet we did become an important change agent towards Malaysia Inc 3.0. The most daunting part of that was standing up to the Malaysian business legend (Tan Sri) Halim Saad.

JAY LE TAXI

Everything was fine until we started to cross the desert. It was the end of a long day. I had flown into Saudi Arabia that evening and was now in a taxi heading to Medina. I was keen to get some sleep. Unfortunately, the same was true for the taxi driver. The boredom of driving on the straight road, in the dark, across a landscape with no distinguishing features must have got to him. As he drifted in and out of sleep the car started to weave madly across the road. I was woken from my slumber in the back by the car coming off the road into the sand. We were in the middle of nowhere. I leaned forward, shook the driver hard on the shoulder to jolt him awake and told him to stop. I got out, shaken and not a little relieved to be still in one piece, and told him to get in the back. I slipped into the driver's seat. My companion on that journey, (Datuk) Zakhir Sidek, moved to the front passenger seat so the taxi driver would have the full luxury of lying flat across the back seat. It wasn't long before he was snoring soundly. I kept my eyes firmly on the road, forcing myself to stay awake while driving along the straight road for the next three hours. Zakhir did his best to make sure that I could stay awake. What he couldn't stop was my mind wandering, and soon strange thoughts and images came to me, including that of a sultry Vanessa Paradis singing 'Jay le taxi' (instead of Joe). All exciting visions evaporated, though, at the thought of what would become of us if we were thrown into a Saudi police cell for driving a taxi without a licence.

It was not a scene I had ever imagined when setting out on a career in banking. Here I was, just after midnight, driving by moonlight across the Saudi Arabian desert in a white Toyota Camry, the vehicle of choice of taxi drivers at Jeddah airport. From Jeddah we had gone up the coast on Highway 55 to Thuwal, then turned north east towards Al Massmamah on Route 15, heading across the desert for Medina at a steady 70 mph. It was January 1998, and I was travelling with our client Zakhir, a UK-trained chartered accountant who is roughly my own age. Zakhir was quiet and unassuming; it only took a brief conversation for anyone to realise he was super smart. He had emerged onto the corporate scene a couple of years earlier, seemingly from nowhere, as the new CEO of the mighty Renong Group.

We had timed our flights into Saudi Arabia so we would land in Jeddah with time to catch the last connecting flight to Medina. The immigration queue wasn't long, and even at the current slow pace, we had enough time to make our flight. But Jeddah wasn't quite like any other airport. Suddenly we heard groans around the room. When we looked at the immigration counter, the officers had put up temporary closure signs. I couldn't tell if they'd gone to pray or to eat. By the time they returned about three-quarters of an hour later and we finally got through, the check-in counter for our connecting flight was closed. There were no more flights that night. The trouble was that we had a meeting in Medina early the following morning and we couldn't be late under any circumstances. The only option was a more than 420-kilometre journey in a taxi. We left the airport carrying our bags and hailed the first cab in line. The driver, a smiling young man from Pakistan, seemed nice enough, and as I said, 'Medina please,' his smile turned into an ear-to-ear grin at the thought of the bumper fare. As it turned out he would get a big payout and a good night's sleep on the back seat of his own car.

We were only going to such lengths for one reason; to meet the legendary Halim Saad, the poster boy of Malaysia Inc. 2.0. Let me say a bit about why Halim mattered so much in those days and so why the fateful choice I was eventually to be presented with also mattered so much to me.

Halim was executive chairman and major shareholder of Renong Group, the conglomerate he had built that had constructed and operated the North–South Highway and owned companies in telecoms, banking, construction, property development, hotels and steel; in fact, it was easier to list the things it didn't do in Malaysia. Renong was the single largest shareholder in Commerce. According to the ownership trail, he was my ultimate boss; and he certainly saw it that way. Halim had summoned Zakhir and me to join him to meet potential investors in the Middle East, who might ease Renong's debt burden. We were to arrive in time to pray with Halim at the Al-Masjid an-Nabawī mosque and pay our respects at Prophet Muhammad's (PBUH) tomb.

Arriving late to meet Halim could be a career-ending mistake, we feared. After a harrowing night of non-stop driving through the desert, we had just enough time to get cleaned up and put on new shirts before presenting ourselves to Halim, who, as usual, looked immaculate. We pretended everything had gone according to plan and followed him to prayers. Our bloodshot eyes told the true story.

Halim was an extraordinary figure who in many ways encapsulated what the Malaysia Inc. system had become. It wasn't the first time I'd met him. When I was appointed deputy chief executive of CIMB two years earlier, I went to pay my respects to him at his office in a rather nondescript building in central Kuala Lumpur owned by the alumni society of MCKK, my father's and his alma mater, which he strongly supported. There was nothing fancy or lavish about his office apart from a large fish tank in the waiting room, which I had ample time to survey because Halim kept me waiting for two hours. When I was finally ushered into his office, he didn't even look up from the paper he was reading. He mumbled something about what was expected of me and thanked me for coming. That first meeting lasted only ten minutes. He never made eye contact with me. I was nervous walking out because I had no idea what my instructions were. My saviour was his faithful secretary Florence, who was at the door and repeated his words to me; it seems that was the standard operating procedure. She must have had bionic hearing.

At least he didn't make me kiss the ring, I thought to myself. Some years later, long after Halim had ostensibly retired, I bumped into him and he said he'd like to come to see me. I immediately said he was most welcome and suggested a time and date. He agreed and with a wry smile quipped: 'Don't make me wait for two hours like I made you.' He knew exactly what he was doing all along!

Halim was powerful without being loud or aggressive. *The Economist* once rather haughtily described him as an accountant (he had trained in New Zealand thanks to a government scholarship) with extravagant tastes (this may have been true: I will never forget the comforts of travelling in his jet), impeccable connections (also true) and dubious business acumen (which was both unfair and inaccurate).

Halim had been born close to the Thailand border, the son of a paddy farmer. He became a classic beneficiary of my father's New Economic Policy, which had given him access to MCKK, a scholarship to study overseas and more career opportunities. Halim was not the inept pantomime villain painted by *The Economist*. He was one of the Malay business icons Mahathir thought the community needed to build its wealth. Billionaires like Halim would create Malay-dominated business ecosystems that would ensure wealth was widely shared among the community. That was the theory, at least. For his part, Halim was on a mission to vindicate his selection, to demonstrate that Malays can succeed and to ensure he carried other Malays with him on his path to success. On paper he personally owned a controlling stake in Renong and many other businesses: what you didn't see but could assume was that most if not all of this was held in UMNO's interest. For many Malays Halim was our corporate hero: he had shown that a Malay could build the iconic North-South Highway, run a multi-billion conglomerate and own a private jet. Halim was a figure of awe.

Yet you can only understand Halim if you also understand the man who created him: Daim Zainuddin.

Halim had worked for Daim at Peremba, a government investment company, and in the mid-1980s, he was handpicked to run Renong, which replaced Fleet as UMNO's investment vehicle. Daim was a controversial figure. This is not the place to go into all the details, but through his roles as MoF and UMNO party treasurer, combined with his private interests, Daim played the corporate conductor for much of the Mahathir era. Daim is not at all like his protégé Halim. There is nothing visibly extravagant about him. He tends to wear old batik shirts and battered cheap sandals. I've come across him several times but never quite got to know him personally. Daim presided over an extraordinarily tangled web of interlinked companies which competed and collaborated with each other but had preferred access to lucrative government contracts. Banks were expected to be supportive with loans. It was the Malaysian equivalent of a Korean *chaebols* and Japanese *keiretsu*, an ecosystem in which larger conglomerates would encourage smaller companies to prosper.

The big difference was that in the Malaysian model government and politics loomed large. In South Korea national economic development was the overriding goal. In Malaysia that had to be achieved while rebalancing the economy in favour of the Malays, and that in turn clouded decision-making and made it easy to disguise political motives and corruption.

The system was extremely opaque. Those of us on the outside could only guess the real owners of the shares and companies involved (as opposed to the nominees). A good example is what happened to Malaysian Airlines (MAS). (Tan Sri) Tajudin Ramli, another Daim protégé, had bought MAS in 1994 from Bank Negara at about twice the market price, apparently to help cover up the massive forex trading losses the Central Bank had incurred in the early 1990s. Tajudin was enabled by loans from local banks to pay over the odds for MAS. In order to pay back the banks he had to squeeze money out of MAS: one famous allegation was that MAS signed a deal to buy eggs for its Nasi Lemak at hugely inflated prices from preferred vendors; another was of huge commissions paid on buying planes. In the wake of the AFC, Tajuddin could not service his bank loans, and the government had to buy MAS back from him at almost 117% above the stock market price, which was equivalent to his cost price. This fuelled the view that Tajuddin was holding shares on behalf of UMNO. Scant attention, though, was paid to the massive damage wrought on the corporate culture in MAS during this time. When the people at the top of the corporation are seen to be abusing a company's coffers, the rest of the organisation tends to either join in or become demoralised. I would even suggest that MAS never quite recovered from this sorry episode.

This highly leveraged and unstable edifice of government contracts, politically linked companies, directed lending and anointed businessmen was badly exposed by the Asian Financial Crisis. Once share prices and currencies started to fall, it didn't take long for the cracks to spread and widen. By the time the crisis hit, Renong was the largest commercial borrower in Malaysia and looked to many like a house of cards about to fall thanks to a bewilderingly complex web of transactions among closely linked companies and questionable deals. In February 1997, for example, Renong was 'made to' take over the National Steel Corporation for about RM2.5bn because another Malaysian company had failed to meet its obligation to the Philippines government, much to Mahathir's embarrassment.[49] The unviable steel project failed soon after and only added to Renong's huge debt obligations as it went into the AFC.

The AFC hit Renong's share price hard: the company's market value fell from RM8bn as at the end of 1996 to RM1.7bn as at the start of

1998. Halim was up against the wall, professionally and personally; he would have borrowed in person against his shares in his companies. That decline quickly created considerable financial and ethical challenges.

In desperation Halim undertook the most extraordinary manoeuvre. At the close of trading on 17 November 1997, United Engineers of Malaysia (UEM), the Renong subsidiary listed on the KLSE, announced that four days earlier it had bought a 32.6% stake in its parent company for RM3.24 a share, a 12% premium on the market price of RM2.90.[50] The transaction cost the princely sum of RM2.3bn. UEM had obviously been instructed to buy shares in its troubled parent; minority shareholders in UEM were up in arms, and the rest of the market was aghast. Unwittingly, CIMB Securities had been the major buyer of Renong shares in the preceding days, executing orders on behalf of a foreign broker. When I was informed of the scale of the buying, I was suspicious that it was an operation to hold up the Renong share price. I never imagined that funds from one of Renong's own subsidiaries were being used to do so.

The deal spooked investors on all sides and was blamed for a sudden fall in the market as a whole: over the next three days the KL composite index fell by 20% which made Renong and its political masters unpopular, to say the least. To pay for the transaction, the cash-rich UEM, which owned the North-South Highway concession, had taken on debt. The inflated price at which UEM bought the shares clearly benefitted those selling the Renong stake: yet who that was remained a mystery. As the Renong share price plummeted, so did the value of the UEM stake; within a week it was worth RM1.1bn or RM1.49 per share, less than half what UEM had paid for it.

Remarkably, given that a subsidiary had been instructed to bail out its parent company without proper authority to do so, and without making a general offer to all shareholders, the regulators did not take serious action against either company. To placate the angry markets, Halim eventually offered to personally buy back the 32.6% block of

Renong shares at the price paid by UEM plus holding cost. That 'put' option to make him buy the shares was exercisable between March 2000 and February 2001, but no one seriously believed that Halim would be able to honour it.

The complex web of desperate deals didn't end there. On 2 January 2001, in a separate but linked transaction, Halim offered to buy 21.56% or 500m Renong shares that were owned by Time Engineering, another one of its subsidiary companies for RM875m in cash.[51] Halim paid a deposit of just RM2m to secure this deal. He owed a further RM873m, and there was no indication how the shares would be paid for. The promise that the cash would eventually materialise was to help Time Engineering stave off creditors demanding for $250m (Rm950) for USD denominated bonds that were coming due.

Halim had until July that year to raise the RM873m he needed to buy back the Renong stake. Clearly, he didn't have the money and was giving false hope to creditors. As his merchant bank CIMB would inevitably be put in a difficult position: whether to go along with the scheme to keep Renong afloat or stick to our principles and the lessons we had learned from the Bakun dam fiasco.

The ethical choice did not take long to arrive. In late June, Lim Tiang Siew of CIMB Corporate Finance was called to a Time Engineering board meeting to discuss whether to grant Halim a further extension in making his payment. The man who had terrorised us to not be late for a meeting was now arguing he should be given another year to pay for the shares he promised to buy. While the board meeting was going on I happened to read an email from Tiang Siew which said the board was moving towards allowing Halim an extension, and CIMB was expected to go along with it. I swiftly called Tiang Siew out of the meeting and told him that under no circumstances were we going to agree to extend the deal. We were not going to put the interests of Halim and Renong ahead of Time Engineering's shareholders and our own reputation. We weren't going to go along with it; we were going to do the right thing. Tiang Siew warned me that everything was interlinked. If we refused to endorse this delay the entire Renong house of cards could collapse. I maintained that we couldn't advise the board to accede to a request that was indefensible.

We were in perilous waters. Halim would be furious, and it wouldn't be difficult for him to bring the guillotine down on my career. At such moments pre-emptive measures are needed; I had to take control of the narrative. I immediately put in a call to Nor Yakcop, then Mahathir's economic advisor, to tell him what I had done. I said I wanted him to know that I did what I felt was right but I fully accepted that there might be consequences. I thought I might be out on my ear. To my surprise he replied: 'Well done. You did the right thing. Come and help the government take over UEM and Renong from Halim.'

That response from Nor Yakcop was a seminal moment for me. It was when I knew the fall of Renong was inevitable and that, despite being within the Renong *chaebol*, CIMB would be all right. To save Renong-UEM from outright collapse the government, through its sovereign wealth fund Khazanah, offered to take over UEM in a RM3.8bn deal that was completed in September 2001, days after the terrorist attacks on the World Trade Center. The takeover removed the systemic risk Renong posed to the entire banking industry as the company in effect became sovereign-backed. I never found out what actually happened to Halim's put option, but in a 2013 legal suit against the government and Nor Yakcop in person, Halim claimed that he was (only) paid RM165m to give up his business empire. If true, the payment was probably apt; however grand his appearance, Halim was created by and for the UMNO-linked companies system. At the end of the day, he was a well-paid employee of the system.

By helping to bring the Renong house down I probably had not made myself popular with powerful figures behind Malaysia Inc. 2.0, but in this game you make enemies whether you intend to or not. In doing so, I felt I was being true to the values my father instilled in me.

I refused to go along with a scheme that would have been politically expedient but unfair for the many other shareholders, investors and lenders involved. It just wasn't right. Renong sat at the heart of the rot which had set into the system linking government, UMNO and corporations; a system that my father had initiated. To defend the second legacy my father left us, I had to disavow what had become of the first. It was not the last time I would be forced to make this choice.

The nationalisation of UEM and Renong was part of the stabilisation of the economy following the AFC. It was also the start of the reform era for corporate Malaysia, the beginning of Malaysia Inc. 3.0, as I like to refer to it. In June 2001, Daim fell out with Mahathir and resigned. Mahathir himself became minister of finance as well as prime minister; in corporate parlance, the CEO was now also CFO. The role of 'conductor' of corporate Malaysia fell to Nor Yakcop, the architect of capital controls, who would have a critical influence on all matters economic, financial and corporate for years to come.

Once capital controls had insulated the economy, Nor Yakcop engineered the nationalisation of several companies that were deemed strategic to national or *bumiputra* interest. Renong and Malaysia Airlines were bought directly by Khazanah; the mobile company Celcom was taken over by Telekom, a subsidiary of Khazanah. Once these companies assumed state backing, it was easier to restructure their debts and refocus them on improving operational efficiency.

Nor Yakcop then identified a cadre of young professionals to helm GLCs, old and new. By 2004, GLCs accounted for 34% of the market capitalisation of Bursa, and their activities and performance were significant to the economy as a whole. As CEO of Khazanah Nor Yakcop chose (Tan Sri) Azman Mokhtar, an accountant I had first met while working on the Tenaga IPO. Azman would go on to spearhead the GLC Transformation Programme to drive the improvement in governance and performance of GLCs. There were careful appointments of board members and CEOs, guidebooks on conduct on everything from human resources to procurement, inter-GLCs collaborative platforms and even regular meetings for CEOs of the top twenty GLCs, and the PM where progress was reported.

At the same time, corporate governance became a mantra for reform across regulators; the SC, KLSE and Bank Negara all placed governance at the top of their agenda. Government Linked Investment Companies (GLICs) like EPF, the Retirement Fund (KWAP) and PNB, which had significant investments in almost all large companies listed on Bursa, started to be activist shareholders insisting on the highest governance standards.

As for UMNO, after Halim's Renong and the like, its investment activities became more dispersed and low-key. The party seemed to become more reliant on direct contributions from businessmen. Politicians started to be better behaved when it came to GLCs and business in general. I remember receiving a call from Nor Yakcop to ask if it was true that I had called default on a minister's personal loan. I apprehensively said yes; to which he said, 'Well done and carry on. Hope you understand that I just have to tell him that I called you as he asked.' 'Politically directed lending has come to an end,' I thought to myself. At the UMNO assembly you would still hear complaints about GLCs not supporting the party, but it was hard to find fault when GLCs were generally performing better and there was an unprecedented degree of transparency and public engagement.

The first decade of the new millennium was a golden period for corporate Malaysia. GLCs were running their business the right way. A new generation of entrepreneur CEOs such as (Tan Sri) Tony Fernandes in airlines, (Tan Sri) Shahril Shamsuddin in oil and gas and (Tan Sri) Liew Kee Sin in real estate were starting to make an impact. Yet the truth was that we had only done half of the job. We had cleared out much of the rot in the corporate sector, but the political system was still unreformed. It still ran on money politics and by accentuating ethnic division. In time, no matter how good the governance of the corporate sector, the frailties of the political system which sat above it would come back to haunt us.

As part of post-AFC financial sector development, the government wanted a stronger, more internationally capable banking sector brought about through consolidation. At the same time Khazanah encouraged GLCs to pursue shareholder value optimisation. I was determined that CIMB would be at the heart of both of these. I prided myself on being a deal maker. It was time for my own company, CIMB, to step up to the plate, do its own deals and be more entrepreneurial.

START WITH
A STUMBLE

When I had returned to Malaysia at the end of April 1999, leaving our two-week-old twins, Arman and Marissa, in London with Azlina (not the most considerate parenting decision), I was in a hurry to get back to CIMB because I had a plan to execute. Although much of corporate Malaysia, especially its financial institutions, was still reeling from the Asian Financial Crisis, CIMB was in pretty good shape, taking its first-ever year of losses in 1998 in its stride. Its balance sheet was strong (no more bad debts), and revenue engines remained sturdy. I was impatient to become chief executive and build CIMB into Malaysia's leading investment bank on the model of the Wall Street banks like Morgan Stanley and Goldman Sachs, which were conquering global capital markets. Once we were successful, I wanted CIMB to be listed on the stock exchange. I had it all written down.

Things didn't get off to the best start. What happened next was reminiscent of what happened to me in 1983 at an inter-schools 100-metre race at Oundle. I had pushed myself out of the starting blocks only to fall with a thud, face-down on the cinder track, sending the crowd roaring with laughter. This felt disconcertingly similar. A few days following my return from London, Robert told me Bank Negara had rejected our application to appoint me as CEO of CIMB on the grounds that I was too young. I would later discover that the central bank officer who made that recommendation was (Datuk) Nor Shamsiah Yunus, who would become governor of the bank in 2018. It was a humbling experience; news travels fast in the small world of corporate KL. Pride comes before a fall, they say, and I had been swaggering around as the very young chief-executive-in-waiting. We appealed, protesting that age shouldn't be a barrier, and that I already had ten years of experience in all aspects of merchant banking. Thankfully, a few weeks later, Shamsiah and Bank Negara relented, paving the way for me to take up the post, two months after my return. I became CEO of CIMB on 1 June 1999. I was thirty-two years old.

When I addressed my first Annual Management Dialogue (AMD – the annual November gathering of senior managers to budget and plan the next year) as CEO, I could look back on an amazing decade for CIMB and only one year of losses in 1998 due to the Bakun debacle. We had earned 20.7% of all advisory fees taken by the twelve merchant banks. We accounted for 22% of IPOs, 30% of new bonds issued and 58% of all bonds issued. We were the undisputed number one capital markets player of the past decade. We had won a string of awards from financial magazines and industry organisations. Many people would have been content with that, and there were plenty who asked me why I was making changes, trying to fix something that wasn't broken. My answer was that we had to think ahead and anticipate the impact of globalisation, liberalisation and technological change. The model might still be working well for the time being, but winners anticipate change and get prepared for it before the competition.

The theme of AMD 1999 was 'Changing Gears'. We needed to benchmark our performance against that of our international competitors, I said, not just the local competition. I officially launched CIMB's new core values of integrity, client service, teamwork, innovation and efficiency. Value statements can come across as trite if they're not followed through; but I always found them an important part of building culture – and we needed to transform our culture as well as our business model.

I wanted to turn CIMB into an investment bank on the US model. Technically, this wasn't possible in Malaysia, which doggedly followed the old British model, in which merchant banks were separate from firms of stockbrokers, which distributed and sold shares. That model had been wiped out in the UK more than a decade before when Mrs Thatcher's Big Bang reforms to the City of London allowed stockbrokers and merchant banks to be bought by banks, including international banks. The Big Bang was like an asteroid hitting the dinosaurs; the British stockbroker all but disappeared. First the firms of stockbrokers merged with one another; then they were bought up by banks from the UK, the US and Europe. The shift was vital to London becoming a global centre for financial services and an important step in the creation of global capital markets. Malaysia, however, had continued with the old model, which had glaring inefficiencies and would certainly be uncompetitive once our own financial market was fully opened up to international players. We were behind the curve; even our 'teachers' from the City of London had moved on.

Investment banks would look after every aspect of finance for a corporate client – advisory, bonds, loans and deposits, equities and mergers and acquisitions. I wanted CIMB to adopt the same hard-driving, high-performance culture as the Wall Street firms. In addition, I wanted us to be able to provide services like funds-management and private banking, not traditionally part of a merchant bank's offering but services provided by the top global investment banks. There were plenty of people telling me it couldn't be done; the authorities would never allow it, they kept saying. I just kept asking why not? If the case is compelling enough, one should believe that change can happen. You just need agents of change.

The mission statement CIMB senior management agreed at AMD 1999 committed to our becoming something that wasn't, strictly speaking, possible in Malaysia: 'to be Malaysia's premier investment bank post-deregulation and liberalisation'. I explained that I thought the authorities would eventually be persuaded to adopt the investment banking model now dominant elsewhere. CIMB needed to start stitching an investment bank together from the ingredients we already had. Even if we had to continue to exist under several separate licences for the sake of the regulators, we should operate as if we were a single integrated business. We could save some costs by consolidating support functions and appear seamless and more efficient to clients. We were working out where the game was headed and getting there first. Before the competitors and before the regulators.

The case was so clear, and I was young and impatient. So I decided to nudge things along in a rather public fashion by taking out a whole-page advertisement in a number of newspapers declaring that CIMB was Malaysia's Number 1 Investment Bank. I realise now this might have been seen as pretty cocky, but I made no apology as I took calls from regulators and competitors telling me I'd overstepped the mark. My defence was that I was not claiming to be a *licensed* investment bank; it was just a description of what we did and how we worked. I wanted to change the rules of the game and I had to start changing the mindsets of both the players and the referee. At almost every opportunity with regulators and on every speaking platform, I would ask why it was that Malaysia was still following a model proven to be inferior?

My persistence paid off. In 2001 Bank Negara issued a 10-year Financial Services Masterplan and included a recommendation for merchant bank and stockbroking companies in the same group to merge to create fully fledged investment banks. CIMB eventually merged with CIMB Securities in 2005 but operationally we brought down the barriers between the two companies as soon as we knew Bank Negara was on board with the concept.

The other critical ingredient to my investment banking plans was the ability to hire and reward talent. So, in early 2001, I went to see

Nor Yakcop, then advisor to Bank Negara, to argue that in order to build an internationally competitive investment bank we had to be able to pay our staff competitively. Bank Negara had a stringent bonus cap, the limit that had so annoyed Steve Wong. During the meeting I took out a huge file of my bonus recommendations for every single CIMB staff member and said that I needed to be able to pay staff according to performance and international benchmarks and I could personally explain the basis of every bonus recommendation in the file before him. If he agreed with my case, then Bank Negara needed either to exempt CIMB from the cap on bonuses or to remove it altogether. Nor Yakcop had a background as a currency trader; he understood financial incentives and made decisions quickly. He said he would do both: he would approve my file with a signature now and he would make sure Bank Negara removed the bonus cap to be fair to everyone in the industry. He knew what it took to get things done.

So that's how we got to call ourselves 'investment bankers'. It took us a while to get the right outfits, but we did arrive, a little late, at the global investment banking party. As it turned out, it was a wild party with all sorts of excesses that would last until the 2008 Global Financial Crisis.

The plan I had developed was now falling into place. We created a Group Management Committee (GMC) for the investment bank, comprising heads of various divisions in the merchant bank and the securities firm. We organised ourselves around our client's needs. An investment banking team would work with clients to understand their needs in full before we proposed the right combination of products. The equities division comprised equities capital markets from the old merchant bank and institutional equities from CIMB Securities. Then we had the corporate banking, corporate finance and debt markets divisions. The enterprise-wide risk-management framework was governed by various specialist risk sub-committees and an overall Group Risk Committee. This was a new practice in Malaysia, copied from the global banks, which again put us ahead of our local competitors. We were trailblazers in the local industry.

As important as these structures was the team that made it happen. Without realising it at the time, now looking back I can see I was following my father's approach. He also liked promoting people who would challenge him, think for themselves and give him honest advice. He liked diverse teams of people appointed on merit rather than because of where they come from. I was very conscious of my young person's temperament and impetuous tendency so I kept two 'grey hairs' close to me: Robert as my advisor and Dr Gan as chief risk officer. Kwan ran Debt Markets and Derivatives; two other key lieutenants from my CIMB Securities days were promoted to head up group functions: (Dato) Hamidah Naziadin became group human resource head in 1999, and Iswaaran Suppiah became head of Group Strategic Risk and Compliance in 2001. My old boss Choon Thye ran Corporate Finance; KC Kok ran Equity Markets; and Noripah Kamso ran Corporate Banking. Yusli Yusof was CEO of CIMB Securities, and Ng Ing Peng was CFO. It was a well-balanced leadership team; some would move on after a few years, but Robert, Dr Gan, Kwan, Hamidah, Iswaraan and Choon Thye stayed for most if not all of my time at CIMB.

Hamidah joined at CIMB Securities in 1991 and remained with the group until 2020. She was the one who least expected her promotion to my management team. We first met when I fancied myself as a high-flying broker and she was concerned with parity and compliance as head of HR. Our relationship was fractious, to say the least. Her first reaction to my appointment as Group CEO was to look for another job. When I summoned her to our first meeting after my appointment, she assumed it would be about her departure. Instead, I asked her to take the top HR job. She had been such a tough adversary back in those days in securities that I knew she would do a great job managing others on my behalf. She would go on to be one of Malaysia's most respected HR professionals. Iswaraan, an accountant, came to CIMB Securities as an internal auditor from BOC seconded for a few months to help clear up acute operational problems. He stayed with CIMB for twenty-two years. He was a 'trusted jack of many trades' to me and would go on to head technology and operations for the group until 2016.

My first three years as chief executive went as well as could have been hoped, aided by the weakened, post-crisis state of our competitors and our transformed, integrated platform. After making a RM87m loss in 1998, CIMB swung to a pre-tax profit of RM189.4m in 1999, followed by RM210.5m in 2000 and RM252.2m in 2001.[52]

As my third financial year in the job came to a close, I felt it was time to take CIMB to the next level, with a separate listing on the stock exchange rather than merely being listed as a part of Commerce Group. I thought we needed direct access to the equity market for capital. More importantly, I wanted staff to be able to own shares in the business and believed that a listing would make our brand more visible and effective, be it for generating revenues, finding partners or making acquisitions.

In 2002, I turned down an invitation to go on the prestigious Eisenhower Fellowship programme in the US to work on the listing. The IPO could be career-defining for me professionally and financially defining for me personally. There was only so much I could earn from my salary and bonuses as an employee. Only through an IPO could I become a fully fledged shareholder in the business I was building. It was the chance to become an entrepreneur chief executive.

I anticipated that the idea would provoke its fair share of opposition. Both my predecessors, Dr Munir and Robert, had pursued it, but Halim had been dead against it. Although Halim was gone now, the Commerce board was likely to resist a separate listing for a subsidiary because allowing investors to invest directly in CIMB might reduce the attractiveness of Commerce shares. And the deal would only have a fighting chance if Commerce could retain more than 50% (and so majority control) of CIMB, which meant that the other founding shareholders, Bank Pertanian, and Japan's UFJ (which had merged with Sanwa), who owned 11.7% and 7.6% respectively, needed to be convinced to sell more shares in the IPO than Commerce. Nor was the value-creation argument very obvious, and the most comparable listing had been a failure: RHB had separately listed its investment bank in 1996, and the shares had traded below the IPO price ever since with damaging effect on the brand and more importantly staff morale, as they had all bought shares via the staff share allocation at IPO. Now, in 2002, RHB Investment Bank was being delisted just as I was campaigning for our listing. This was not going to be straightforward.

My first move was to bring in a partner to strengthen my case and help me navigate the corridors of power. I approached (Tan Sri) Azman Yahya, who had just stepped down as the hugely successful first chief executive of Danaharta. Prior to that, Azman, a first-class LSE graduate and chartered accountant, had been at two other merchant banks, where he proved a tough competitor.

The idea was that Azman would become executive chairman of CIMB, I would remain CEO, and the pair of us would drive the business forward. We thought that an option to buy 5% of the company each at a fair price would provide the right amount of incentive for us to commit ourselves to the business for the long term. Through the listing, the rest of management and employees would be offered equity options to align their interests too.

We thought this structure was a novel and clever way of achieving both stronger management commitment to the company and the NEP's aspirations to increase *bumiputra* ownership. Enabling *bumiputra* management to own shares made a lot more sense than allocating shares to politically connected businessmen. And granting options was a more sustainable way of maintaining *bumiputra* ownership. If we borrowed money to own shares outright, we would be at the mercy of the vagaries of share price movement; when the shares fell below a certain price the banks would demand a cash or collateral top-up or force-sell the shares. Countless *bumiputra* individuals had either prematurely sold shares or got into financial trouble by borrowing to take up what seemed like attractive share allocations. Indeed options on 5% of shares at the right terms could even be worth more than a 30% allocation of fully paid shares in the same company.

Our first challenge was to obtain all the necessary consents. We decided to start at the top. Commerce's major shareholder was now Khazanah, and since the PM was Khazanah's chairman, and as Dr Mahathir dominated all the meetings he chaired, he was going to have the final say. Azman and I went to see Nor Yakcop. He liked our proposal and agreed to take it to the PM. We left his office feeling optimistic. A few weeks later, however, he came back to us saying that the PM's decision was that the IPO could proceed but that only I should be allocated options on 5% of CIMB. He said that they were concerned about the precedence of a non-employee being granted share options in the company. I always suspected that the true reason was that they didn't want Azman otherwise engaged, so they could call on him for further stints of national service. In my view he is the best minister of finance we never had.

Once the ultimate shareholder had endorsed the deal, I went to the Commerce board for approval. I added a 'sweetener' by proposing that the IPO should take the form of a rights entitlement to Commerce shareholders, as opposed to being offered to the public at large. This made it much harder for the board to object, as Commerce shareholders would benefit not only from the sale of its stake, but also from that of the other shareholders who were selling. UFJ Bank was distracted by its own multi-bank merger back home so it decided this was an opportunity to take a profit on an investment made by one of its legacy banks (ironically they would return to buy 5% of CIMB at a much higher price in 2006). Bank Pertanian, the original controlling shareholder, was hesitant and only agreed after several painful rounds of negotiations. My pitch was that they needed to agree to sell just over half their stake in order to be able to sell the balance on the market later at a big premium (which luckily turned out to be the case).

In June 2002, with all the approvals in place, I signed an agreement with Commerce for the chief executive's options. That gave me options to buy up to 42m CIMB shares (equivalent to 5% of the company) at any time over the next five years at an initial price of RM1.63, equivalent to CIMB's book value[53] at the time (RHB was trading at below book). The exercise price of the option would increase at a rate of 5% per annum. What that meant was that over the next few years, if CIMB shares did well, I would become wealthy. If CIMB shares did very well I would become very wealthy. The downside risk to me was mitigated, as I would only exercise the options when I could sell them for a profit. My financial upside was squarely aligned with all shareholders and especially Commerce with the biggest stake in CIMB.

At CIMB we saw ourselves as masters of the IPO. We had done many listings for clients and now we were to do the same for ourselves. I was confident the listing would be a great success. Commerce (for itself and on behalf of Bank Pertanian and UFJ) was offering 128m shares in CIMB at a price of RM1.75 each to its shareholders, as well as to Commerce and CIMB board members. An additional 41m shares, just under 5% of the company, was set aside for an Employee Equity Scheme (EES) for management and staff to be given options to buy shares at IPO price (learning from the RHB experience). In addition, we set up an Employee Share Option Scheme (ESOS) to issue up to another 10% of the company in due course. I was determined that the staff would share in the growth of the business they were building. I wanted CIMB to be a mutual gains business. Staff would own or have interest in almost a fifth of the company over the next few years.

After we launched the prospectus, we went on an international roadshow to meet Commerce shareholders and explain our story so they would take up their rights entitlement and thereafter hold on to our shares. While not all shareholders took up the offer, some actually applied for excess shares, so the offer worth RM225m was fully subscribed.

When the listing day dawned, 8 January 2003, we nervously made our way to the stock exchange for the traditional ceremony of hitting the gong to start the day's trading. Then came the moment of truth – watching the buying and selling of the stock on the screen. Sometimes a stock that's listed for the first time jumps in value by 30–40%: great for new shareholders, who make a big gain, but a sign that the offer was priced too low. A good rule of thumb is that there should be a 10–15% premium in initial trading. That would nicely reward investors for taking the risk of buying the shares while the company or selling shareholder would feel it had got a fair price. I was nervous but I thought that we'd structured, valued and marketed the deal as well as we could, so we should get the right premium.

Nothing of the kind happened. The shares hovered at just above the IPO price all day. Worse still, I knew it didn't drop below the IPO price only because I had a lot of help from friends and clients: I literally begged them to help stem the price fall by buying up shares. My own IPO was the only one I was ever involved with where there was no celebration dinner; the mood afterwards was sombre. It was a big helping of humble pie. Things got no better in the coming weeks. For the first three months the share price was as flat as a pancake. Whatever I thought of my amazing skill in creating Malaysia's leading investment bank, it had clearly left investors distinctly unimpressed. They could see no reason for the share price to be trading at anything above the basic book value of the company. Some investors pointed out that even at book value we were at a premium to the nearest comparable stock, RHB Investment Bank.

There followed a series of rueful post-mortems as we debated: what had we got so wrong? The first conclusion was that we had got too cocky. We had listened too avidly to our own hype and too little to what the external benchmarks were telling us. We thought we knew best. We had seen it from our point of view, rather than that of the investors, who needed to believe that we would create value. That started with demonstrating that we were good at managing our capital and optimising return on equity, not with focusing just on profitability. We had retained a lot of capital without it being clear how we would use it. Once we had pinned down the problem, we needed to do something to regain the trust of investors. We needed to make a bold gesture to create a chance to tell our story once more.

We decided to surprise the market by paying a large special dividend only four months after the IPO. Investors who had paid RM1.75 per share got back 40sen or 23%. Investors who owned the shares jumped with joy; those who didn't wanted to know which company did such a strange thing; such payments should be done before, never right after listing. On the back of that dividend we promoted the stock again, admitting our error, and after that, we never looked back. On the first anniversary of listing, the stock closed at RM4.64, up 165%. In 2002, we made a pre-tax profit of RM180m ahead of our prospectus estimate of RM160m. In 2003, the number jumped to RM351m, and the following year to RM385m, when our net return on equity hit 21%. When CIMB was delisted from the stock exchange in 8 January 2006 we had returned, through capital appreciation and dividends, a phenomenal 343% to those that invested in the IPO in 2003.[54]

People say that you learn more from the setbacks and failures than from the successes and triumphs. The initial IPO was a very public setback. No one who tries to do something complex, difficult, demanding and rewarding is going to get away without getting some things wrong. When you make a mistake, you have to recognise it, rather than brush it under the carpet. If the mistake affects someone else, you have to apologise and then do something to put it right. A mistake then becomes an opportunity to rebuild and even strengthen a relationship. That's what we did with our IPO. We listened to what investors were telling us. We acknowledged our mistake. We did something very tangible to put it right, which restored our relationship with the market.

That repair of our relationship with investors was critical to what happened next. At the end of 2004, thirty years after its incorporation, CIMB was at the top of its game and the darling of investors. The company's share price was RM5.35, giving us a valuation of RM4.6bn and 3.3 times book value compared to RM1.5bn and 1.0 times book value at IPO just two years earlier. That made us one of the most highly valued investment banks in Asia. We increased our market dominance and started seeing earnings contribution from new business lines, such as Islamic capital markets, private banking and funds management in private equity and real estate. We had weathered the AFC, resisted the merger with RHB, done the right thing over the collapse of Renong, turned ourselves into an integrated investment bank and pioneered the rise of the Malaysian corporate bond market, all in the space of a few years. While the Malaysian economy after the AFC did not grow at the rate it did in the 1990s, we were at least in calmer waters. And CIMB became a good exemplar for the much-needed reform of the Malaysian corporate sector to make it more professional and accountable. To top it all off, after a big false start, we eventually managed to get our listing right and reward the shareholders and staff who had put such faith in us.

By making our luck and by making the most of the luck that came our way, we found ourselves in a great position but we could not rest on our laurels. In the CEO's Annual Report statement of 2004, I wrote: 'CIMB has arrived as Malaysia's premier investment bank and outgrown its current vision statement.' It was time to start Act II.

SECTION THREE

UNIVERSAL BANKER

THREE-IN-ONE

After our first two years as a listed company, we were flying high by most measures and as seen by fund managers, clients, staff and even our regulators. It seemed everyone expected us to continue at high altitude. I felt the kind of pressure that was probably the ultimate cause of many bank crises over the ages; desperate to continue to grow, to show good results, bank CEO decides to take higher risks, lend more and leverage more. We did not do any of that. Instead, in 2005, we did three massive acquisitions that completely transformed our business; we morphed from investment banking to universal banking. One deal started towards the end of 2004, another completed in 2006. But 2005 was the seminal year.

There was a palpable sense of optimism running through the Malaysian corporate sector at the time. The AFC was squarely behind us, the bursting of the dot.com bubble only slowed momentum briefly, and by 2003 GDP per capita had exceeded its pre-Crisis levels. In October 2003, Mahathir stepped down, and, despite widespread praise for how he had navigated Malaysia out of the crisis, the country euphorically welcomed the new PM, Abdullah Badawi, affectionately known as Pak Lah, whose image was softer, more thoughtful and amiable.

Badawi was an antidote to twenty-two years of increasingly authoritarian leadership. With his talk of Civilisational Islam, rebuilding institutions, good governance, multiculturalism and greater press freedom, he contrasted sharply with his predecessor. The manifesto on which he and BN campaigned for the 2004 election – creating a Malaysia of Excellence, Glory and Distinction – was full of good intentions. Malaysia, he promised, would become a more dynamic, knowledge-driven economy, in which private-sector entrepreneurship would play a critical role (there was no mention of the large state-driven projects favoured by Mahathir). Education would be improved through better national schools, computers in classrooms and better teaching of english. Corruption would be attacked at all levels in both the public and private sector, with much stronger checks and balances between the executive, judiciary and legislature to prevent the over-centralisation of power. Malaysia would be a model Islamic country, one that practised tolerance and welcomed diversity. The avuncular Badawi wanted a country that would be civil, kind and yet economically successful. His manifesto paved the way for one of BN's greatest electoral victories. In the March 2004 general election Badawi won a thumping victory, with 64% of the popular vote and 90% of the seats in parliament.[55]

Yet as the mood in the country was becoming more optimistic, at CIMB things started to look more challenging.

At the Annual Management Dialogue in November 2004 I outlined three severe threats on the horizon which would impact not just our financial performance but the competitiveness of our business model. In other words, working our guts out wasn't going to be enough. We could not win no matter how well we played; we needed to find, or better still create, a different game to play.

The first threat was an imminent change in accounting rules. Companies would be required to declare profits as soon as they were earned; in the past we could hold back profit recognition to smooth our earnings record, to show steady growth. It wasn't completely logical; investors knew investment banking earnings were volatile, but they didn't like that showing up in accounting profits. If the quarterly earnings we announced became volatile then the premium attributed to our shares would collapse, in my view. The second threat I identified was that globally more commercial banks were entering the fray and using their bigger balance sheets to attract, and even demand, investment banking mandates for themselves. Investment banks operating independently, like us, were at a disadvantage. And the third challenge was simply the flip side of our large market shares in Malaysia: we could only grow with the market at best.

Even before that AMD we had already made some moves to shift our model. Earlier in the year we tried to take over TA Securities, Malaysia's largest retail brokerage, to improve our brokerage margins (retail clients paid much higher commission than institutional) and equities distribution capability. The deal fell through, and there was no other entity in Malaysia that could make a material difference to our stockbroking business. So we started to look overseas, and by coincidence I knew Goh Yew Lin, whose father founded and controlled the well-respected eponymous Singaporean brokerage firm GK Goh. GK was getting tired and had told Yew Lin that he would consider selling out, 'but only to the right buyer'. Yew Lin was someone you knew you could trust as soon as you met him. I guess I met his dad's criteria of 'a good buyer'. I hadn't met GK, but his reputation as a gentlemen preceded him. 'I've met the apple, the tree can't be too different,' I mused to myself.

Everything about the deal seemed to fit. We were buying a profitable, well-run company which would give us a pan-Asian platform and fully fledged brokerage operations in Singapore, Hong Kong, Jakarta and Bangkok as well as sales units in London and New York. GK Goh only had a small research outfit in Malaysia, so there was minimal duplication. We would become the largest home-grown investment bank in ASEAN overnight. There was compelling logic to it – but still, one never quite knows what will swing a deal like this. Even in a deal that was going as smoothly as this there are tensions, uncertainties, hidden obstacles, bumps in the road. I was blissfully unaware of what was going on on the other side. Only years later did I learn that GK had been about to call it off at the eleventh hour, actually on the day of agreement signing. What saved the deal was a lecture he was given that very morning by a thirty-something regulator about an operational lapse. I would love to find the young lady to thank her!

The deal caused something of a sensation: a Malaysian buying a Singaporean business when most foreign direct investments seemed to go the other way, from the regional financial centre into domestic markets in the region. To this day, people still ask me how much of GK Goh we bought, believing that it must only have been a minority stake. We bought the whole company. It was one of those deals that people think is impossible simply because no one had done such a thing before. Malaysians had set up small brokerage outfits in Hong Kong and Singapore as offshoots of their home-grown business or bought minority stakes in other companies, but this was the first outright acquisition. And GK Goh was one of the venerable names in the industry.

The purchase of GK Goh, which we announced in January and completed in June 2005, was the most pleasant deal I ever did. There was no rancour or bad feeling, no surprises afterwards. GK was wonderful to deal with: honest, straightforward and helpful. He genuinely wanted us to do well with his business. Years after we bought the company, he would insist on talking to anyone who was about to leave for a job elsewhere in an effort to persuade them to stay. He wanted me to be happy with what I'd bought; he was very personal about things. His only grumble was that the SGD233m price we paid was only 1.38 times the book value.

Even today, whenever I meet him, he doesn't fail to claim that he sold the company too cheaply because we earned the $53m premium back in less than two years. Not only was GK already profitable, but quickly we realised synergies with CIMB clients trading via GK units and vice versa. The enlarged equities distribution platform enabled us to win more investment banking mandates and earn more from every IPO and share placement that we did. With CIMB's backing the ex-GK platform started to win more corporate finance and equity placement mandates in other markets too.

The purchase of GK Goh took our investment bank regional, giving us new markets to grow in. However, it also further amplified the other two threats – competing with much bigger banks and the volatility of our brokerage income. To address those, we went in the opposite direction, deeper into the heart of Malaysian business, and invariably that brought me face to face with what had become of aspects of my father's legacy.

There was a growing contest in Europe and the US between pure investment banks, like us, and universal banks that combined investment banking and commercial banking to serve all customer segments. The commercial banking platforms were able to obtain cheaper funding and write larger corporate lending cheques because of their reach and economies of scale. After the Great Depression, investment banks and retail banks were kept separate by the Glass Stegall Act 1933, but those regulations were repealed in 1999. The likes of JP Morgan and Citibank jumped into investment banking. Soon they and the Europeans such as HSBC, Deutsche and Barclays were tying up lending with investment banking mandates; even interest charged on loans became tied to how much in investment banking fees they earned. It was clear to me that the universal banking model was superior, and so to continue to be a successful investment bank we needed to become a universal bank. Universal banking would also bring more stability to our earnings, reduce our dependence on deals and create regular streams of income from banking small businesses and retail customers.

On paper, the solution seemed to be right in front of us. Our parent company Commerce had all the ingredients of an all-singing, all-dancing universal bank if CIMB were to be combined with its other wholly owned subsidiary, Bumiputra-Commerce Bank. Yet CIMB and BCB operated independently and cooperated rarely, not least because the cultural differences were stark, and no one wanted to do the hard work of making investment and commercial bankers work closely together.

BCB was created by a merger between Bank of Commerce and Bank Bumiputra in 1999. Bank Bumi, as it was known, was a part of my father's legacy, and it became a striking example of how parts of that legacy were abused and misused. Bank Bumi did not have a happy history. It was created in October 1965 under Abdul Razak's direction in response to demands made at the first Bumiputra Economic Congress earlier that year. Amongst the frustrations expressed by aspiring Malay businessmen was that capital was too difficult to access when banks in Malaysia were all foreign- or Chinese-owned. Creating Bank Bumi to address that need was a major national project; amongst Bank Bumi's initial board members were Tengku Razaleigh and Robert Kuok. Bank Bumi grew rapidly on the back of strong support from government agencies, most notably Petronas. The bank's remit, though, was both commercial and social; it was profit oriented but also prioritised helping Malay businesses. Bank Bumi's CEO sometimes had to go to the annual UMNO General Assembly to defend how much it had lent to Malays.

In the early 1980s, the bank which had become Malaysia's most international bank, with offices in New York, Tokyo, London, Bahrain and Hong Kong, proudly announced that on the basis of assets it was the biggest bank in ASEAN. Unfortunately, in banking exponential growth in assets is actually easily achieved by lending easily. Not long after Bank Bumi faced financial ruin. The initial growth of Bank Bumi said everything about the power of government to mobilise resources at scale; the financial ruin said everything about the downside of government being in business without the proper checks and balances and safeguards against political meddling.

The cause of the collapse was the 'BMF scandal', as it became known, Malaysia's first modern major financial scandal. Bumiputra Malaysia Finance (BMF) was Bank Bumi's Hong Kong subsidiary which grew its loans at an astonishing pace, from RM82 million to RM1.8bn between 1978 and 1982. When Bank Negara auditors looked into its books, they were shocked to find that 84% of the loans were to three property companies linked to one developer by the name of George Tan, of the Carrian Group. The then governor of Bank Negara, Aziz Taha (who would become my father-in-law), in a letter to the bank's board called it 'imprudent and highly irresponsible of management'.[56] Shortly afterwards, in 1982, the Hong Kong property market crashed, following the announcement that the territory would be handed back to China in 1997, and the Carrian Group defaulted. The scale of the losses threatened the solvency not just of BMF but the parent bank as well. Growing concerned, Bank Bumi bosses sent their trusted internal auditor Jalil Ibrahim to go through BMF's books. On 19 July 1983, Jalil's body was found in a banana plantation in Hong Kong with a bathrobe cord around his neck. The trouble at BMF was not just bad loans. It transpired that staff at BMF had extended massive lines of credit to Tan without getting much by way of collateral; Carrian profits had been siphoned off into Tan's private accounts, and BMF senior staff had paid themselves consultancy fees to arrange the deals. There has never been a fully convincing account of what transpired. Although several BMF directors did end up in jail, suspicions remain that some of the money received by the directors and Tan ended up flowing through the Malaysian political system.

The government simply could not allow Bank Bumi, by then owned by Permodalan Nasional Berhad in trust for millions of *bumiputra* unit holders, to fail. In 1984, Petronas was mobilised to bail out the bank, buying 90% of its shares for about RM2.5bn. In 1989, Petronas would once more have to inject substantial funds, after which ownership of the bank was sold to Khazanah. The bank never quite recovered from the BMF scandal, the stigma it created and the impact it had on staff morale. Although it returned to the black, poor lending practices continued, and the AFC hit the bank hard. Bank Negara was desperate to find a long-term solution, and in 1999 the Commerce Group, having avoided the RHB merger, stepped forward with a merger proposal to create BCB. Khazanah became the single largest shareholder when Commerce issued it with new shares in exchange for Bank Bumi. Through the merger with Bank Bumi, Commerce Group became a GLC, whereas through its previous owner, Renong, it was linked to UMNO. That shift in ownership, however, did not alter the chain of command above the company: a GLC ultimately reported to the prime minister, who was also UMNO president.

The BCB merger was a huge operational undertaking. Bank Bumi had scores of branches all over the country, millions of customers, over 12,000 employees, and a reputation for financial mishaps. Bank of Commerce had just 2,700 staff and was tightly run. The merger created Malaysia's second-largest bank by assets, but it didn't go down well with financial analysts, who worried that the culture of the larger Bank Bumi would swamp BOC. It didn't help that, right after the merger was completed, Md Nor, then BOC chief executive and de facto Commerce Group CEO, was whisked away to become an advisor to Daim at the Ministry of Finance. Analysts were soon proven right: by the end of 2003, if you stripped out the value of Commerce's stake in CIMB from its share price, the 'see-through' value of BCB made it the least-valued bank in the market, at a price to book value of about 0.9 times. In other words, the market thought it was worth less than the net assets recorded on its balance sheet.

Md Nor's role as de facto Group CEO was assumed by the soft-spoken, pipe-smoking former Tenaga engineer Dr Rozali. He was analytical and strategic, whereas Md Nor was more gut intuition and bold action. One of Rozali's first decisions was to bring in McKinsey & Co, the management consultants, to advise on how

BCB could be turned around. The project was internally led by (Dato')Shukri Hussin, former CEO of CIMB Securities during my time there. This was in line with the more rigorous performance-management framework introduced by Khazanah in its push to transform GLCs. Azman Mokhtar, Khazanah's managing director, initially suggested that I should take over as BCB's chief executive and spearhead a turnaround. That was out of the question; I had just led an IPO for CIMB with an implicit promise that I would be around for the long term. Moreover, BCB needed a complete overhaul; if I went in alone it was more likely that I would be the one turned around. The conversation with Azman did, however, trigger me to wonder if there was a way to square the circle: could I help to turn around BCB *and* create value for CIMB shareholders?

In early 2005, when the team from McKinsey got around to asking for my views on what should be done I told them that what was needed was 'discontinuity', in other words, a big shock that forces absolutely everyone to recognise the need to change. I joked that with my help perhaps for once McKinsey would have an actionable plan: 'You should go back to Commerce and tell them that CIMB should take over BCB and operate the combined entity as a universal bank.' By that stage Kwan and I had already kicked the idea around in private. He was confident we could get a significant uplift in the treasury and bonds side of the business just by what CIMB was already doing but with cheaper funding and bigger transactions. I was confident that there were synergies between BCB's corporate banking and our investment banking platform, both in Malaysia and in other markets, especially Singapore, where we had just bought GK and there was a BCB branch doing not much. These were important starting points, as I was unsure how long it would take for us to turn around banking for small and medium enterprises (SMEs) and the retail operations. I wanted to be sure we could show progress to get everyone behind the merger, especially the staff. There's nothing like unambiguous financial improvements for that.

Once McKinsey had bought into the plan, I brought Kenny Kim into the loop to work on the 'how to'. Kenny was one of the crop of highly talented corporate financiers that joined CIMB in the early 1990s. He and I had just worked together advising Telekom Malaysia on its takeover of Celcom a few months earlier, part of the 'nationalisation' of strategic assets after the AFC. I found him more aware of the issues involved in integrating two businesses than most deal makers I had worked with. That mattered because this was not a deal we could execute, get paid fees and walk away from; this would be ours to nurture and grow thereafter; we would own the successes but also the setbacks.

Our plan for the merger was quite simple: set up a new company – we called it CIMB Newco – which would be a wholly owned subsidiary of Commerce, to acquire 100% of both CIMB and BCB. CIMB shareholders would be offered new Commerce shares in exchange for their CIMB shares, ending CIMB's separate stock market listing after only three years. The economics boiled down to CIMB shares being valued at RM5.50 or a 10.7% premium to its market price (compared with the RM1.75 IPO price less than three years earlier). CIMB shareholders received Commerce shares valued at RM4.80 per share, equivalent to a 4.3% premium to the market. We had to make it slightly more attractive for CIMB shareholders, because its minority shareholders had to vote in favour of the deal and some were reluctant to switch from a 'battleship to an aircraft carrier', as one put it. (CIMB's majority shareholder, Commerce, had to abstain because it had an interest in both sides of the deal.) Our pitch was that the synergies from the two banks being able to operate effectively as one would make the Commerce shares worth even more in the future.

By the time Commerce board of directors had accepted McKinsey's advice and invited me to present the plan, I had done the necessary ground work. I had tested the plan with Azman so I knew it had the endorsement of the single largest shareholder. I didn't need to go higher up this time, because the proper institutional processes were working: Azman would get his own board's clearance. The deal was approved and then announced on 6 June 2005. I immediately got to work: I was thirty-eight years old and brimming with energy and determination.

My first major decision was to select the management team for the combined bank. I wanted to do it quickly to minimise uncertainty for staff. I was almost phobic about periods of leadership uncertainty because it prolongs staff anxiety and tends to make the best ones vulnerable to temptations of working elsewhere. In line with the rationale for the deal, most positions were filled by CIMB management: BCB's Corporate Banking department was absorbed under the Investment Banking division headed by Charon Mokhzani, our former external legal advisor who had joined CIMB as deputy CEO; Kwan, Gan and Hamidah headed the combined version of their existing portfolios; Iswaraan headed the combined Technology and Operations, and a young Islamic investment banker, (Dato') Badlishah Ghani, headed the combined Syariah banking franchise. Ex-BCB management took on SME banking (Bakar Buyong) and Consumer Sales and Distribution (Dato) Sulaiman Tahir; areas in which CIMB had no expertise. We brought in a new head for retail banking products, Peter England (ironically, an Australian), from Hong Leong Bank, and (Dato') Faiz Azmi from Pricewaterhouse (who would go on to become executive chairman of PwC Malaysia) worked for us temporarily as a consultant in the role of chief financial officer. A cadre of CIMB corporate-finance-trained professionals Kenny, Tiang Siew and Effendy Shahul Hamid, took on Group Strategy, Group Internal Audit and Group Marketing and Communications respectively. Tengku Ahmad Burhanuddin, the larger-than-life personality known to one and all as TAB, took the executive director position at the bank, while Robert Chiem stayed on as my advisor.

It was a huge leadership challenge for every one of us; almost everyone stuck with it for years. There was a sense of a mission; we were building a new banking icon, which we all wanted to see succeed. I suddenly had responsibility for thousands of staff, including hundreds of bank tellers who earned in a year what some of my traders earned in a week. At CIMB I was used to negotiating packages with my managers one on one. Now I had trade unions to deal with. I had to get used to speaking to big crowds in Bahasa, rather than in English to a tight-knit team of people I knew by name. My first foray into these town hall meetings proved instructive. At the end of a meeting in Kuala Terengganu, on the east coast of Peninsula Malaysia, I asked staff if they had any questions. A couple of people stood up and read their questions from a piece of paper. From there I went a hundred miles down the coastal road to Kuantan, close to my ancestral home of Pekan, to address another large gathering of staff. Towards the end the same questions came up, worded in exactly the same way: the staff were reading from cards written for them by their managers! There was obviously an unhealthy culture of fear and hierarchy, which I immediately wanted to break. I made it very clear there and then that I was not happy, and the new culture I wanted was one where everyone could say as they pleased, including to the CEO. 'Ask me anything as long as it isn't about my personal life,' I would say; a slice of humour also helps to ensure attention.

I used these meetings to lay out how I wanted things to work. The SME and retail operations were underperforming because the culture encouraged people to care about neither customers nor results. One of Faiz's first jobs was to try to work out how many non-performing loans the bank had (no one knew) and to sort out which we might get some money back on. This was a revolutionary idea apparently: Bank Bumi had simply given up on billions worth of lending that had gone wrong, and no one really bothered to try to reclaim the lost funds. Faiz found that some of the borrowers, when approached in the right way, would pay up willingly. Faiz, always one for dark humour, coined a name for the effort to chase down these non-performing loans: 'Project Living Dead.' It wasn't rocket science; it was a grind, but in the past no one was motivated to do this kind of work. At CIMB if there was money to be made we made sure staff would be motivated to do the work by a combination of financial rewards for themselves and a sense of contribution to the overall mission.

We found that there was a pervasive sense of drift in many parts of BCB. Everyone was paid the same bonuses and seniority always seemed to take precedence over performance when promotions were being decided. I wanted a culture in which people would be differentiated and rewarded, for performing and working hard. It came as quite a shock when I announced that we would no longer be paying standardised bonus multiples; there would be a big range starting at zero for underperformers. Both bonus and salary increments were to be determined based on each individual's report card on their performance and future potential.

Stories about my hard-driving style started to spread. Most were true, but I do hope that one story that still makes me wince didn't spread too far. At about 9.30 p.m. one night I was on the phone berating a senior manager in the loan recovery department when she eventually picked up the courage to say, 'Sorry sir but it is Christmas Eve, and I am at Mass.' Later I would reflect on that moment and wonder if in my determination to succeed I had started to resemble my old boss Steve Wong. Obsession with competition and success can change you; countless times I had to reacquaint myself with my own values. I wanted to be tough but fair, I wanted to drive people to work hard but with compassion. Raising my voice on Christmas Eve to a Christian at Mass was simply way out of bounds.

My new order would not be for everyone, and it was best for those who did not like it to leave, so we set up a separation package. I did not like the standard approach used by companies, the Voluntary Separation Scheme (VSS), because it was made available to everyone and the best staff tended to take up the offer, as they would most easily find another job. I worked with Hamidah to create an alternative, which we called a Mutual Separation Scheme (MSS). Under the MSS the employer retained the right to reject applications so we could tell the better staff not to bother applying. In addition, the MSS was made available for a six-month period (a VSS was usually just open for a few weeks) to give staff ample time to decide if they could accept their new roles and the new organisational culture. In practice, poor performers were encouraged to take the MSS by being told their bonuses were likely to be zero. About 12% of BCB staff took the package, more than we expected. The MSS went on to become the common separation scheme for many Malaysian companies. The only laxity was that we didn't test the acronym first; staff mocked that MSS meant 'Masa sudah sampai' in Malay, meaning 'Your time has come', usually in reference to someone about to die.

To say there were plenty of sceptics about the merger is an understatement. Quite a lot of people thought it sounded a disaster in the making. We had no experience of running a mainstream bank with branches, ATM machines, credit cards and overdrafts. Some people pointed out that deal-junkie investment bankers were the worst possible people to charge with turning around a conventional banking business, which is all about systems and processes. I can imagine that plenty of our many detractors were rubbing their hands in gleeful anticipation of our impending comeuppance.

I was confident we were not going to fail. I wasn't sure we could turn BCB into a fantastic bank. But we didn't need to do that. We just needed to make it a better bank. We were determined to prove that you can turn a tired state-owned business into a well-run, customer-focused organisation. We needed to create a culture in which people want to work harder for the team and to serve the customer. However, we soon realised that turning around the SME and retail business was going to be a very long haul. We had to recruit and train large numbers of new people, exit large numbers of weak ones, overhaul some existing businesses like credit cards, which was a total mess; remake processes, and so the list went on. I was worried that if it took too long we would lose momentum, resistance would build up, and we would end up settling for mediocrity.

With the BCB deal done, any sensible person would probably have drawn breath. But deals, like London buses, tend to come along in twos and threes. And if you don't catch one of them you could end up waiting a long time for the next one.

A few months before the CIMB-BCB merger was announced, my brother Johari invited me for a coffee at the Concorde hotel in KL with HRH Sultan Sharafuddin Idris Shah of Selangor. Prior to ascending to the throne, HRH had been active in business. I had never really spoken to him, but Johari felt that as I was now a senior banker I should get to know him. It was only a coincidence at that point that HRH and his partner (Tan Sri) Syed Yusof Syed Nasir were part-owners of Southern Bank, one of the last independent Chinese family-controlled banks. In 1999, Southern Bank had merged with Ban Hin Lee Bank to be one of the ten banking groups to survive the AFC. At the end of a very pleasant conversation about the prospects for the Malaysian economy and banking, His Royal Highness patted me on the arm and told me that if he and his partner were ever to sell their Southern Bank stake, they would like to offer it to me to see if I could engineer a merger with CIMB's sister bank, BCB. I was flattered and I wasn't going to say no but I read no more into it; in these situations people often say things, and nothing ever comes of it.

In this instance that was not the case. A few months later, in October 2005, Ganen Sarvananthan of Khazanah told me that the Sultan had fallen out with (Tan Sri) Teong Hean Tan, (TH for short) the founder and CEO of Southern Bank, and that his stake was probably for sale. Ganen was one of Azman's first hires when he took over at Khazanah. I had known him since his days as a mergers and acquisitions banker at UBS; he could smell a deal a mile away. We always worked well together on deals and also on how Khazanah oversaw CIMB: I kept him briefed on what was happening at our company, and he in turn would make sure that Azman knew enough not to fuss. According to Ganen, dissatisfaction among the minority shareholders centred on TH's plan to buy a Singapore-based insurance company, which would consume a lot of capital and serve almost as a poison pill to deter potential bidders for the bank. HRH's remark at the end of our tea came back to me.

It took no more than a quick look to see the obvious synergies and opportunities. Southern Bank was entrepreneurial and had some particularly good business units – credit cards, direct (phone) banking, SME banking and micro-lending. It was strong where we were weak. With its geographic base in Penang and its large Chinese customer base, Southern Bank would be a great complement to BCB; and it also had a stronger performance-based culture. I could see how an infusion of its staff into the larger bank would help drive the cultural transformation I was seeking. What was left unsaid was that a merger would make us less Malay and more Malaysian. It would have been near-suicidal for me to say publicly that we wanted to see more non-Malays in the company; but the lessons I had learned from my early days at CIMB had stayed with me; there was power in diversity, we needed to tap into it and to do that we had to become more Malaysian.

As good as the deal sounded, there was a major problem: TH had no desire to sell or to merge and he was not ready to stop being CEO. We were undeterred. Following initial behind-the-scenes courtesy conversations with TH, we moved quickly to obtain Bank Negara's approval for a formal bid. Bank Negara's endorsement was straightforward, since despite whittling down the number of banks from fifty-eight to ten clearly demarcated financial services groups in the aftermath of the AFC, it still wanted mergers to create fewer, stronger banks. TH felt obliged to explore a deal; he couldn't brush us off, knowing that a group of major shareholders were keen to sell and had specifically mentioned us as a potential buyer. Syed Yusuf was also chairman of the bank at the time. Once we had Bank Negara's approval, TH was at a significant disadvantage. Bank Negara's rules forbade competitive bidding wars for banks: it was an old rule based on a fear that such contests might destabilise not just the bank in question but the banking system as a whole. We had the first shot at the deal; other suitors would get a chance to come in only if our negotiations failed. That meant that Southern Bank couldn't entertain a competing bid, even though there were strong indications that Maybank would be willing to pay a handsome price. The deal was ours to lose.

Our bid turned out to be hugely controversial. Communal loyalties were stirred up. A Malay royal and his business partner, who had been allocated their shares in Southern Bank to comply with the NEP, were selling out and putting it in play. A plucky, private, family-owned bank was now at the mercy of a state-backed bank with much greater resources at its disposal. I recalled how angry I had been when RHB had come knocking at our door in 1998. I could imagine how affronted TH felt. KL's small business community was soon divided into warring camps. You were either for CIMB or for Southern Bank; for Nazir or for TH. Both sides had connections and networks which they tried to bring into play. TH and his wife, for example, were close personal friends of PM Badawi, who quite wisely refused to get drawn in, saying that it was a matter for market forces to determine. We were in the business news nearly every day for weeks. Thankfully there wasn't yet any social media; I dread to think what it would have been like in the era of the hashtag. As it was, it was bruising: punch and counter-punch, each side denouncing the other, often through proxies.

For me personally, the bid was further complicated by family connections. Long before this, TH was 'Uncle TH' to me. He and his wife, Puan Sri Lim Swee Lay, were once close friends of my in-laws, and Azlina and her family sometimes stayed at the Tan family home in London during school holidays and exeats. Swee Lay was the daughter of (Tan Sri) Lim Goh Tong, my grandfather's business partner. They had set up the Genting Highlands Resort together. My maternal grandfather Noah had transferred much of his wealth to the Noah Foundation, a charity run by my cousins, and which had accumulated a significant stake in Southern Bank. Even my cousins initially indicated that they were backing TH; I had to plead with them to change sides. Genting was now run by Swee Lay's brother, and they were one of CIMB's top clients. And there was a generational dimension: I was the young upstart daring to take over a business built up over many years by someone who was my elder and better. TH was known to his staff as 'Emperor' for his imperial style of leadership. The Emperor was facing a whippersnapper.

TH dug his heels in. We kept him under siege and worked hard at winning over other shareholders of Southern Bank. We were assisted, behind the scenes, by several Chinese tycoons. I like to think that the reason we managed to get them on board was that they could see that CIMB was a well-run multiracial Malaysian bank with an entrepreneurial mindset. This was not a deal being stitched up by politicians. We were not being parachuted in at the behest of the Ministry of Finance to do a political favour. Yes, we were state-controlled and part of the establishment, but our motives were purely about business. We wanted to create a better bank, and most of them could see that.

Ong Beng Seng, the Singapore-based property tycoon and close friend of the Sultan and Syed Yusuf, consistently advised them to stick to the plan. (Tan Sri) Khoo Kay Peng, the owner of MUI Group (and Laura Ashley) lent us his vast house on Jalan Ampang to meet in secret, saying that he 'didn't want to see friends quarrel'. On several occasions our negotiations got extremely heated; it was just as well that we were safely behind the high walls of his mansion. The decisive figure, though, was Chua Ma Yu, Rashid Hussain's former partner at RHB.

I had known Chua for many years, not well, but he seemed to enjoy sharing with me his views on markets and corporate personalities, which I always found helpful. And he absolutely loved to be part of the action when a deal was going down. So we encouraged him to enter the fray by taking a significant stake in a company called Killinghall

Malaysia Berhad, which held a 17% stake in Southern Bank. We had gathered that at a reasonable price Singapore's OCBC Group was a seller of its 14% stake in Killinghall. We showed Chua that at that price he stood to make a lot of money in quick time if he bought Killinghall shares and then made sure that Killinghall sold its Southern Bank stake to us and returned to shareholders the proceeds from the sale. And to see the plan through once he had the stake he should demand to be made chairman of the Killinghall board. For some reason our opponents didn't realise the significance of this manoeuvre, even when to accompany him onto the board of Killinghall, Chua proposed Lai Kok Peng, who had previously worked at CIMB, for ten years reporting to Kenny, who was my key person on this deal. Killinghall was historically controlled by Swee Lay; she called the shots on behalf of her and TH's stake in the company. Its board, however, was divided between those who thought the merger was in Killinghall's best interest and those who supported TH. Chua's entry as chairman tilted the balance decisively in our favour. That they did not deny or delay Chua and Lai's appointments was the decisive moment in the saga.

Once Chua took control of Killinghall's board, the company demanded a general meeting of Southern Bank shareholders to appoint a majority of new directors on the basis that the current board of the bank was against the merger with CIMB. Killinghall nominated four individuals who were already sitting on boards of other (non-competing) financial institutions, so there was little risk of not obtaining regulatory approval for their appointment. If the general meeting voted in the new directors, it was game over for TH, as they would form the majority of the Southern Bank board. It was a hostile, aggressive move but at that stage there was no turning back. I did what was necessary to win.

A few days after Killinghall's intentions were made public, TH reached out to me for the first time; before that I was always the one asking to meet. We both knew we were getting close to the end: he was in a corner. He wanted to meet in complete secrecy, so I organised it to be at a most extraordinary place: the Queen's bedroom at Carcosa Seri Negara, the former British governor's residence, which for a time became a six-star boutique hotel. Queen Elizabeth had stayed in the suite during the Commonwealth Games in 1998. It had the ultimate trappings of colonial power; from the balcony you could look down on the Malaysian parliament building.

We talked for more than four hours in the suite's living room, pausing only to call for the waiter to refresh our drinks. In the end we agreed a price that allowed TH to feel he got a good enough deal. I could have squeezed more out of it, given that we had the upper hand, but I wanted him to be able to hold his head up high and be helpful during the deal transition period. We would close the deal valuing Southern Bank at RM 6.7bn; and TH would be paid a gratuity of RM20m in recognition of his past services to the company.

The period when you have agreed a price but have yet to assume control is always tricky, and TH's cooperation would make a difference to how smoothly things went. I would inherit his staff and I wanted them to know that the contest had ended amicably. Southern Bank had not been conquered, it was a merger. When we finished our negotiations, it all became a little weird. TH and I instinctively hugged, for what seemed like quite a long time. It was cathartic for both of us after having said many things to or about each other that we wish we hadn't.

The day after the Carcosa meeting, 14 March 2006, we held a press conference to announce the deal and the cessation of hostilities. TH and I shook hands and smiled at the throngs of cameras and reporters. Relieved, I came home in daylight for the first time in ages. I was exhausted. I had been working flat-out for weeks, starting early and often finishing well after midnight. It was a draining, bruising battle played out in public. I had barely seen Azlina and the kids for weeks. I slumped in my chair at my desk in my study, loosened my tie, but just as I wanted to close my eyes I saw an envelope sitting in the middle of the desk. It had been hand delivered; whoever had brought it had instructed our maid to give it top billing amongst all the items waiting for me. When I opened the envelope and read the contents I was astounded. It was from our landlord: she was evicting us. I ran to show the letter to Azlina; she was livid. It didn't matter that I'd just pulled off a historic takeover making my bank one of the biggest in the country. We no longer had a house to live in. She wanted to know why I'd allowed my family to find itself in this position, and what I was going to do about it.

Perhaps I should have seen it coming. Our landlady was Siew Lay! Our tenancy agreement with her was loosely drafted, a deal between family friends. It had been kind of her to offer us the house when she heard we were looking for temporary accommodation, as the rent definitely wasn't going to make any difference to her cashflows. Now, she was being anything but kind.

The personal had intruded upon the professional. I decided that I too had to push the boundaries a little. I called TH and gave him a choice: either his wife retracted the eviction notice or I would do whatever was in my power to make his parting with the bank unpleasant. I remember thinking I sounded more like The Godfather's Don Corleone than a bank CEO. A few hours later, we were told we would not need to move out after all. Azlina was pacified but still annoyed, as the dignified thing to do was move out, which we did as soon as we found a new house to park ourselves.

Over the next two days, I had one-on-one meetings with senior managers at Southern Bank to make sure key people felt welcomed and could put the recent hostilities behind them. For those who could not, we agreed that it would be best if we went our separate ways, but the majority were offered positions. Key appointments were Jean Yap, to run credit cards; Tan Leng Hock, to run SME lending (replacing Bakar, who retired); and Aaron Loo, to run a new micro-credit business as part of retail banking.

At the enlarged Group Management Committee we now had people who had worked at the whole range of legacy banks that made up CIMB: Bank of Commerce, Southern Bank, Ban Hin Lee, United Asian Bank and Bank Bumiputra, as well as CIMB itself. It was quite a mix. I made my decisions on who should be part of the senior team based on a combination of merit and many diversity criteria including to ensure that all staff could look to the senior management line-up and feel connected in one way or other. My job was to make them a team and drive them to succeed in their own divisions but also as a group.

In two helter-skelter years we had gone from being a newly minted investment bank with about 1,000 staff and assets of about RM15bn to a universal bank with commercial and retail customers in their millions, an extensive branch network, more than 20,000 employees and assets of about RM152bn. When we started, we were a tenth of the size of Maybank, Malaysia's biggest bank; now we were a mere 10% smaller. What we had created, so it seemed to me, was a combination of the best of the diversity that Malaysia had to offer. Through imagination and hard work we had built a universal bank, combining investment and commercial banking to give us scale and reach. In the process I like to think I had taken over and started to clean up one of the abused and mistreated aspects of my father's legacy, the bedraggled Bank Bumi, which had started life with such promise. There would be many more deals to do, but we had all the main pieces in place.

The most visible part of the integration of the three banks was the branding and the revamp of the 'look and feel' of the branches. We decided to go 'out of the box' and hired a Singapore-based two-man outfit called Mind Wasabi to design our new brand architecture, the chevron with the tagline 'Forward Banking' in three colours: blue for investment banking, red for consumer banking and green for the Islamic banking franchise. Once we had become better at consumer banking, we would harmonise all our operations under one colour – red. The template of new CIMB branches was modern and fresh and brought in all the new protocols on encouraging the customer to do as much as possible on machines instead of facing the teller. A new online banking proposition was launched called 'CIMB Clicks'.

On 7 September 2006 we welcomed PM Badawi to launch the new CIMB brand and its very first branch at the Starhill Gallery in Bukit Bintang, KL. Whenever the prime minister comes you tend to see everyone you invite and more. Unfortunately, I didn't cater for a large 'more', and the ballroom of the Marriott hotel was overcrowded. But other than that, meticulous preparation paid off. It remains the proudest moment of my business life standing on stage next to Badawi and my mentor Md Nor, who had just returned to assume the chairmanship of CIMB Group.

The Malaysian merger was an unambiguous success, and the Malaysian operations would underpin the Group's regional expansion and financial performance for years to come. We turned Bank Bumi into the core of a successful universal bank with high standards and aspirations. As part of the rebranding exercise in 2006 we renamed Commerce as the Bumiputra Commerce Holdings Berhad, a temporary measure so as to avoid any political backlash for dispensing with the word *bumiputra* completely. BCHB's net return on equity, which had been below 9.0% in 2004 and 2005, jumped to 14.0% in 2006 and 15.6% in 2007 (not including a one-off gain from the sale of BCHB's insurance business, which took return on equity to 20%). Net profit from operations in 2004 was RM 0.73bn, rising to RM2.1bn three years later. At the end of 2007, BCHB's market capitalisation was RM37.1bn, compared to RM12.5bn in June 2005 when the CIMB–BCB merger was announced; over that period its share price was up 68%. Investors stopped worrying about being on the aircraft carrier.

In 2009, by when CIMB had become a well-known brand, we quietly renamed the holding company CIMB Group, dispensing with BCHB. It's always good to minimise the number of politically sensitive fronts you open up, especially since towards the end of 2006 we had decided to take on another highly politically charged deal.

When I returned to Malaysia after university I had applied for a job as a graduate trainee at Sime Darby, the giant palm oil plantation owner. Now it was time to revisit Sime Darby with an altogether more daring proposition.

SYNERGY DRIVING

On 27 November 2006, some of the most powerful chief executives in Malaysia gathered in a suite at the Meridien hotel in the KL Sentral district to wait anxiously for their major shareholder to arrive to talk to them. They were unsure about what. Alongside (Datuk Sri) Zubir Murshid, the CEO of Sime Darby, one of the oldest plantation-based conglomerates in the country, were his counterparts from two slightly smaller, old-school palm oil companies: (Tan Sri) Wahab Maskan, from Guthrie, and (Tan Sri) Sabri Ahmad, of Golden Hope. Each company had a venerable history that went back to the colonial era. Permodalan Nasional Berhad, the massive government fund management company and instrument of the NEP, had controlling stakes in each.

Although I was already the chief executive of the enlarged CIMB Group, I was still in awe of the giant, historic planter companies, which between them had 107,000 employees in Malaysia and Indonesia. I felt excited but also slightly queasy as I walked down the corridor and into the room. After being introduced by (Tan Sri) Hamad Kama Piah, the chief executive of PNB, I went straight to the point: 'Gentlemen I am here to offer to buy all your companies, together with all their subsidiary companies.'

The assembled CEOs were stunned. It was the opening move in what would become the most audacious deal in Malaysian corporate history.

CIMB would set up a shell company with just RM100m in cash and capital to take over three of the country's biggest companies for RM31.4bn. At the time our market capitalisation was only about RM15bn. How did we think we could pull it off – and why would we want to?

It had become our stock-in-trade to take on complex deals. We grew not merely by responding to requests for advice, but by proposing deals to potential clients, deals they would never have thought of on their own. I like making things happen, especially when other people doubt they can be done.

In the course of my career I have advised on scores of deals: buying, selling and merging companies. My brother Nizam suggested I work at a merchant bank because I would learn about the Malaysian corporate scene. It was in M&As that you learned the most; IPOs and other equity issuances tended to be more about compliance with rules and regulations. Our regular clients included most of Malaysia's top companies such as Petronas, YTL, Genting, Nestlé, Telekom and Sapura. For the group controlled by Ananda Krishnan, the prolific Malaysian international entrepreneur and philanthropist, we listed Astro, the satellite television group, and Maxis, the mobile telephone company, then took them both private and relisted them both again. At one time we were handling M&As for all three mobile companies – Maxis, Axiata and Digi – yet no one minded, a reflection of our reputation as *the* deal maker. We also advised many smaller, less-well-known companies. Every deal had its own war story, and I savoured them. Nizam was right, I did learn a lot. So much so that I developed an instinct for deals.

The first years of the new millennium were a fertile time for M&As. Companies that survived the AFC had to look at themselves afresh: could they continue as they were; should they merge; should they sell the business? The potential for synergies was key to answering those questions. The Government Linked Companies Transformation programme placed pressure on GLCs to think like private companies; we were being measured on the same scales of shareholder value creation. The programme was the most visible and successful part of the effort to clean up the mess left behind by the collapse of Malaysia Inc. 2.0 in the AFC. Khazanah showed the way with its stable of companies, including CIMB, transforming themselves domestically, and many aspiring to become regional champions. PNB, which had the largest portfolio of strategic listed companies, took its time, keeping rather quiet for the first few years of the programme. But when it finally moved, it shook corporate Malaysia not least because the deal involved three legendary names.

Sime Darby had been set up in 1910 by a young Scottish adventurer, William Sime, and his older, wealthy banker-partner, Henry Darby. Sime Darby started in the still fledgling rubber industry and then shifted, very successfully, into palm oil production. It was acquired by Malaysian investors in the 1970s in line with the government's agenda of repatriating flagship companies. Guthrie, created in 1821 by Alexander Guthrie, was one of the oldest British trading companies in Southeast Asia, and introduced to Malaysia rubber in 1896 and palm oil in 1924. In 1981, in a dramatic dawn raid on the London Stock Exchange, Guthrie was taken over by PNB buying up a majority of its shares in a matter of minutes. Golden Hope, meanwhile, had been created through the merger of several smaller, equally venerable, tea and coffee plantations, and had been taken over by PNB in 1990.

It was a poorly kept secret that PNB wanted to merge the three companies into a single operation to achieve economies of scale and synergies. When CIMB started looking into the deal, we calculated that a 1% reduction in costs would generate a 10% increase in profits; there were plenty of ways to cut costs by eliminating wasteful duplication, especially in administrative functions and procurement. Privately owned plantation companies were already significantly more efficient, delivering double-digit returns on equity rather than the single-digit returns provided by these PNB companies. The sheer scale of the combined group was also attractive. With more than 600,000 hectares of palm oil plantations, it would control between 5 and 6% of the world palm oil market, making more than 2.5m tonnes of palm oil a year. That would give the merged group more influence over supply and, possibly, prices. The merger to create a larger, more efficient, powerful and profitable company was compelling – yet it had also proved far more difficult to pull off than one might expect.

I had heard that PNB wanted to push ahead with a merger and had asked banks to advise how best it could be done. PNB owned Maybank, our main competitor; I knew that they'd be in pole position to get the business. I had also heard that Arab and RHB had been consulted. For whatever reason CIMB had been left out. This would be the largest merger deal in Malaysia ever. Our market share in M&A work would suffer badly if we weren't part of the deal. My deeply competitive instincts kicked in: how could we barge our way in, I wondered?

I asked our PNB relationship manager in investment banking (Datuk) Wan Razly Abdullah to look into the matter. He quickly reverted: my intel was correct, PNB had been asking around for advice, but the deal looked impossible for a very simple reason; PNB's own role in the transaction.

PNB was the major shareholder in all three companies. So if one of the three companies were to take over the other two, PNB would be playing for both sides at the same time. In situations such as this – technically where there are 'related parties' involved in the deal – the rules were that the party in question could have no say in the deal; they had to abstain. Yet without PNB's votes, there was no guarantee the deal would go through. The deal looked unlikely without PNB's involvement and impossible with it. Moreover, the CEOs and boards of the individual companies had little interest in a merger that could lead to job losses and cost-cutting, so they were likely to encourage minority shareholders to reject a merger. PNB was stuck. Lawyers and corporate financiers had been scratching their heads for months trying to find a solution, with no success.

I cobbled together a team comprising Wan Razly and a couple of our best corporate financiers, plus (Dato) Sreesanthan Eliathamby, one of the most creative corporate lawyers in town. We gathered in my favourite meeting room, Room Two in the ten-storey Bangunan CIMB building on Jalan Semantan. It was light and airy, with a good view of the greenery beyond. The sliding doors to the balcony could be opened, so we could sneak outside for a cigarette break. It was perfect for long meetings. I announced at the outset that we weren't going to leave the room until we had a solution to PNB's conundrum. It took several hours of intense brainstorming and countless cigarette breaks before we had something that might work.

What we came up with sounded, on the face of it, like a crazy idea. PNB could be either a seller or a buyer, but not both – so it needed an intermediary to whom all three companies could be sold and who would then hand back the merged group to PNB. We racked our brains to think who might play that role, and then it struck me: why couldn't we be the intermediary in question? CIMB could buy everything and then hand it all back to PNB. We tried to poke holes in our own idea, and eventually I concluded: 'Not fail-proof but this has legs.' I told the team to map out the details, and that we could now finally leave Room Two.

CIMB would set up a shell company to buy all the assets and liabilities of the three planters including their four listed subsidiaries. In exchange all shareholders including PNB would get pro-rata shares in the shell company; so PNB would become comfortably the single largest shareholder. PNB would not, however, technically be the buyer, nor legally in control of the buyer, so this was no longer a related-party transaction. The only risk was that regulators might object on the basis that, in substance, if not form, PNB was the buyer; but we hoped they wouldn't, as it was such a compelling proposition and in the national interest. To avoid valuation arguments, we decided that we would value all the public companies at their current market prices plus a 5% premium. The same for everyone. Of course, there were plenty of reasons why companies deserve higher or lower valuations, but I was firm that any deviation from this simple basis would open a Pandora's box, and the deal would fall apart. Many great deals in which everyone stands to gain fall apart because people argue about who is making more. We had to govern the whole deal with some strict rules which applied to everyone. No company should be allowed to even tweak any of the key terms. The other danger was, of course, a leak which would move share prices and disrupt the whole deal. Quite incredibly, we moved in stealth for weeks, and there was no unusual share price movement at all until the deal was formally announced.

Once we had developed the plan, we went to search for names of shell companies to buy off the shelf. (Incorporating a new company from scratch can take time, so lawyers create 'oven-ready' companies which one can buy in order to speed the process up.) One name stood out for me: Synergy Drive. For all that it sounds like a road on a suburban business park in the US, it summed up what we were trying to do: drive down costs and drive up profits by realising synergies between the three groups of companies.

Even before I put the proposal to the flabbergasted chief executives in the Meridien, I was confident they would come around to supporting it. I had already done the groundwork. I knew they would be apprehensive and reluctant but they would take the steer of PNB's chairman, (Tun) Sarji Hamid. Sarji was rather feudal in the way he ruled the PNB group of companies. He was also key to getting the support of PM Badawi, as they were contemporaries as civil servants during my father's era. Sarji used to live next door to my mum in Jalan Eaton, so I had met him a few times, but the former chief secretary to the government was always stern and serious. When I went to see him to explain our proposal, I gathered quite quickly that he wasn't sure how much he could trust a young deal maker. Thankfully I had the foresight to bring CIMB chairman Md Nor along – Sarji would be comforted by seeing someone older and more conservative next to me. Still, just to make his priorities clear to us, he started with a one-hour lecture about PNB, the Razak legacy and the NEP, and only when he believed that I understood all that did he allow me to present my proposal. Sarji just listened, but from the body language I knew he liked the substance of what we would be able to achieve for PNB. Synergy Drive with all the companies inside would end up being 45% owned by PNB and its various unit trusts. PNB would have control of the new plantation giant and be in a position to enjoy better returns.

Once it became clear that key stakeholders wanted the Synergy Drive deal to succeed, the executives and boards of the three companies fell into line. It wasn't all plain sailing: the boards of four listed subsidiaries of Sime Darby, Guthrie and Golden Hope also had to give approval, and some of the minority shareholders complained about being forced to swap their shares in individual companies for shares in the combined group. The battleship and aircraft carrier analogy was aired once more. Thankfully, the share price of all seven listed companies went up, indicating that analysts and investors supported the deal, making it hard for anyone to claim the status quo was preferable. It also meant that those that didn't believe in the deal could always sell their shares in the market at a higher price.

The remarkable deal that turned Sime Darby, Guthrie and Golden Hope into Synergy Drive was completed in January 2007. Synergy Drive, the shell company we started with, was subsequently renamed Sime Darby and took its place as the world's largest listed palm oil producer. That was all achieved through an off-the-shelf company and dreamed up in Room Two in the CIMB offices. It felt pretty audacious.

The Synergy Drive deal was important for us at CIMB in ways we hadn't expected. The shares we held as a result of setting up the new company surged in value to such an extent that I came to feel guilty for profiting too greatly. By the end of 2007, Sime Darby's market capitalisation had risen from RM31.4bn when we announced the deal to RM59.6bn, up a phenomenal 80%, driven in part by the jump in palm oil prices from RM1,600 per tonnes to over RM4,000 per tonne in a year.[57] I reported to Nor Yakcop, now Minister of Finance II, that the bank had made a gain of between RM300m and RM400m (depending on the Sime Darby share price). We had risked RM100m in terms of upfront expenses, but I still thought we had made too much money from the deal and felt the need to own up and suggest some mitigation. I felt we should somehow give back some of the profits and proposed that CIMB set up a foundation, which, over the next few years, would give out at least RM100m to various charitable causes. CIMB Foundation went on to become the centrepiece of our corporate social responsibility programme, and the company would contribute much more than the initial commitment over years to come.

I learned many things from doing the deals we did – and those that we did not – but the most important lesson from all of this is that, even when you go ahead, a deal is only as good as the follow-through.

It was one thing to have come up with a clever idea for a deal, another to execute it. The real value of Synergy Drive would lie in how the merged company was run subsequently. That was another story. Zubir, the CEO of Sime Darby, was chosen to be CEO of the merged group. A long-serving Sime executive, Zubir certainly had the credentials, but I suspect his ego got the better of him: there were all sorts of stories of over-ambition and conflicts of interest. In 2010, Sime Darby incurred massive losses in its energy and utilities division; he was removed from his job and charged with criminal breach of trust. It all got very messy.

Zubir didn't follow through with phase two of the plan that we had mapped out, to dispose of the many peripheral businesses the planters had acquired in sectors ranging from healthcare and energy to motor vehicle services, in order to focus on the core palm oil business. Instead, the merged group continued with the same slightly chaotic mix of businesses as before. The plan to create a focused palm oil group was eventually implemented ten years later in 2017 at the behest of (Tan Sri) Wahid Omar, Sarji's successor as PNB chairman. The opportunity to create a dynamic, integrated and innovative palm oil group that could operate both upstream in plantations and downstream in added value applications and products was missed for many years at great opportunity cost, in my view, not just for the company but for Malaysia. As to whether the deal was a success, *The Edge* best summarised it in a '10 Years On' report when it wrote 'All said, has the merger delivered on its major objectives as outlined in 2006? The short answer may be that the critical mass has proved useful but much potential synergy seems to have remained unrealised.'

The Synergy Drive deal was the largest and most audacious I was involved in. There were many more that were less prominent, but each had its own story. What I learned from my career as a deal maker is that it's never enough for a deal to add up on paper. Deals are often very personal; they come down to decisions made by a handful of people. And the deal has to make sense to the people involved, who have egos to nurture and reputations to protect. To turn a deal from idea into reality you have to understand who those key people are and what makes them tick. Once talks start in earnest, something slightly strange has to happen. The two sides have opposing interests, they both want the best possible price: for the buyer that means the lowest possible, and for the seller the highest. Talks can quite easily get heated, as they did for us with Southern Bank. But a deal starts to work when a degree of trust builds up between people who start out as adversaries. Then a deal acquires a certain rhythm of back-and-forth, credible proposal and credible response. Then the chances of an agreement becomes high. People are often selling companies they have put their heart, soul and family name into, like GK. Deals are never certain. A lot can go wrong, people can just change their minds, as GK almost did. And never be too scared to pull out; some of the best deals were the ones we decided not to do.

CIMB went round the course with RHB three times – in 1998, 2012 and 2014. The first time, we opposed a bad deal in which they were proposing to take us over on outrageous terms. The second time, their major foreign shareholder (an Abu Dhabi SOE) set a ridiculously high price. In 2014, there was huge momentum behind a proposal to merge CIMB with RHB and Malaysian Building Society Berhad (MBSB). Our shareholder Khazanah was in favour; the Employees Provident Fund, which had a major stake in RHB, wanted it to happen; the regulators were happy; and the advisors were pushing us on. It was going to be a big deal, we would become the largest bank in Malaysia. But the more I looked at it, the less I liked it: making MBSB part of a banking group would have required us to set aside much more capital to cover its relatively riskier loans. Meanwhile, banking was changing rapidly, and I felt we would be paying a premium to acquire a branch network that we would sooner rather than later have to close down at some cost. Our advisors were showing gains from synergies that I simply could not believe in. So eventually we called the whole thing off. It was a tough decision to take – certainly, it was disappointing to many people, but it was the right thing to do.

Just as you need to know when to pull out, you also need to know when to go all in. That helps explain why the 2010 proposed combination of AirAsia and Malaysian Airlines did not come to pass. Had it done so, we might not be in the mess we are today with a national carrier still haemorrhaging money. Yet the reasons for the failure of that combination go to the heart of the way politics influences business in Malaysia, and it brings the story to another, fateful, shift in the political environment we operated in: my brother's rise to the pinnacle of power.

ENTER THE
TRANSFORMER

It did not take long for Prime Minister Badawi to find that opening a Pandora's Box of reforms was one thing, delivering on them was quite another. He tried hard to build consensus and in search of compromises found himself having to back down on many of his promised reforms. He created a Royal Commission that publicly recommended the establishment of the Independent Police Complaints and Misconduct Commission, but when the police resisted, Badawi caved in. He tried to tackle corruption and, while he largely kept his own reputation for being a clean politician, critics alleged that that was far from true of those around him. He introduced new processes to check and balance power and delegated authority but could not avoid being seen as slow and indecisive. He encouraged free speech but as online media and blogs took off, he was the recipient of unprecedented levels of criticism.

Mahathir, who had grown disenchanted with his successor, took full advantage of the power of blogging to launch extremely hurtful attacks. Badawi was often caught napping on camera, due (we later found out) to sleep apnoea, which inevitably left him tired the next day. When Mahathir accused him of being asleep at the wheel, it didn't seem like a metaphor.

Badawi went from leading BN to its greatest victory to presiding over its worst-ever result in the general election of 2008, when its share of the popular vote fell to 51% and the party lost its coveted two-thirds share of seats in parliament. It was a stunning reversal. (Tan Sri) Kamal Badawi, his Cambridge-educated son, said later: 'My father promised change but in the name of consensus building and a less PM centric administration, let go of control at the same time.'[58] Malaysians wanted reforms; they voted for it in droves. But Prime Minister Badawi's fate showed that the process of reforming needed to be carefully steered or people can quickly turn against the reformer.

Immediately after the elections Badawi was pressed to resign; the most powerful voices were Mahathir from the outside and (Tan Sri) Muhyiddin Yassin, then the most senior vice president, from inside UMNO. Within months the premiership was passed to his deputy, my brother, Najib, who took office in April 2009 and appointed Muhyiddin as his deputy.

Arriving at the pinnacle of political power after a thirty-year career climbing to the top, Najib hit the ground running. His opening gambit was a well-choreographed inaugural television address which he closed with the slogan: '1 Malaysia. People first. Performance now.' That became the tagline for his incoming administration. He was brimming with energy and determination to transform the country; he was attracted by innovative ideas and novel ways of doing things.

I was enthusiastic about Najib's approach. I helped to organise first an international road show for fund managers in New York in 2010 to promote his transformation agenda, and then a speech at the prestigious Sheldonian Theatre at Oxford University in 2011, when he launched his 'Movement of Moderates', in which he urged moderates from all sides to come together to develop the centre ground of global politics. The speech won plaudits around the world. It looked as if Najib could become a star on the international stage as the leader of a democratic, economically successful, West-leaning

Muslim-majority state. It was just the story that many people wanted to believe.

At home he appeared to have ambitions to reform almost every aspect of Malaysia. Najib understood the clamour for reforms and where Badawi had fallen short. He branded his reforms 'transformations' to connote follow-through and action. He enjoyed being called 'the Transformer' after the toy robots and sci-fi movies.

The first to be transformed was government itself. In January 2010, Najib launched the Government Transformation Programme (GTP), which identified six National Key Results Areas (NKRA) – crime, corruption, student outcomes, living standards, rural infrastructure and urban transport – and a seventh, cost of living, was added a few months later. Report cards were prepared to monitor progress of reforms to achieve the key milestones specified; ministers and ministries were to be held to account for their performance. The GTP was driven initially by Khazanah and then by Pemandu, the Performance and Delivery Unit led by (Dato Sri) Idris Jala, former CEO of Malaysian Airlines who had cut his teeth at Shell. Bringing a high-flying corporate CEO into the cabinet to lead transformation was a radical move that excited everyone who had been frustrated by bureaucracy.

The second part would be the economy. One of Najib's first acts as PM had been to set up a National Economic Advisory Council, chaired by (Tan Sri) Amirsham Aziz, former Maybank CEO, to devise a New Economic Model to take Malaysia from a middle-income economy to a high income, developed economy by 2020. Where Badawi's promises were vague and lofty, the NEAC produced a long, detailed and thoughtful report. Not only did it set high aspirations for what Malaysia should become; it was frank about the country's weaknesses, and systematic in proposing conceptual solutions.

The NEM called for the speedy removal of the multiple barriers that had held Malaysia back from reaching its full potential. This, the report said, would require more than incremental tweaks; it would mean a major overhaul of the way Malaysia did business.

The analysis behind the NEAC report has stood the test of time. Malaysian economic growth was slowing. Too little of what growth there was reached the bottom 40% of the population. Too much of the economy depended on low-cost competition, and on employing low-wage, often foreign labour in low-value-added activities. Productivity, innovation and investment were all below potential.

Malaysia could only break out of this trap by ending the economic model dominated by the state, which directed too much of what went on in the economy through its ownership of GLCs, subsidies, permits, licences, price controls and preferential treatment of favoured industries and businesses. State domination would have to give way to a model in which economic growth was led by private sector investment, entrepreneurship and innovation, if Malaysia was to move into the higher-value-added markets of the future in biotechnology, green services and digital technology.

Achieving those aims would require dismantling much of the machinery through which the state managed the economy, the NEAC concluded. It would demand improvements in the quality of governance in the public and private sectors so that they matched international standards. And it would mean reforming the education system to create a more entrepreneurial, creative and collaborative workforce that would be capable of engaging in continuous innovation. The country's position with regard to human capital was concerning, the report warned: Malaysia was not developing enough talent, and too many of those with talent were packing their bags and leaving, at an accelerating rate, while the number of skilled expatriates was also in decline. The NEM was farsighted enough to see that environmental concerns would also become a big factor for Malaysia: its reliance on palm oil and petroleum could become a vulnerability in a world trying to respond to climate change. Malaysia needed a new Green Growth model, it recommended.

The most striking aspect of the NEM was its willingness to confront the issue of affirmative action. The report could not have been clearer that the NEP needed a far-reaching overhaul: 'The NEP has reduced poverty and substantially addressed inter-ethnic economic imbalances. However, its implementation has also increasingly and inadvertently raised the cost of doing business due to rent-seeking, patronage and often opaque government procurement. This has engendered pervasive corruption, which needs to be addressed earnestly.'[59] Not only that, the report went on, but the NEP was proving ineffective in reducing inequality. Malaysia had all but eradicated extreme poverty, but about 40% of the population were still only just hovering above the poverty line.

All of this chimed with the conclusions I had reached myself based on my own experience. The machinery which had grown out of my father's first legacy, the institutions and programmes of state-led development and affirmative action, with the NEP at their heart, had become dysfunctional and ineffective. Worse, their diversion from their true purpose had created fertile conditions for corruption and patronage which undermined my father's second legacy, the values and principles he believed should guide good government. It seemed to me, and I was not alone, that Najib, the eldest son, was now going to offer a credible, comprehensive package of reforms to put the country back on the right path.

The NEM proposed that instead of imposing conditions on business to meet specific ownership quotas, or targets to employ *bumiputra*, help would be based on need and merit rather than ethnic identity. Affirmative action would be market-based: it would encourage people to build up the skills they needed to earn higher incomes or run their own businesses. This would allow the economy to become less unequal, more productive and more competitive at the same time.

The authors of the NEM were well aware of the obstacles. A wave of linked reforms would be needed; such sweeping changes would not be possible without the political will to overcome the resistance of vested interests. 'The most important enablers of the NEM are political will and leadership to break the log-jam of resistance by vested interest groups and preparing the *rakyat* to support deep seated changes in policy direction,'[60] the report concluded. 'Resistance is likely to come from the business community, including protected industries, employers of foreign labour, licence holders, beneficiaries of subsidies and experts at doing business the old way.'

The NEAC report, dated 30 March 2010, conceptualised the most ambitious reform programme for Malaysia since my father had introduced the NEP back in 1970. The report concluded with a warning: Malaysia would lose its way unless urgent action was taken.

That was, it turned out, exactly what happened.

One test of Najib's commitment to transformation, with business driving innovation and higher productivity, was the possible merger of loss-making Malaysia Airlines (MAS) with the rising force that was AirAsia. I was at the heart of the negotiations.

The possibility of that merger had first arisen in 2009, when Idris Jala, then MAS CEO, came to see me to discuss whether the two Malaysian companies should stop undermining each other in what was already a tough market. I knew (Tan Sri) Tony Fernandes, the CEO of AirAsia, would jump at the deal, because it would appeal to his thirst for glory and excitement. And he would see the commercial logic.

I first met Tony in early 2001 when he came to my office with his partners, looking for finance to purchase a low-cost airline, AirAsia. I couldn't see why he thought it was a good idea for him to own an airline when he didn't have deep pockets and only had experience in the music business. I didn't want to sound condescending, so I made the excuse that MAS was a sister company of ours (through Khazanah) and my former boss, Md Nor was its chief executive at the time. Tony had already written off the meeting as pointless even before he came along. Afterwards, he let everyone know he thought I was a cocky princeling. (That was the polite version.) I meanwhile was trying to think if I had heard a more ridiculous business idea.

Only three years later, in 2004, AirAsia had become a huge success and was contemplating an IPO, so I beat a path to Tony's door to pitch for handling the flotation. I couldn't bear the thought that this high-profile offering might not involve CIMB. Reluctantly, at the behest of an old friend, Tony agreed to see me over a Japanese lunch. I was in terrible shape, with a sore throat and temperature, but I was determined to make CIMB's case in person. He took some relish in getting his own back, making it plain we would not be getting the business. I suppose that meant we were all square and somehow we agreed that we'd play some squash together.

I was impressed by what he had done with his airline and, along with some squash, I got an insight into his sense of competitiveness, which wasn't unlike my own. Our first contest was like something from *The Hunger Games*; we flung ourselves around the court in what felt like a fight to the death. I liked him because he was such an outspoken, energetic, creative, plain-speaking outsider. I gather he saw me as a classic product of the establishment, but with a rebellious and irreverent streak.

When I suggested that AirAsia should merge with MAS, Tony was enthusiastic. 'If you can turn around Bank Bumi,' he said, 'why can't I turn around MAS?' Azman Mokhtar at Khazanah was always sceptical whether the deal would work but he knew the loss-making airline was Khazanah's Achilles' heel and was open to more radical solutions. Azman and Tony were among a group of senior Malaysians who came to Oxford for Najib's speech in May 2011 when he launched his Movement of Moderates. As the three of us got talking, the deal moved from being merely an idea to seeming a real possibility.

When we got back to KL, I put the idea to Najib, who was also the chairman of Khazanah. This kind of deal, injecting home-grown private-sector entrepreneurship to turn around a struggling state-owned enterprise, sounded just the kind of thing the NEM had in mind. Yet from the outset Najib sounded a note of caution. He thought it wouldn't look good to his core Malay support to have AirAsia take over the national flag carrier and he wasn't ready to relinquish control of a strategic national asset to Tony. So instead of either going all in or calling it off altogether, Najib said he preferred the more cautious idea of an initial collaboration between the two airlines, through an exchange of shares, to test the water. If that worked, the companies could go for a full-scale merger.

These awkward compromises rarely work with deal making, as we found out the hard way. In August 2011, Tony and his partners took a 20% stake in MAS and gave Khazanah a 10% stake in AA in return, and the two airlines began trying to collaborate. The partnership provoked fierce opposition, especially from MAS staff, consumer groups and Malay activists. Staff on both sides tried to assert their superiority: after all, the two tribes had fought each other for years, and now they were being asked to work together. Consumer groups screamed accusingly every time prices went up or flight frequencies were reduced. The ethnic communalism that played a role in CIMB's Southern Bank takeover was also a factor in this deal. As if all that wasn't enough, we were taken by surprise by the newly created Malaysia Competition Commission (MyCC), which saw aspects of the collaboration as anti-competitive. This was the Commission's first case; ironically, it wouldn't have had an issue if the two companies had merged completely. The moment I knew the deal's days were numbered was when MAS announced its sponsorship of Queens Park Rangers, the English Championship football team Tony owned. I am not sure whose idea this was, but perception is reality, and the perception was that Tony had used his new-found clout for personal gain. The deal's opponents made the most of it. We had misjudged the public reaction to the deal; everyone seemed to have a reason to dislike it.

In May 2012, Najib asked Azman to unwind the share swap. Afterwards, Najib told me: 'The deal made economic sense but, unfortunately, not political sense.' It was proof that despite the coherence and ambition of the strategy set out in the NEM, politics was still the decisive factor. As MAS continues to flounder, I can't help thinking that we, by which I mean the entire country, missed the opportunity to build a great airline combining a low-cost, no-frills offer with a full-service airline, while exploiting huge synergies. It was a reminder that the political backdrop for the economy and business was largely unchanged, despite the rhetoric to the contrary.

The failure of the MAS–AA partnership was just one instance of the failure to follow through with the NEM. The NEM was never just about the economy; reforming the NEP, corruption and education could never be just that, it had to reach into politics. Najib would lament that without his own electoral mandate he could not take on political reforms. Barely six months after the NEM report was released on 21 September 2010 Najib launched the Economic Transformation Plan (ETP), again spearheaded by Idris and Pemandu, with the aim of transforming Malaysia into a developed world economy within a decade by reforming key economic sectors and facilitating private investment in them. Many important multi-billion-ringgit infrastructure projects trace their inception to the ETP, including the KL–Singapore High Speed Rail link and KL–MY Rapid Transit system. Idris listed a total of 131 so-called Entry Point Projects worth RM800bn that he said would propel Malaysia to become a high-income nation by 2020.[61] The thought of such a massive surge in economic activity was mouth-watering and Idris' regular engagement programmes caught the public's imagination. Yet as the ETP gained momentum, the rest of the NEM's reforms took their place on the long shelf of great unimplemented plans. Whether Najib would have implemented the NEM if he had won a stronger mandate in 2013 we will never know. It was never enough to transform just government and the economy, there had to be a third leg – a 'Political Transformation Programme'. On more than one occasion I would point out to Najib you cannot just mend two of three broken legs of a table.

Although I was sharing my "two sens" on national issues from time to time, they were nothing more than the kind of ad hoc suggestions a PM gets from friends and family members. I was more focused on CIMB's continued transformation. We had gone from investment bank to universal bank. Now another calling presented itself. It was time to get to know our neighbours.

THE ASEAN
ADVENTURE

The timing was a coincidence, the consequences were fateful. On 6 November 2006, I became CEO of the entire Bumiputra Commerce Holdings Berhad group of companies (soon after renamed CIMB Group).[62] Three months later, on 15 January 2007, at the twelfth ASEAN summit, the heads of state brought forward the implementation date for the ASEAN Economic Community (AEC) from 2020 to 2015. From that point on my career became inextricably connected to ASEAN. Our ambition would be to become one of ASEAN's leading universal banks, with operations all across the region.

At the beginning of 2007, CIMB Group included the third-largest commercial bank in Malaysia (after Maybank and Public Bank), ASEAN's largest investment bank and Indonesia's sixth-largest bank (thanks to a stake we had taken a few years earlier in Bank Niaga). Just five years later, at the end of 2012, CIMB was ASEAN's fifth, Malaysia's second and Indonesia's fifth-largest bank by assets. We had universal banking capabilities in Malaysia, Indonesia, Thailand, Singapore and Cambodia and ASEAN's widest branch network, with 1,079 branches from Chiang Rai to Bali. As well as being ASEAN's top investment bank, CIMB was also the world leader in *sukuks*, or Islamic bonds. It was an amazing run.

We had been both pushed and pulled to pursue an ASEAN strategy.

The push came from the fact that in the long term we couldn't rely on our small domestic market, of just over 30 million people, for the scale necessary for a universal banking operation. The landscape was shifting in no small part due to technology: good banks would be less about human relationships and more about online and mobile applications, and technology-enhanced processes, from risk management to credit assessment to trading of financial products. Creating those digital platforms would be expensive. We could continue for a while on the path we were on. But sooner or later we would need economies of scale to reduce unit costs, invest in new technologies and compete in increasingly open markets.

The pull came from the attraction of ASEAN: more than 630m relatively young people, in fast-growing economies, well endowed with natural resources and strategically located between the fastest-growing large economies of the twenty-first century, India and China. For me there was something almost romantic about building an ASEAN banking group. I wanted to show that Southeast Asians could do it for themselves. And there was a family dimension too: a more integrated ASEAN was another part of my father's legacy; he was one of the 'original five' who negotiated and signed the 1967 ASEAN declaration; he spoke often about the importance of regional collaboration and independence in the midst of the Cold War.

ASEAN has been vital for peace and stability, enabling regional dialogue and collaboration, all of which have been the basis for the extraordinary prosperity of the region over the past four decades. The 1992 ASEAN Free Trade Area Agreement started the process of economic collaboration amongst countries to show that regionalism could deliver economic as well as political benefits. The plan to create the AEC, launched in 2007, was the big leap with a vision of a 'single market and production base, characterised by the free flow of goods, services, investment and skilled labour as well as the freer flow of capital by 2015'.[63] Across ASEAN, barriers to trade were coming down, and movement of goods and services, people and information, was getting easier. We wanted CIMB to be the bank to make all that work for ASEAN companies, consumers and investors.

We had already taken some small steps outside Malaysia. The first had come, at the turn of the century from Md Nor's long-held ambition to take the group into Indonesia.

Md Nor subscribed to the notion of *serumpun*, that Malaysians and Indonesians were of the same ethnic roots and therefore should collaborate and integrate more. The corporate carnage left behind by the AFC created opportunities to buy what had been good banks. Md Nor eyed Bank Niaga as the best choice; the 'local Citibank', as it was known, because many of its staff were well-trained ex-Citibankers. Bank Niaga was similar in complexion to Bank of Commerce in that its roots lay in corporate banking. Coincidentally Niaga also means Commerce in Bahasa.

Niaga was the second bank (after Bank Central Asia) to be sold by IBRA, the Indonesian bank restructuring agency, in the wake of the AFC. We first indicated our interest early in 1999, but I had meetings with five different president commissioners (chairmen) of IBRA before they finally launched the tender in 2002. We were nothing if not persistent, and when we were told that it was a very competitive situation we put our best foot forward. Shortly afterwards, when bids closed, IBRA called me to say that we had been shortlisted. Naturally, I was overjoyed. 'Who else is shortlisted?', I asked, keen to know who we were competing against. 'You're the only bidder,' came the reply. 'Actually, you've won it.' At that point my heart sank. I wondered what everyone else knew that we didn't.

My worries only intensified when the deal went down badly with our investors. We bought Bank Niaga for what we thought was a good price – less than 1.5 times its book value – for a large bank with all its bad debts cleaned up. But analysts were predicting the Indonesian economy would not escape from a downward spiral. Prem Manjooran, the Malaysia specialist at Capital International, our largest foreign investor, came to our office demanding to know what we were doing throwing money away in Indonesia, which he described as a failing state. Within a week of the deal being completed, the Commerce stock price was down 25%. Prem would go on to be a good personal friend, but there was no room for pleasantries then; he wanted us to know he was annoyed, so he placed his orders to sell our shares through his dealer at CIMB. For days I could only watch helplessly as we hammered down our own share price on Prem's instruction. It was not an auspicious start to our ASEAN expansion.

For the first few years Commerce didn't do much with Bank Niaga beyond taking its seats on the board. Contrary to what many were expecting, Indonesia stabilised and recovered rather quickly, and Bank Niaga rode the rising tide while other much larger banks were still beached and under repair. Economic recovery, the potential of its huge population of 220 million and the emergence of a stable democratic politics got everyone excited about Indonesia. Valuations of Indonesian banks shot up: in 2008 Maybank paid 4.6 times book for its control of Bank Internasional Indonesia (BII). Our early investment looked smart, as even Prem later acknowledged.

When I took charge of the whole group, Niaga came under my purview, and I moved to increase collaboration between CIMB and Niaga, to find cross-border synergies. In investment banking we started to channel all of Niaga's equities-related business to CIMB GK Indonesia. In treasury, CIMB structured more sophisticated products for Niaga to sell to its clients. CIMB's ex-Southern Bank team helped Niaga launch its new premium credit cards. And in branch banking the learning went the other way: Bank Niaga was much better at branch customer service, so we seconded a squad of young Indonesians to various CIMB branches in Malaysia..

Our investment in Indonesia deepened when Khazanah was required to sell its stake in Bank Lippo, a well-regarded mid-sized bank once part of the Lippo Group, to comply with Bank Indonesia's policy that no investor should hold stakes in more than one bank. The sale of Bank Lippo to one of our competitors (Maybank made an attractive offer) was contemplated; but Khazanah decided that the best way for it to maximise the value of its stake was by enhancing the value of its shares in CIMB and allowing us to merge Lippo and Niaga to create the fifth-largest bank in Indonesia. The RM8.6bn merger was signed on 2 June 2008, and the combined bank was renamed PT Bank CIMB Niaga.[64] In tune with the scale of the new bank, a 'heavyweight' corporate figure, Arwin Rasyid, was appointed CEO. He was previously a corporate banker with Niaga but had also been CEO of PT Telkom and vice chairman of IBRA.

We sent a large team to Indonesia for months to help with the integration of the two banks. They were confident. The BCB and Southern Bank integration had been a great success, comfortably exceeding the synergy targets we set ourselves. But soon they realised that things were different there; understandably the locals liked to do things their way. Despite my insisting that this was a merger not a takeover we couldn't stop Niaga staff asserting themselves as the 'winners', and, as a result, we lost quite a few Lippo staff and customers. We then launched the CIMB regional operating model, where divisions were integrated across the region, but the Indonesian team never quite embraced the idea of being directed by Kuala Lumpur. Since the OJK (Otoritas Jasa Keuangan, the new Indonesian Financial Services Authority) regulations prohibited shareholders from being involved in operations, we had to rely on moral suasion instead of directives. Without properly integrating divisions across borders, we couldn't maximise synergies nor exercise sufficient oversight.

The effects were not evident in the early years, during which CIMB Niaga posted great results. CIMB Niaga profits grew from about RM400m in 2008 to RM1.9bn in 2012, and net return on equity reached as high as 21% in 2012.[65] As Indonesia became flavour of the season during the commodities boom, and CIMB

Niaga contributed as much as 32% of the entire Group's profits in 2012, our shares became a proxy for the Indonesian market, especially for investors who couldn't invest in the country directly themselves for one reason or other.

Having bedded down Indonesia, we started to look for banks to acquire in other markets. We were in a hurry to build a complete ASEAN platform, ahead of the arrival of the AEC. Where there were scant acquisition opportunities, we devised other strategies.

In Singapore, through our acquisitions of BCB and Southern Bank, we already had two branches. However, we were not going to be getting any more; I got the hint from 'well-informed' friends that unless the Singaporean DBS Bank was able to acquire a bank in Malaysia we couldn't expect any concessions from the Singapore authorities. We could sing all the sweet ASEAN tunes we wanted; to Singapore Inc. we were part of Malaysia Inc.

Our strategy in Singapore was to turn the constraints we faced into an advantage. In 2008, we launched a 'direct' retail bank, which would rely on telephone, online channels and mobile sales staff. A number of investors questioned the logic of starting a new retail offering in a saturated market dominated by giant banks. However, by sharing cost savings with customers via better pricing and focusing on superior standards of service, we were very successful: by 2012 we already had 44,000 retail customers and by 2017, 125,000 customers. At the same time, we continued to grow the rest of our businesses riding on investment banking, the ex GK Goh platform and the large Malaysian diaspora in Singapore.

We appointed Mak Lye Mun, one of the best talents we inherited from GK Goh, as CEO of the bank. Lye Mun fully subscribed to the regional operating model. In contrast to Indonesia, Singapore was fully integrated; there was a seamless flow of information, people and funding. CIMB Singapore's net profit grew steadily from SGD 6m in 2008 to SGD75m in 2012 and SGD154m in 2017, which accounted for roughly 10% of the Group's profits.[66] Lye Mun was promoted to head CIMB's entire wholesale business (treasury, investment banking and private banking) in 2016, the first time a major regional business head was based outside of KL.

In Cambodia, we chose yet another approach; we took on a completely new licence to create a new bank from scratch. The central bank had a laissez-faire attitude: So long as you met all the requisite criteria you could get a licence. After applying for the licence on a trip to Phnom Penh in 2009, I requested to make a courtesy call to the governor of the Bank of Cambodia. To my surprise he insisted on coming to tea with me at my hotel and brought our licence along with him; you don't get a warmer Central Bank welcome than this, I thought to myself. We launched CIMB Cambodia on 19 November 2010 (by coincidence on my birthday). A small but very successful start-up, it became profitable within five years, and grew to have thirteen branches and pre-tax profits of more than $10m by 2017.

Thailand was a story of clever acquisition but frustrating operational execution. CIMB was still relatively little known outside southern ASEAN countries when we came to bid for BankThai in 2008. Indeed, when our acquisitions team first went to make a presentation to officials at the Bank of Thailand (BOT), they were taken into a side room and asked to explain which bank they came from. Our hosts hadn't heard of us. Yet ironically this lack of a presence in Thailand became an advantage. Almost everyone else who was interested in BankThai – HSBC for example – already had a stake in one of the country's banks, and BOT regulations stipulated that a foreign bank couldn't own more than one Thai bank. Everyone else had to make conditional offers that depended on their being able to sell their other business or merge it with BankThai. We were free from those entanglements and so could make a straight cash bid.

We were delighted to pull off this deal, paying RM1.8bn for a 93.1% stake which translated to a valuation of 2.3 times book value. But BankThai turned out to be a really tough slog.

The bank had a troubled history, having been born out of the merger of fourteen distressed finance companies shoehorned together by the BOT's Financial Institutions Development Fund (FIDF) in the wake of the Asian Financial Crisis. Each of these finance companies had its own legacy system and lots of legacy people. The bank had a vast network of ATM machines, but half of them weren't working, and some were only used for a handful of transactions a day. Costs were high from the top down, the CEO even had a string of personal advisors on the books. Our first decision was to appoint a new CEO, another 'heavyweight', Dr Subhak Siwaraksa, who previously headed Thai Military Bank (and remove all the personal advisors!).

We described CIMB Thai as a 'turnaround' situation, and while it has had its moments, overall it fell short of expectations. The bank needed to see itself as an upstart challenger as it was sub-scale, the eleventh-largest in a market dominated by giants Siam Commercial Bank and Bangkok Bank. Yet its strategy was much the same as CIMB in Malaysia and Indonesia, where we were among the largest players.

It didn't help that Thailand was beset by one problem after another after we went in. There were terrible floods in 2011 and long bouts of political turmoil, as rival groups of protestors wearing red and yellow T-shirts took to the streets in 2010, 2013 and 2014, often right outside CIMB Thai's head office on Langsuan Road in Bangkok.

It was often hard for the regional team to even be in Bangkok, as we were insistent on the complete safety of our staff. On one occasion we heard that the red shirts in huge numbers had seized Suvarnabhumi airport, so I took no chances. I hired and despatched a private jet to the old airport at Don Muang to bring home our Malaysian staff. As the plane was landing, the pilot could see red shirts swarming down the road towards it. He calculated there was just enough time to land, pick up the team and take off again. Our team ran to the plane as soon as it landed. But at the foot of the aircraft steps, inexplicably, they paused. The pilot was consternated. The crew were shouting at them to get on the plane. The Malaysians carried on, milling about at the foot of the stairway. It was their first experience of boarding a private jet. Never mind the angry rebels breaking through the barriers, heading straight for them, nothing was going to stop them taking selfies!

In 2013, CIMB tried to enter the Philippines. Based on our Thai experience, where it was hard to break through as a small bank with little brand recognition, we looked for a partnership model with one of the conglomerates that dominate the Philippine economy, and in that sense we found probably the best partner in the San Miguel group, the country's most diversified conglomerate, which wanted to find someone to run its bank. Coincidentally, its subsidiary was also called Bank of Commerce. It seemed like destiny! Unfortunately we couldn't close the deal, as it proved difficult to agree partnership arrangements that could weather all eventualities. In 2017, once Bangko Sentral ng Pilipinas (BSP) liberalised issuance of new licences to foreigners, CIMB went back to create a pure digital bank, which was launched in December 2018, just after I retired. By all accounts CIMB Philippines exceeded expectations, reaching 2 million customers in just fifteen months.

The pure digital bank was also the strategy eventually pursued for Vietnam, where CIMB was awarded a new licence in 2016, some years after its initial application. Advances in technology and the success of new digital banks, especially in China, had totally transformed banking, and the economics of cross-border expansion. Building banks from scratch need not be a slow process. CIMB Vietnam was initially launched on a traditional banking model, so its strategy had to be recalibrated, and its development fell behind CIMB Philippines.

By the end of 2018, CIMB was present in all ten ASEAN countries. Aside from the major operating units, CIMB Investment Bank had set up an advisory unit in Brunei in 2008, BOC had kept a representative office in Myanmar ever since the early 1990s, and CIMB Thai set up a branch in Laos in 2014.

How should the ASEAN strategy be assessed with the benefit of hindsight?

If we start with ASEAN itself, the AEC fell well short of being the land it promised to be. The AEC isn't anything like the single production base that was envisaged, even though it was launched with great fanfare at the beginning of 2016 (one year late). As sharply as tariffs came down, non-tariff barriers went up. Intra-regional trade and travel didn't grow very much as a percentage of the totals but intra-regional investments did, underpinned by regionalisation of companies like CIMB, Ayala, Siam Cement, Capital Land and Salim Group. One of the reasons the AEC fell short was the lack of consultation between bureaucracy and industry. For instance, banking regulators spoke of encouraging regional banking: what ASEAN banks needed was easier flows of information, people and operations across borders to facilitate operational synergies, yet all ASEAN central banks ended up agreeing was that central banks should negotiate licences bilaterally – a somewhat ironic outcome for a multilateral platform.

Although AEC wasn't the enabler we hoped, ASEAN did resonate with customers. For all its domestic struggles, CIMB Thai excelled in channelling business from Thai companies operating in other markets to the rest of the Group. ASEAN also helped bring the organisation together. One of my favourite events was the CIMB ASEAN Games, when we gathered staff to compete in various sports: the sense of camaraderie was powerful. It also brought a greater sense of purpose to our work, the mission to catalyse regional integration.

CIMB would have regionalised with or without AEC. In investment banking we needed new markets for growth, whereas in commercial banking we needed the scale. There were synergies every day in making revenues and in reducing costs. In procurement, for example, the single core banking system CIMB bought for about RM1.0bn in 2009 would have cost 70% more if its various banks had to buy their own. However, the cost savings generated were considerably less than we hoped, because we could not get rid of the duplication of senior staff, systems and processes due to local regulations. And regulators would restrict the extent of integration. Indonesia, for instance, would not allow secondment of staff below a certain seniority or the hubbing of operations overseas.

They say diversity defines ASEAN. At the start, we underestimated the implications of that statement; we had to learn for ourselves, sometimes the hard way. Even a simple 'yes' in a reply from staff can mean quite different things; in some countries staff mean: 'Yes, your instruction would be carried out promptly'; in others, staff just mean: 'Yes, I heard you,' so if you didn't follow up, it just wouldn't be done. There were things it took time for us to 'get': our corporate mascot for online banking was the Octopus, affectionately known as Octo: He was one of the first things that greeted a new visitor to Malaysia on the trains at KL international airport. I issued instructions that Octo needed to be used consistently across all territories. Only after thousands of Octos had gone out did someone point out that in Indonesia "octo" is a term of abuse reserved for corrupt politicians. We had to recall thousands of Octos! I was livid that no one from CIMB Niaga had bothered to warn me beforehand, but it was just symptomatic that in Indonesia there is a greater reluctance to question the boss than there is in Malaysia and Singapore.

Cultural and language differences made it much harder. In Thailand, for example, the language barrier was troublesome, but the cultural differences were even more serious. People in different cultures respond to pressure differently, and I think I underestimated how our Thai colleagues would react when I kept pointing out that Singapore was much smaller yet so much more profitable. They became determined to prove themselves, which in turn proved costly at times. To generate high growth, they grew their loan book too rapidly, and in time credit defaults rose. In Indonesia it took me years to figure out why so many of our bad loans were due not to poor credit assessment by staff but to siphoning of funds by borrowers. It eventually dawned on me that ultimately it was the lack of fear of the legal system and the threat of imprisonment that allowed people to behave that way. Being incarcerated just doesn't have the same social stigma as in, say, Malaysia and Singapore.

Looking back now, would I do it again, knowing what we do today? The challenge was to get the right balance between operating as a single integrated ASEAN company and being multi-local; there is never a solution that covers all situations at all times. However, the basic premise of ASEAN expansion remains solid: a fast-growing, increasingly connected market right on our doorstep made up of millions of people with aspirations to live better, longer, richer lives. And it was those stories that kept inspiring me on what was also a personal journey.

I will never forget talking to Bun Yin, general manager of CIMB Cambodia, about his traumatic experience surviving the Killing Fields, Pol Pot's reign of terror and genocide in the early 1970s, which killed an estimated 2 million people in a population of only 5 million. He had been listed for execution and survived only because the invading Vietnamese arrived on the very morning he was due to be killed. The fact that we played a role in our manager's journey from fighting for his life to running a bank left a deep impression on me. It is not just the numbers that count in banking, it's the people. Banking at its best can help people transform their lives, as it did for Bun Yin. The real purpose of banking is to help people live better lives, in better homes, to gain a better education and to increase their livelihoods. Across ASEAN that story is being played out in tens of millions of families every day. I wanted CIMB to support these people, to make their aspirations real. The big story of ASEAN is actually made up of millions upon millions of these micro stories of hard work, saving, aspiration and persistence. I am glad that CIMB decided to be a part of that story.

If I could do it again, I would, but the strategy would be different, especially knowing what we do about banking today. It would be primarily about building new digital banks from scratch rather than buying legacy operations and branch networks. It would have been slower but much less capital-intensive. In general I would opt for a slower pace of growth as the rush to success ahead of the AEC proved costly in areas where our risk oversight was less developed and I would also not have such high hopes about ASEAN as an enabler for business. ASEAN will always be a fabulous political platform, but economics will always be just an addendum to that.

At the end of 2012, the effects of our regionalisation were clear: CIMB's non-Malaysian operations accounted for 41% of profits. No other regional banking group came close. All country units were profitable; even CIMB Thai returned 7.4% on our invested capital. CIMB Niaga's profits were up 31.8% from the previous year; Singapore profits had doubled, albeit from a small base. Across the region consumer banking (SME and retail) was up 24% while wholesale (treasury, corporate and investment banking) was up 23%. From 2010 to 2012, CIMB Group recorded three consecutive years of record profits and return on equity exceeding 16%. There was a triumphant feel about the place.[67]

There were clouds on the horizon, though. Bank Negara was introducing a new capital adequacy framework on 1 January 2013; the CIMB Annual Report for 2012 noted in passing that CIMB had introduced a Dividend Reinvestment Scheme (DRS) as part of its dividend for the year. The DRS allowed shareholders to receive new shares at an attractive discounted price instead of cash. I didn't like the DRS, as it was unfair to shareholders who needed annual cash payment, but it was the simplest way to add capital to our base. Conceding on introducing the DRS was a reflection of how concerned I was about the impact the new rules could have on us, even though a lot of details were still being finalised. We had come through the 2008 global financial crisis almost without a dent, but in time we would get caught by its aftershocks. The crisis did not get us; the response to the crisis did cause us trouble.

THE GFC CAME LATE

In my annual letter to shareholders in early 2009 I described the previous year as 'the most traumatic year in the history of modern world financial markets', reflecting the devastation it brought to the most venerable names in international banking and finance. Lehman Brothers, the bank I was tempted to join back in 1993, was just the most high-profile casualty. Of course, ASEAN was not immune to the shockwaves, yet in contrast to the Asian Financial Crisis ten years earlier CIMB's financial performance was barely dented. In 2008, CIMB Group's net profit dipped 26% to RM2.69bn. The following year, CIMB's net profit jumped 43.8%, to RM3.79bn, and net return on equity Return on Equity hit a then record high of 14.9% as improvements from our Malaysian mergers started to come through and our international operations did well. Not only did we brush off the Global Financial Crisis (GFC) operationally, we seemed to be beneficiaries of the surge in capital flows to emerging markets made possible by the quantitative easing (QE) strategies of the developed economies, which meant that interest rates were kept low and banks had their balance sheets bolstered. In 2009, CIMB's share price jumped 119%, outperforming the top thirty companies on the Bursa Malaysia by 74%.

Yet the GFC had a delayed but profound impact on CIMB and its heady expansion fuelled by mergers and acquisitions. In 2012, we were sorely tempted into buying a piece of Royal Bank of Scotland (RBS), a once-mighty global bank that was retreating in disarray after the GFC. Our stock was trading at more than two times book, we had ample capacity to do lots of things. Or so we thought. For at the same time, financial regulators were collectively developing new rules and regulations for banks to make them safer and even boring. In many ways CIMB epitomised the aggressive bank that re-regulation after the GFC was designed to tame.

The RBS deal seemed to make perfect sense. The bank had grown to become one of the largest banks in the world, in part through its takeover of NatWest in the UK. It had, however, become ridiculously overstretched, and it was now so desperate to sell its Asian stockbroking and corporate finance business that it was making it available at 80% of its book value, RM850 million. This was tempting: we could merge the business with our own investment banking and stockbroking business, already the largest across ASEAN, making it the largest investment banking operation in the whole of the Asian Pacific region excluding Japan. The deal would enlarge our presence in Hong Kong, take us into Australia and give us access to markets in South Korea, Taiwan and India. We could help RBS clients to access ASEAN markets, and, in turn, RBS could offer our clients access to Australia and other large Asian markets. It was compelling, at least on paper.

Once the deal was done, we started grappling with making it work in practice. We knew that margins in the traditional stockbroking business were thinning due to liberalisation and competition eating into commissions. We didn't factor in the near disappearance of those margins as more trades went online and more trading went through algorithms requiring systems that we could not afford to develop. Some key RBS staff had left, and only a trickle of deals was coming through. The engine was out of gas. The CIMB brand did not help them. We were not well known in Asia beyond ASEAN, and completely unknown in Australia. When it did work, the new platform delivered impressive results: for instance, in 2013, we led the $1.3bn IPO for Asian Pay Television, a Taiwanese asset, owned by Australians, that was to be listed in Singapore.[68] We had headline deals in Australia, Taiwan and Hong Kong. But there were too few such deals, and margins continued to dwindle while costs remained stubbornly high.

A toxic culture had taken root at RBS in the heady run-up to the 2008 crash. People there assumed that they were entitled to be well paid even when they were making losses. They didn't seem to mind that the accounts were awash with red ink. CIMB, in contrast, had pulled itself up by its bootstraps in part by turning around loss-making banks. We *hated* red ink. We could never get that message across to the team in Sydney in particular. Some would say our senior management was too gentlemanly to take on the big egos of the alpha-male culture in Sydney. But the truth is that the problem went deeper. The RBS staff would always ask what was in it for them before they'd do anything: raw self-interest was dominant. At CIMB we had striven to create a culture where people worked for one another in the cause of the shared enterprise in a spirit of mutual gains. As one of my colleagues put it, CIMB staff in Kuala Lumpur who had been used to doing long days, day after day, to get deals done, would look at the RBS guys and wonder how they got away with being paid so much for doing so little. The RBS guys in Sydney would look down their noses at their ASEAN colleagues, wondering why they were so diligent and hard-working.

The RBS acquisition only added about 4% to overheads in 2013. The deal was small relative to CIMB as a whole but it came at a bad time and left a sour taste.

They say thirteen is an unlucky number; 2013 was a turning point for CIMB as the operating environment soured for emerging markets and ASEAN in particular. Funds were leaving our markets as the West began to recover from the GFC and the commodities market suffered an abrupt downturn. That year, global markets rose 24%, but emerging markets fell 5%, and ASEAN 7%.[69] Indonesia was badly affected, with the ruppiah losing 21% to the USD while domestic interest rates jumped by 1.75%, slowing growth and sharply increasing our share of bad loans. CIMB Niaga, which had been our most powerful growth engine, was spluttering.

In 2013, CIMB Group's profit dropped 2.2% (excluding one-off items), but overheads had jumped 11.1%, and loan losses also doubled to RM660m.[70] Our net return on equity of 15.5% fell short of our target of 16%. Fortunately, profits from Thailand and Singapore grew well, as did overall consumer banking in the region. We were not in trouble, but our performance was decidedly mixed.

Looking ahead, I began to worry about the Group's prospects. We had set high standards, achieving record profits and rates of return on equity in the mid-teens every year since 2009. But we had accumulated costs with our acquisitions and, with overheads totalling RM8.5bn for the year, our cost-to-income ratio was 57.6% in 2013, much higher than those of our main competitors.[71] Growth at CIMB Niaga was stalling, and the bad debt ratios suggested that it might get a lot worse.

In 2012, we had hired Dave Thomas from RBS (separately from the acquisition) as head of Group Risk to take over from Dr Gan. In his phrase, it was time to 'fix the plumbing'. Dave was a veteran of the global financial crisis and brought energy as well as experience to this job. He had seen it all before and was concerned about the quality of many of our Indonesian loans, the impact of new regulations and our high cost base, which becomes an acute challenge when revenues slow sharply. There could be no quick fixes, and we had to do things methodically. I agreed and pulled together a team to develop what we called the Target 18, or T18, plan, which would set targets for three years ahead to allow us to make decisions for the long term. The idea was to force ourselves to set aside the near term, disrupt whatever part of the business necessary as long as shaking it up meant better and more sustainable results in the long run.

Our capital situation could not wait for the new plan, though. At the start of 2014, we raised RM3.55bn of new capital by private placement, the first and only time in my career as CEO that we tapped shareholders for funds. The new capital adequacy framework applied by Bank Negara applied not just to CIMB the bank but the CIMB Group as a whole. And under the new methodology, goodwill on our balance sheet (the premium we paid to acquire companies at above their tangible assets) was to be deducted when calculating capital. It was a massive hit due to our many acquisitions: we had RM8.1bn in goodwill, almost 28% of RM29.3bn of shareholders' equity. Meanwhile, the way to calculate Risk Weighted Assets was also changed, which meant you needed more capital for any given asset. Suddenly, from a situation where we thought we had excess capital, we had barely enough. Our own minimum target for our main Common Equity Tier-1 (known as 'CET1'), was 8% of risk-weighted assets; at the end of 2012, we were only just slightly ahead at 8.1%. After the new private placement shares were issued, we were still only at 9.5%.[72]

In 2014, the operating environment took a further turn for the worse. The slump in commodity prices continued to undermine the rupiah and businesses dealing in commodities. The Group's operating income dropped but only by 1%; however, with our high cost base and loan loss provisions, the Group's net profits fell by 23% to RM3.1bn. Our return on equity fell to 9.2%, well below our target of 13.5%, and our stock underperformed the stock exchange index by 22.3%. CIMB Niaga's profits declined another 45% in 2014, and you could tell from the rise in impaired assets that its results were not getting better soon.[73]

I knew the T18 programme was the right thing to do. But I questioned whether I was still the right CEO to see it through. The programme might have to undo many of the things that I'd put in place. I might be too swayed by history or emotion. More to the point, T18 would require intense energy, and I felt quite burned out. Anyway, the

March 2013 *Harvard Business School Review* that I had read claimed that optimal tenure for a CEO is about 4.8 years;[74] whatever the right number may be, I had done way more – fifteen years! If I stayed in position, I was in danger of becoming an obstacle to the growth of the bank I had put so much into. On the other hand, CIMB was so huge that I also questioned the ability of any one person to lead the company. I felt incredibly lonely at times, often burdened by the weight of so many decisions and responsibilities. I discussed the dilemma with Md Nor over a number of weeks, and he came up with the solution: I would step into his shoes to become a non-executive but a more active chairman, and we would appoint a new CEO. That meant Md Nor would step aside, which was incredibly magnanimous of him.

Managing succession is tricky, but it's the truest test of whether you've created something successful: can you hand it over to other people? In 2013, Najib had made Wahid Omar a minister, thereby creating a vacancy for the role of chief executive at Maybank. The bank went through a semi-public competition between the main candidates to replace him. I knew this would create an opportunity for us, because those who lost out would be frustrated and tempted to leave. I put feelers out to one of those candidates, (Datuk Seri) Tengku Zafrul Aziz, whom I had known for years. Zafrul was also a Bristol University alumnus, seven years my junior. He was then head of Investment Banking at Maybank but he had worked for me at CIMB earlier in his career. I saw him as my potential successor, and the opportunity to bring him came when Charon, our Head of Investment Banking, moved to Khazanah at the end of 2013.

On 1 September 2014, I became chairman, and Zafrul took over as initially acting and then Group CEO. I was conscious that I'd need to play a quite different role as chairman. No incoming chief executive really wants the ghostly presence of his predecessor hovering at his shoulder. I had to be very clear about what I could and couldn't do. I told the staff that no one was going to have a bilateral conversation with me, bypassing Zafrul. My job now was to support him to make decisions. I also consciously decided to spend quite a lot of time out of KL, which gave him more space in which to operate. I found it all much easier than most people expected, mainly because Zafrul and I established a good working arrangement. We were helped by the fact that we are quite different. Zafrul has run all six of the major marathons in the world: Tokyo, London, Berlin, New York, Chicago and Boston. I had been a sprinter in my time; but these days I prefer a gentle jog around the park followed by a cappuccino, or two. My only reservation was whether he would stay long enough. He stayed on for six years until March 2020, his longest at any company, and his excuse for leaving was reasonable enough: to become Minister of Finance.

Zafrul and the team got down to implementing T18 methodically by cutting down costs and improving processes, while I forced myself to stay strategic, focusing on what I was best at, deals. I spent a lot of time on monetising CIMB's stakes in Bank of Yingkou in China, CIMB Principal and CIMB Securities, all of which realised significant value on companies I had earlier set up or acquired and then helped to grow. The sale of 50% of the group's combined stockbroking business to China Galaxy Securities, a Chinese state-owned enterprise, enabled us to realise gains from many of the units acquired from both GK Goh and RBS, at about 1.5 times book.[75] We spotted the chance to sell the stake to Galaxy at a perfect time, in 2017, just as they had been mandated to build an international broking franchise. The RBS deal was a failure but we managed to recoup the losses and lay the foundations of a franchise that has the potential to rise to become an Asian champion. The combination of Galaxy's China domestic operations and CIMB Securities instantly made it one of the top three brokerages in Asia ex-Japan.

At the Annual Management Dialogue in 2017 I congratulated the entire senior management team, describing it as the year that 'CIMB got its mojo back'.[76] The three years between the start of 2014 and the end of 2016 had been financially difficult (though always still profitable), but now CIMB would finally hit record profits again; its market capitalisation had exceeded RM60bn, the previous high back in 2012; investors, clients and staff were all saying the right things about the company again. T18 had successfully brought down costs, improved capital adequacy ratios and raised return on equity.

Banking, though, had changed a lot in those years: the post GFC re-regulation had successfully made it boring. Board meetings became all about the demands of complying with regulators. At the same time technology was beginning to dominate strategy, and investment banking was becoming less and less profitable. I began to wonder if banking was still my calling. As for CIMB, I had transitioned leadership to Zafrul, but with my oversight. Perhaps it was time for me to go a step further by handing over the chairmanship? I began to think that the end of August 2019 would be a nice time to retire completely from CIMB, almost exactly thirty years after I joined and at the end of my current three-year tenure as approved by Bank Negara.

As I thought about my eventual exit, I asked myself, what would I be most proud of?

First, the overall story. CIMB went from being a mid-tier merchant bank in Malaysia to its top investment bank, and then a leading ASEAN universal bank. That was a phenomenal achievement – beyond anything I had imagined when I joined or even when I took the reigns as CEO ten years later. We did not do one thing well. We excelled at three quite different things, evolving between them: first, creating a fully fledged investment bank, then engineering domestic mergers to become a universal bank and finally expanding regionally to emerge as a pan-ASEAN bank.

The second aspect of all this that makes me very proud is that thousands of people worked with me. At the start, when I was employee number sixty-nine, we could have just about all fitted onto a squash court; at its peak the bank had over 45,000 employees, enough to fill a big football stadium. Wherever I go, I meet people who have worked at CIMB, and who have powerful, affectionate feelings towards it. I stayed at the firm for all those years because CIMB was my community; I was rooted there, connected to the people who made it what it is. The core team that drove CIMB was highly professional: all were very good at their jobs. Yet there was something more than that which was critical to our success. We were bonded together, like a family. What we did at CIMB was not just work, it was our life for a quite a while. We were not hired hands, doing a job because it paid well. We were committed to a common cause and to one another. All organisations, large and small, public and private, need skilled professionals who can do a good job, whether in marketing and sales or finance and human resource. We need those professionals to give us their detached and objective judgement. But if you really want to grow something you need a team which is committed to one another and the job at hand almost like a family. And like a family they want to protect their joint reputation, the name they share.

I am enormously proud of CIMB's diversity. We created a sense of shared commitment in an organisation that, from the outset, valued difference. In the corporate finance team that I joined in 1989, I was the diversity employee. Later on, I was always proud to hear the joke that CIMB actually stood for Chinese Indian Malay Bank. We always saw diversity as a dividend, providing different ideas, insights and knowhow, and enabling us to be more creative and innovative. We grew from a small, marginal player to become one of the biggest banks in ASEAN by being more creative, by anticipating and making change before the competition. Innovation drove our growth, and diversity drove our innovation. We were never content with the status quo. CIMB was a disruptor, even before the term became cool. We didn't live up to all the expectations placed on us. We didn't always get it right: RBS was a bridge too far, CIMB Niaga got too gung-ho, and CIMB Thai fell short of expectations. It was not perfect by any means but it was never going to be. If there was one thing that I would have changed if I could, it would be to have embraced long-term value creation wholeheartedly from early on. I should have been less concerned about short-term imperatives of investors and analysts. That would have guided me to have invested in more sustainable operational improvements early on. It would have made the early years less exciting, the later years less difficult and the long term more sustainable. But shareholder value and share prices were all the rage then, and I might have lost momentum or tested our shareholders' patience.

What we achieved together at CIMB can be measured financially, in profits and market share. CIMB never made a loss in any of the years I was chief executive or chairman, we comfortably weathered the dot.com and commodities boom and bust, as well as the Global Financial Crisis. Shareholders who invested in our IPO in 2003 and stayed with us till 2017 would have enjoyed a robust 22% per annum return on their investment in combined dividends and capital appreciation. In 2003, we listed with a market capitalisation of just RM1.5bn and total assets of RM9.6bn; at the end of 2017, CIMB's market capitalisation was RM60.3bn and it had RM506.5bn in assets. In our IPO prospectus we forecast making RM112m in net profit in 2002; fifteen years later, in 2017, we made RM4.5bn.[77]

Numbers aren't the only measure of success, however. The truth is that money is a crude and imperfect measure of value. I never wanted to maximise profits at all costs; I wanted to make sure people working at CIMB felt proud of the organisation they worked in, not only because we were all making money, but also because we were giving back to society. In 2017, as we celebrated the tenth anniversary of the CIMB Foundation, I had the pleasure of announcing that going forwards we would commit to an annual spend of at least 1% of profit before tax on philanthropy the first Malaysian company to make such a commitment. Based on 2017 earnings, spending on Corporate Social Responsibility was to be RM60million in a single year.

By joining up the dots backwards, I can now see that much of what made me proudest at CIMB reflected the values and methods my father had relied on and sought to inculcate in us. He was a nation builder; I was merely an institution builder. But we were both builders, deeply passionate about our chosen mission. I tried to copy his recipe to be both consultative and bold and yet to take small steps and big leaps. He was a rooted cosmopolitan; a part of his heart was still in the *kampong* where he grew up. I was rooted in CIMB as a Malaysian first, even when it grew to be all over ASEAN. I was unusual among my peers, who generally had several different jobs at different organisations. I stood out by sticking with the same organisation; my father did the same. I believed that success begins with understanding one's own limitations and weaknesses; my father did too, which made him so self-assured. I like to reflect on both my successes and failures, as I am sure he would if he had been given more time on this earth.

I was lucky in my career to see with pride Malaysia unfold and grow. And there was much that would have made my father immeasurably proud. Yet the setting in which we worked and succeeded was also highly imperfect. The story I have just told is littered with too many examples of bad practices which were condoned, ignored or even encouraged. Whenever I think about my father's legacy of values and methods, I feel an unease about the way that the other side of his work – the system of institutions, policies and programmes he created – had been serially abused and misused, twisted and contorted out of all recognition.

I saw that first-hand in the completely opaque way shares were allocated to a select few *bumiputra* investors under the NEP; in the Bakun dam scandal, when a politically linked company made off with the proceeds of a rights issue with impunity; in the cruel injustice meted out to Tommy Ng and his family after he was scapegoated to pander to political interest. I saw the consequences of the corruption in the demoralised state of Bank Bumi, which had been brought to its knees time and again, and in other companies too. And, of course, I had a front-row seat in the wheeling and dealing that was significantly to blame for the AFC.

The collapse of Renong's house of cards ushered in the GLC transformation programme of the early 2000s, which coincided with the rise of a new generation of entrepreneurs and executives. Yet bold and professional though these efforts at corporate reform were, they did not touch the core system linking politics, government and business, which was left largely intact. In 2014, when I was looking forward to helping chart CIMB onto the next wave of growth from the chairman's seat, I had little idea that I was about to be plunged headlong into an intense conflict between my father's twin legacies: the remnants of the system of institutions, policies and programmes he laid the foundations for, against the values, principles and methods he stood for. This would be a conflict played out on an epic scale, involving billions of dollars. Yet it also touched me personally and professionally in ways that went to the core of what I stood for, which side of the fence I would come down on. My tenure as chairman was dominated by events beyond CIMB, and beyond my control. To understand why, I have to take you back to an oddly priced bond that we had noticed in 2009 and which came back to haunt us, all of us.

SECTION FOUR

1MDB

SOMETHING FISHY

I don't remember the exact date, but I will never forget the moment. What seemed like a routine discussion with one of my senior staff turned out to be the first step on a long journey that took me deeper into the realm of politics than I had ever wanted to go and to clash with another Razak, my brother Najib. It must have been sometime in May 2009. I was at my desk in my office on the top floor of Bangunan CIMB when Kwan came charging into my room with an incredulous look on his face. As head of Debt Markets and Derivatives, he had seen the details of a bond being offered by a company called Terengganu Investment Authority (TIA) and he was certain that there was something fishy going on. The government was involved, so he knew I would want to know about it straight away.

The state of Terengganu, which was rich in oil reserves, had decided to set up a sovereign wealth fund. To create this fund TIA was raising money by issuing a thirty-year bond, nominally worth RM5bn.[78] The idea was straightforward enough: investors would buy the bonds; TIA would use the money to make investments; the return from the investments would pay bond-holders interest (or profits) and ultimately their capital back. To investors what was really attractive about this investment opportunity was that the federal government was guaranteeing the bonds. In the last resort it would repay the bondholders. That made this bond a credit risk-free proposition.

While it was unusual for a state as small as Terengganu to set up such a fund, it wasn't unheard of, especially for one so rich in oil: the Canadian state of Alberta has such a fund, as does Alaska. In the Malaysian context it seemed odd for the federal government to back it, as other states might well demand similar support. Still, Terengganu occupied a privileged position: its Sultan was serving as HM the Agong, and the Terengganu state government was hotly contested between UMNO and PAS. Following UMNO's poor showing in the 2008 general election, it might well have been seen as expedient for the government in Kuala Lumpur to back such a fund in order to secure the support of the palace and local voters.

What Kwan came to tell me was that the pricing of the bond was extremely odd. It was offering a rate of return far higher than an equivalent Malaysian government bond would have to offer in order to attract investors. In addition, the placement method, how the bonds were being sold, was also unusual. When offering a bond like this, you would want to put it out to tender to get the best possible price for the issuer. Yet this bond was being sold to selected parties first who were now offering it on to other investors, almost instantaneously. They were flipping it. From court proceedings years later, we would find out that there were two primary investors, Country Group Securities in Thailand and Aktis Capital in Singapore. They had agreed to buy the bonds from AmInvestment Bank (formerly Arab Malaysian Merchant Bank), which was managing the deal, and were now selling them at fair value to Malaysian banks, asset managers and pension and insurance funds. Kwan calculated that the sale price equated to a 13% premium to what they had paid for the bonds. He estimated that this flip gave Country Group and Aktis a combined one-off, same-day profit of RM559m.[79] In other words, TIA gave away RM559m in a discount to a select group of investors; so some people involved made off with that sum. To this day it is unclear who ultimately benefitted from this mispricing as the ultimate investors behind Country

Group and Aktis have yet to be revealed, or the complete money trail for that matter.[80]

Kwan and I were protective of the ringgit bond market. CIMB played a major role in developing the market after the Asian Financial Crisis, and we dominated it both in advising on bond issuances and the daily trading of bonds. We had worked with the industry and regulators to create many of the conventions, norms, rules and protocols, as well as many of the innovative product structures. The bond market was our operating space, and we liked to keep it neat and tidy. To thrive, the market needed things to be kept above board, and participants had to follow the rules and conventions or be made to do so. TIA's flagrant flouting of those norms was a danger to a market that had become so important not just to us but to the Malaysian economy as a whole.

When I asked around, I discovered that TIA was the brainchild of a twenty-eight-year-old from Penang by the name of Jho Low, who was fashioning himself as a financial whizz kid and international deal maker. He had apparently persuaded HM Sultan Mizan Zainal Abidin of Terengganu, the then Agong, to create TIA and assemble an impressive list of heads of GLICs to advise on the project and sit on the company's board, including: (Tan Sri) Azlan Zainol, the CEO of Employee Provident Fund; (Tan Sri) Bakke Salleh, the CEO of FELDA; (Tan Sri) Ismee Ismail, the CEO of Tabung Haji (the Pilgrim's Fund.); and (Tan Sri) Lodin Wok Kamaruddin of Lembaga Tabung Angkatan Tentera (LTAT), the Armed Forces' retirement fund. The bond was devised by top-drawer investment bankers: Goldman Sachs and AmInvestment Bank.

To his credit, His Majesty grew suspicious of Jho Low – perhaps after he learned about his questionable antics in earlier deals – and pulled out. Low and the banks pressed ahead with the bond nevertheless, despite the state government's instructions not to do so. On top of the guarantees provided by the federal government the fact the issue went ahead reinforced the impression that the bond had the approval of powerful people in the federal government, and it created an extraordinary situation: TIA, a company with assets and liabilities relating to a thirty-year RM5bn bond, had no home. The money had been raised in the name of a state that no longer wanted it. MOF officials then inquired if Khazanah would step in to take over the company, but its management baulked at the idea of being accountable for money raised at such high costs with no plan for deployment.

When Najib became prime minister in April 2009, succeeding Badawi, he retained the minister of finance position that he had assumed in September 2008. Apparently at Jho's suggestion, Najib decided to turn the 'homeless' TIA into a new national investment agency called 1MDB. Najib saw it as an opportunity. By renaming the company '1 Malaysia Development Berhad', after his new administration's tagline '1 Malaysia', he knew he would 'own' 1MDB's success. He would not have contemplated any outcome other than success. He was PM and MoF, he had the might of the state in his hands. How could he not succeed?

1MDB's objectives were never very clear. Its publicity material suggested the fund would invest on behalf of Malaysians in projects that would create the good jobs of the future, in green energy and eco-tourism. There was also mention of 1MDB attracting foreign investors to take part in domestic projects. As if to distract from the hazy rationale, a high-profile advisory board was set up, including among others Bernard Arnault, chairman and CEO of LMVH; His Excellency Khaldoon Khalifa Al Mubarak, CEO of Mubadala Development Company of Abu Dhabi; and Mr Chang Zhenming, chairman and president CITIC Group of China. Najib made himself chairman of the advisory board.

It was also unclear why and how Jho Low had practically unimpeded access to the PM. Najib seemed smitten with Jho Low, who had assiduously courted his wife (Datin Seri) Rosmah and her son Riza Aziz, whom he knew from their student days in London. He certainly knew how to charm people and could impress anyone with his access to powerful people (whether genuine or paid for) from heads of government, to CEOs and Hollywood celebrities. Such apparent closeness to power made it hard for others to second-guess any accounts that Jho Low gave about what Najib wanted or had instructed. The concentration of power in the office of the PM, which was significantly amplified during the Mahathir era, was near absolute; so whenever the PM chose, or allowed it, a close confidant could also become extremely powerful. Rasputin-like figures in the court of the PM had become a regular feature of Malaysian politics; Jho Low would take that to a whole new level.

What was clear to me was that the bond issue had been unusually priced and placed, quite deliberately. I went to see Najib to tell him that I was worried about 1MDB based on the bond issue and explained how I thought money had been siphoned off. I told him such practices were not only unethical but also risked undermining trust in the bond market, which was a pillar of our financial markets. We had seen such practices in the early days of the market, and new norms and rules were in place to stamp it out, so regulators needed to act against this, I said. If the board had sanctioned the deal, it was either dangerously incompetent or complicit in giving away money. He expressed genuine concern and said he would look into it.

Emboldened by my conversation with Najib, I raised the matter with senior officials at Bank Negara and the Securities Commission and with Nor Yakcop, by then minister in charge of the Economic Planning Unit. I also called the CEO of AmBank, Cheah Tek Kuang, whom I had known for many years and liked (he always seemed to me to have the manner of an obliging uncle); nonetheless, I gave him a piece of my mind, saying that whether or not this deal was illegal, it was unethical, and what's more would damage the reputation of our bond market.

I wasn't sure quite what my badgering would achieve but I assumed there would have to be some investigations, be it at AmBank or by the authorities. This assumption didn't last long. Minutes after I put down the phone to Cheah I received a call from (Datuk) Azlin Alias, the PM's special officer. Azlin was an old friend who had been seconded to the PM's office from a subsidiary of Khazanah. We had met in the early 1990s, when he was with Tenaga Nasional, and we understood each other very well. He was obviously uncomfortable having to pass the message to me. 'The PM wants to know why you are querying the CEO of AmBank,' he said. My only response was a grunt of irritation. Unmistakably, the message was that 1MDB was off limits. Cheah had obviously communicated to someone powerful that I was asking questions about the bond. I wondered if Azlin was acting on Najib's direct instructions or Jho's orders in the guise of Najib's name. I never found out, and never will: sadly, Azlin died in a helicopter crash in April 2015.

What we did find out later was that a financial calamity of vast proportions was only just beginning.

Financial markets can seem horrendously complex to outsiders. At heart, what happened at 1MDB was quite simple, but the execution required considerable sophistication, and the contingency planning on the part of Jho Low was brilliant. Even until today, with everyone supposedly looking for him, his whereabouts still remain officially unknown.

1MDB used the explicit backing of the Malaysian government to make bankers and investors feel secure. Ownership by the Malaysian government gave those behind the fund the 'calling card' they needed to meet and deal with the 'who's who' across the world. And they used the clout of the PM to avoid scrutiny from 1MDB's own board members, auditors and regulators, and later investigators.

1MDB was a Government Linked Investment Company and as such it should have been subject to the oversight of the GLCT programme as was Khazanah, EPF, PNB and the like. In at least two of the regular meetings between GLIC and GLC chiefs and the PM, to discuss progress of the GLCT programme, I asked the prime minister why 1MDB was not required to attend or indeed comply with the various guidelines the rest of us worked under. I never got a proper response. Instead, after one of the meetings the CEO seated next to me asked if I could avoid sitting next to him in future. 'I don't want the PM to glare in my direction ever again,' he told me. To be fair, 1MDB was not the only exception but all the others like Petronas and Felda were long established.

Many of 1MDB's projects were in whole or in part financial scams. They entailed 1MDB paying inflated prices for assets bought from private parties (such as oil fields and power plants) to the benefit of those selling or paying hugely deflated prices for Malaysian Government assets (such as the huge tract of land that became the Tun Razak Exchange). In addition, cash was invested in fake fund management companies that gave false accounts of how the funds were being invested. The people behind 1MDB diverted money raised on the bond market through a series of shell companies in Singapore, Switzerland, Hong Kong and Australia into accounts they controlled in places like the Seychelles, the Cayman Islands and the Middle East, making it difficult to trace. Sellers of assets would presumably also find ways to channel the inflated sums they were paid into accounts such as these. The cheap assets 1MDB managed to buy from the government were in due course revalued to create the impression in the accounts that the fund was making profits and to cover up losses when the fund's assets deteriorated in value or funds disappeared.

While 1MDB could get away with showing profits by juggling valuations of its supposed assets, cashflow deficits which involve actual money were more difficult to hide. 1MDB raised more than $6bn of bonds (excluding the original TIA bond).[81] These bonds had to be serviced; money had to go back to bondholders. There were operational expenses too. To cover these outgoings, they borrowed from banks or the government. They got away with it for a while because they were clever at covering their tracks and they knew how to entice, bluff and bully their way through a complacent and self-interested financial system, in which most people didn't ask difficult questions because they didn't want to risk losing their slice of the deal. There were eye-watering sums to be made from 1MDB for those who were prepared to look the other way.

It is worth repeating. The basic ideas behind the scheme were simple: raise money on the bond market; siphon it off through shell companies; juggle the valuation of assets to create the impression that everything was going well; borrow money from banks and the government to cover cash shortfalls. The execution was extremely well thought through and sophisticated. The complete trail is extremely hard to trace, to this day.

One of the fund's first ventures was with a company that sounded as if it was linked to the Saudi royal family. Yet when I asked around about Petro Saudi International Ltd and the oil fields it was supposedly developing with 1MDB, I was told the oil field in question was in no-man's land, in territory that was disputed by two neighbouring ex-Soviet states. It could not be accessed, let alone drilled for oil. Petro Saudi sounded like an arm of the Saudi government, but in fact its offices in London seemed to be little more than a brass nameplate on a door. When I went to see Najib to raise these doubts, I asked why a sovereign wealth fund dedicated to Malaysian development was investing in some questionable oil fields in middle Eurasia. 'Has anyone consulted Petronas on these fields?' I probed further. As usual, Najib said he would look into it.

I also turned to people I knew on the 1MDB board; Bakke, the chair, and Azlan who I met most weeks as a member of the EPF Investment Panel, and warned them that something was surely amiss. Bakke is a reserved and punctilious chartered accountant whom I got to know during my first few weeks at CIMB in 1989: he was our client as CFO of Island & Peninsular, a PNB subsidiary. Bakke had a well-earned reputation for playing a straight bat.

Original incarnation. In September 1974, Abdul Razak officiated
Pertanian Baring Sanwa Multinational Merchant Bank
that would later become CIMB.

Work hard, play hard. With my CIMB Corporate Finance colleagues at
karaoke in October 1990. Left to right are Ng Pin How, Angie Ng,
Karen Keh, Raymond Fam, Ng Kok Teong and me.

"Raja sehari". As the Malay saying
goes, "King and Queen for the day".
Azlina and I on the night of our
wedding reception at Shangri-La
Hotel on 11 January 1992.

Over The Top. Cover of the
Men's Review magazine
of December 1994.

New CEO and the Board. First Annual Report Photo as CEO of CIMB taken
in January 2000. I had recently had my head shaved in Mecca during my Hajj
pilgrimage. Seated is CIMB Chairman Dr Rozali Md Ali. Standing on my left
are Dato' Robert Cheim, Shuzaburo Eto and Dato' Mohd Rosli Ahmad Aziz.

Young family. Family portrait at home in July 2004.

CEO of the Year. I was recognised as the American Express/ Business Times CEO of the Year in 2004. The award was presented by Nor Yakcop, Finance Minister II and Dato' Sri Syed Faisal Albar, CEO of New Straits Times.

Universal Banking Beckons. Announcing the merger between CIMB and BCB in June 2005. Left to right are Shukri Hussain, Executive Director of CAHB, me, Tan Sri Mohd Desa Pachi, Chairman CAHB, Dr Rozali Mohamed Ali, CEO CAHB and Datuk Azmi Abdullah, CEO of BCB

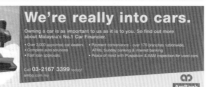

Read all about it. Cover of *The Edge* on 31 October 2005. The CIMB unwelcomed bid to take over Southern Bank was extensively covered in the media. Over the course of my CIMB career, I appeared on the front cover of *The Edge*, the leading business weekly on 25 occasions.

Proudest moment. The launch of the new CIMB Group brand on 7 September 2006 by Prime Minister Badawi who is flanked by me and Chairman Md Nor Yusof.

Innovative Banking. On the cover of the December 2006 edition of Euromoney, one of the most prestigious international finance magazines. In 2012, Euromoney would go on to award me special recognition for my "Outstanding Contribution to Asian Finance"

RM100 million for CSR. Najib and Rosmah; Azlina and I at the launch of CIMB Foundation in November 2007. Far right is (Tan Sri) Siti Norma Yaakob, the first Chairperson of the foundation. The funds were set aside from the profits we made from the Synergy Drive deal.

CIMB Classic 2012. At a photoshoot with Tiger Woods in front of the Petronas Twin Towers. The CIMB-sponsored annual event was then the only men's PGA tournament held outside the Americas. There were 9 editions from 2010 to 2018.

The Last Supper. At the CIMB Hari Raya Open House in July 2015 where Najib sat awkwardly in front of his DPM, Muhyiddin, who he would sack the next day. On Muhyiddin's right is Tun Mohd Khalil Yaakob, Governor of Malacca, on his left is Tun Musa Hitam, former Deputy Prime Minister. On Najib's right is my brother Johari.

Ar-Rahah. With my mother looking on as HM The King, Tuanku Al-Haj Abdul Halim Mu'adzam Shah officiates the mosque named after her in October 2016. Located in Kampung Kerinchi, Kuala Lumpur, the 17,500 square metre wide mosque accommodates up to three thousand people for Friday prayers.

Chairman and the CEO's. At the CIMB Group AGM in April 2017 with Zafrul (Group and Malaysia), Mak Lye Mun (CEO Singapore), Khun Kittiphun (CEO Thailand) and Tigor Siahaan (CEO Indonesia)

Trailblazer in philanthropy. At CIMB Foundation's 10th Anniversary in November 2017, I announced the commitment to spend 1% of CIMB's annual profits on corporate social responsibility.

Farewell speech. At CIMB Thai head office in Bangkok, in November 2018. CIMB kindly organised farewell events in every major country where it had significant operations.

Back with the family. In the garden of our home in Oxford, in 2018.

We later found out that at a specially convened 1MDB board meeting on 3 October 2009 Bakke questioned why $700m of the $1bn to be invested in a joint venture between 1MDB Petro Saudi had been paid to an offshore company called Good Star Ltd instead of the joint venture company.[82] He called for the whole joint venture to be properly audited, not just the flow of funds but also the true value of Petro Saudi's contribution to the partnership, an oil field supposedly worth $2.5bn. Had the board followed through with this, the whole project might have been stopped in its tracks.

Bakke resigned from the board without fanfare a few days later. Azlan, as the then-CEO of the EPF, saw the bond pricing from both sides; I remember being in the EPF Investment Panel meeting at which he saw the price of the TIA bonds offered to EPF and asked me where the difference had gone. I replied: 'I told you there was something fishy.' He wanted to resign at the same time as Bakke but was persuaded to delay, since losing two board members would have raised eyebrows. He left in January 2010. Since then, they have both thanked me for my timely advice, but I can't help but wonder what would have happened if they hadn't resigned quietly, if they made public their concerns instead. But having said that, if I had been in their shoes I might also opted not to incur the wrath of the all-powerful PM.

From the outset, I was determined CIMB wouldn't get involved in 1MDB in any way. I told to my management team we would never have anything to do with the fund because of its poor governance practices. In the years to come, 1MDB would become one of the main players in the mergers and acquisitions and corporate bond markets, paying huge fees to bankers. I made my team sit on their hands as they watched some of their competitors earn vast sums in bonuses courtesy of 1MDB. One year at a performance review they produced a chart showing how well they would have done had the CEO (me!) allowed them to be involved in 1MDB's bond placements. But I stuck to my guns: a reputation can be as much about what you choose *not* to do as what you do. Yet in the circumstances, did I myself do enough? Sometimes I wonder if perhaps in my CIMB capacity I should have formally (instead of verbally) complained to the regulators about the TIA bonds, and other seemingly questionable practices at 1MDB which I had noticed, even if it might not have made a difference.

As 1MDB got going, my relationship with Najib became somewhat strained. I wouldn't put it more strongly than that. My criticisms of the TIA bond issuance set a pattern that would repeat in the years 2009 until 2013: I'd become concerned about an aspect of 1MDB's conduct; I'd warn my brother; I'd leave reassured that action would be taken – only to find out subsequently that nothing had actually been done. Over time, Najib would have less and less patience with my questions. After a while 1MDB became almost a taboo subject for us. I couldn't get through to him, and a couple of times he even quipped that I must be jealous or just have a personal dislike of Jho. Of course, Najib had every right not to listen to me; he would not be the first powerful person to ignore advice from a family member. I dearly hoped I was wrong about 1MDB. At the time it seemed that Najib was carving out a new centre ground in politics at home and around the world, and I was eager to support him, not just because he was my eldest brother but because he promised reforms that I believed were desperately needed.

The fact that 1MDB became a huge financial scam was probably the most blatant testament of a failing system. At the heart of that failure was the fact that the PM was simply too powerful; his actions easily avoided the scrutiny of his peers or the public. By extension, the people around the PM were very powerful too, and it was difficult to keep a check on what they were doing in the PM's name. When he returned power to Parliament in 1971, my father had warned about the perils of having too much power: 'Even if you do not intend to misuse it, you may do so inadvertently … especially through delegation. You cannot check everything yourself. You may be sincere, but can you be sure that all your officers who act in your name are sincere?'

The scam was opaque and superficially plausible, it had the backing of arguably the world's leading private-sector financial institution – Goldman Sachs – and association with some of the world's most famous business-people on the advisory board. Top Malaysian and other international banks were also involved – not just AmBank but Maybank, RHB, Standard Chartered, Deutsche Bank and Affin Bank provided 1MDB with large borrowing facilities. 1MDB board members with grave doubts felt it was best to go quietly. The regulators preferred not to look too hard. People were simply too afraid of the PM and his power, and given the perception that the enforcement arms of the state seemed fully under the PM's instruction displeasing him risked losing one's place in the upper echelons of Malaysia Inc, or something even worse. The 1MDB affair took off as Najib sat at the pinnacle of a highly centralised system of power. He had worked all his life to get here. It is worth understanding what that must have meant to him.

NAJIB'S RISE

There had always been an air of expectation surrounding Abdul Razak's eldest son. When Abdul Razak died, there was clamour for Najib to succeed him, although my father himself thought Najib was probably too gentlemanly for the rough and tumble of politics and instead should become an accountant or go into business. He took the Pekan seat uncontested in February 1976 at the age of twenty-three. After that, the family saw much less of him: his political career was all-consuming. He soon became a deputy minister, got married and moved out of our family home. We were proud of him, the eldest son picking up the torch from Dad. Leadership and responsibility were thrust upon him at a very early age when he had very little experience to prepare him for it and protect him against what was to come.

There was no doubt that being Abdul Razak's son defined Najib politically in the early years and cast a long shadow thereafter, for better and for worse. It gave him significant advantages, but also the aura of a political princeling. Thanks to his name, Najib didn't need to struggle for public recognition, yet his rise to the top was by no means assured; he had to shed his soft image and navigate the often vicious infighting in UMNO. Najib was very much a creature of the political party he eventually came to lead and the system of patronage on which it works.

After its creation in 1973, BN dominated in the polls, and UMNO dominated BN. Whoever led UMNO would lead the coalition and with it the government. As a result, the competition for positions in the party hierarchy were proxy contests for the best jobs in government. The UMNO leadership was decided in party elections held (usually) every three years. The voters were delegates from all the UMNO divisions. These people, about 2,000 of them (the precise number depending on the number of divisions at the time), in effect decided who held power. The UMNO president would be prime minister. There was also fierce competition for the position of deputy president and for the five vice-presidencies (which included the chiefs of the women's and youth wings). Where you came in these contests was a sign of where you stood in the party pecking order. For those vying to become an UMNO cabinet minister, the standings in elections for the Supreme Council also counted. A good result in Supreme Council elections made a senior ministerial post likely. Once in power, the victors in these contests could reward those who had supported them. Needless to say, becoming a delegate was very valuable.

This near-constant round of internal party elections created a dense pattern of patronage. To put it bluntly, a lot of money was needed to oil the machine. Allegations of vote-buying date back to at least 1981, during the first modern contest for deputy president between Musa and Razaleigh. Candidates would 'invest' in their election campaigns with the hope that they could recoup the outlays once their government post had been secured. Delegates also invested to win their selection at branch and then division level and would seek their returns. The mechanisms to provide those returns were all in place: the government dictated licences, expenditure and share allocations and influenced even bank lending, making the merry-go-round of support-and-reward toxic especially since the rules regulating money politics were light and enforcement sporadic. As Malaysia became wealthier, larger sums were at stake.

Najib rose through this system, becoming a member of UMNO Youth Exco in 1976, its deputy chief in 1982 and chief in 1988. He ran successfully for the vice presidency of UMNO in 1993, 1996 and 2000. He couldn't have achieved all this simply by virtue of being Abdul Razak's son. Along the way he developed loyalists, forged alliances, won victories, had setbacks and made enemies.

Success was not a foregone conclusion for Najib, despite his name. His career even almost came to a premature end.

After Mahathir sacked Anwar in 1998, he chose Badawi as his deputy despite the fact Najib was the most senior UMNO vice president; Badawi had come behind him in the 1996 party polls. Najib felt humiliated – it was a public slap in the face. In true Mahathir style, he announced his decision during an UMNO Supreme Council meeting without any warning or explanation. Najib put on a brave face but he was demoralised. In the general election the following year he almost lost his seat in Pekan, winning by just 241 votes out of a total of 26,797 votes counted (in the 1995 general election his majority had been 10,793 votes). He was forced that night to contemplate the end of his political career. All his brothers were in the room with him, agonising as votes were counted box by box. For several hours his career hung by a thread. We were sat in the living room of the wooden *kampung* house by the Pekan river that Abdul Razak had built; the fear of dropping the torch handed to him will have preyed very heavily on Najib's mind.

Najib's subsequent rise to become prime minister was a dogged comeback from this near-disaster. He paid much more attention to his constituents, visiting Pekan almost every weekend. He would stay in Abduk Razak's house, where previously he preferred the Hyatt Hotel, thirty miles away in Kuantan. He then built a new house on the same piece of land for himself. He set up the Rahah Foundation to support the underprivileged in the constituency. He strengthened his base within UMNO and was re-elected the top vice president and de facto number three. He developed the strongest network of support within UMNO, apparently stronger than even Mahathir and Badawi. When Badawi became prime minister in 2002, somewhat reluctantly, he chose Najib as his deputy. As he dithered, Mahathir publicly implied that appointing Najib as deputy had been agreed as part of the power transition.

After BN's dismal performance under Badawi in the 2008 general election, Najib finally made it to the top of the very greasy UMNO leadership pole. Once again Mahathir was hugely influential. In retirement he had criticised Badawi vociferously, even leaving UMNO in protest. In a very public show of endorsement Mahathir rejoined UMNO soon after Najib became Malaysia's sixth prime minister in April 2009.

As I've explained, Najib hit the ground running, offering wholesale transformation of the way government and the economy worked. Yet he also came into office caught on the horns of a painful dilemma. He believed in the agenda for transformation and the imperative of sweeping away the old ways of working. Yet he sat at the top of a political party stuck in its ways, consuming vast amounts of cash to fund its system of patronage. There was no plan to transform how money politics worked, in UMNO or more widely. Najib was at the pinnacle of a system of power where the interests of the party and the work of the government were inextricably entwined. Previous UMNO presidents may have been able to rely on funds coming from their own companies, such as Fleet and Renong. But with Renong's collapse and much greater scrutiny over the conduct of GLCs, that route was now cut off. At the same time Najib was loathe to be beholden to tycoons and oligarchs whose contributions invariably came with expectations of a *quid pro quo*. He had to find another way to fund the money politics machine that was UMNO. As UMNO was supreme within BN, it was also incumbent on the UMNO leader to carry the burden of funding the coalition partners too. It was in that setting that 1MDB came into play.

For a long time, I was proud to be associated with Najib. The five of us always saw ourselves as a band of brothers. We helped one another out. My brother Nazim was an architect; if any of us needed help with renovating a house we called first on him. Johari was a lawyer; we turned to him for legal advice, at least unofficially. Nizam was the clever one we could consult on anything. Najib, though, was the eldest, and we respected the hierarchy, the special role that gave him. Although none of us got much involved in politics, we would help out at election time. It became a tradition that we would follow him on the campaign trail for the last few nights and help put up posters all over Pekan town. Whenever concerns were raised about Najib's conduct, my natural inclination for family loyalty meant I gave him the benefit of the doubt. When Najib was accused of wrongdoing, I couldn't believe it could be true of a brother of mine. When he became PM, I would disagree with him on more than one issue and though I had serious concerns, about 1MDB especially, I would only raise them in private. I continued to believe in his premiership. It was in this context that my brother asked for my help in the run-up to the general election of 2013.

He was in full fundraising mode. I knew from my friends in business that many of them had contributed money to the election campaign, as usual. What was unusual was that under Najib they were asked to transfer funds into bank accounts rather than giving raw cash, as in the past. This was a good sign; much easier and safer for the donor and traceable. One day, when my brother needed to turn some of those contributions into hard cash, he turned to me. He was under pressure to win his first general election as UMNO leader, and it was a small ask, I thought, to help him. After all, he was not asking for a loan from CIMB or for money from me personally; he just wanted me to help him to be able to get cheques turned into cash quickly when he needed it.

He told me the cheques would be drawn on his own bank account at AmBank. I said the only way I could help was as an individual, not as CIMB, so I would set up a dedicated account to handle his transactions and, for ease of administration, put the account in my name. As the cheques were coming from AmBank, I knew the bank would have undertaken the mandatory checks on the money's origin to comply with anti-money laundering regulations. Anyway, I had no reason to doubt that he had legitimately accumulated substantial contributions for the elections. My brother asked me to convert into cash four cheques worth a combined RM25.7million. He would notify me how much cash he required at any time and send someone to collect it from staff at the branch. I neither retained nor used a single sen of the funds. I thought I was helping my brother, doing my bit without compromising any laws or rules. It never for a moment crossed my mind to think the funds could be of questionable origin. Of course, with the benefit of hindsight I regret agreeing to be involved at all.

The 2013 election was the big test of Najib's strategy to reach into the non-Malay community, to build up the middle ground and undercut the opposition coalition of the Parti Keadilan Rakyat (PKR, or People's Justice Party), the DAP and PAS. It was widely assumed that BN could do no worse than it had in 2008; it was expected to do considerably better. On the eve of voting day Najib's inner-circle were even touting the possibility of regaining the two-thirds majority lost in the previous election. Yet GE13 was a humiliating setback befitting the coincidence of unlucky thirteens for the superstitious (as most Malaysians are!). BN went down from 140 seats to 133 (another 13!) while the opposition went up from 82 to 89 seats. BN won less than half of the popular vote, only 47%: the majority of Malaysians voted against it for the first time ever. Opposition leader Anwar Ibrahim lost no time in alleging that Najib had stolen the election through gerrymandering.

Najib's centrist, modernising strategy hadn't worked. Even before he'd analysed the results, on election night itself, he announced that BN's poor showing was due to a 'Chinese tsunami'; Chinese voters had turned their backs on BN to cause the awful results.

Najib would later hold post-mortems on the elections, but the die was cast: he blamed ungrateful Chinese voters who'd refused to back him even though he'd done so much for them. In his mind, he was the PM who even dared to talk about a new needs-based affirmative action. At one formal post-mortem, someone did raise rumours about dodgy dealings at 1MDB as a factor in the defeat; he was told 1MDB wasn't talked about outside corporate circles. That was probably true. In the general election 1MDB's influence was more indirect. According to DAP leader Lim Guan Eng, Jho Low had actively campaigned in his Air Putih constituency, in Penang, by offering envelopes of cash to voters, with a promise note of more if BN won. It was really crude and only had the effect of further motivating the opposition. Jho Low's other crude antic was to bring Psy of 'Gangnam Style' fame to sing at one of Najib's rallies in Penang. That Najib would even think Jho Low could be helpful in politics was baffling but also symptomatic of how money politics had reached a new, distasteful low.

Having held onto power by his fingertips, Najib needed to rethink his strategy. His transformational agenda hadn't won electoral support. His attempt to occupy the centre ground had failed. He'd spent lots of money on the 2013 election to no avail. He decided the only way to secure his position was to go back to basics. He had to rally the Malay vote with an appeal to Malay nationalism and he had to combine that with traditional money politics to secure his position, be it in the party and with the voters. 'Cash is King,' he would say. That cash had to come from somewhere.

The 1MDB affair was not a consequence of the failure of Najib's political strategy. The fund had already been in operation for four years and from court proceedings we now know that monies allegedly originating from 1MDB arrived in Najib's account before GE13; the debate is over the true origins of the funds, whether the bulk of it really came from political donors or from 1MDB, and what Najib did and did not know about the origin of the funds. But the failure of his moderate, modernising transformation agenda to generate electoral results led him to double down on divide-and-rule, cash-and-carry politics. The scene was set.

REBEL OR
DRAMA QUEEN?

In the wake of the May 2013 elections, lurid tales began to reach us of the antics of Jho Low and his crew as they partied their way across the world. A few months later, Tony Fernandes was buying a suit at one of the most exclusive fashion houses in Paris – he was about to receive an honour from the French government and didn't own a suit (he has famously bad dress sense) – and when he told the assistant serving him that he was Malaysian, the man replied: 'Oh, you must know Jho Low. He's one of my best clients.' Tony had never heard of him. Then some friends from New York who were in the music business told Tony they had been to a lavish party in a hotel owned by Robert De Niro that had been thrown by a Malaysian prince going by the name of Jho Low. Soon after, Tony got a call from Lakshmi Mittal, who was eating at one of the most exclusive restaurants in St Tropez to tell him a Malaysian guy at the next table had just spent close to a $1m on a lunch for the group he was with, which had included the most expensive champagne in the house. 'Don't tell me,' Tony cut in, 'is his name Jho Low?' These were just some of the stories we were picking up. It was unseemly for Najib to be closely associated with Jho, of that I was sure. And the contrast with the frugal Abdul Razak could not have been starker.

The chatter in financial circles was that 1MDB had placed some of its funds with an unknown fund manager called Bridge Capital. I was curious, so I asked one of my officers to look into the fund. The firm's website gave little information, but we noted that its purported investment strategy completely contradicted the list of stocks it appeared to hold. We called Bridge to see if it was interested in managing some of CIMB's funds. Any normal fund manager would have jumped at the opportunity; Bridge was completely uninterested. It appeared to be no more than a front. Another warning sign.

Things took a turn for the worse in late 2013, when I took a call from Mohamed Raslan Abdul Rahman, the managing partner of KPMG, which was then 1MDB's auditor. Raslan was an accountant who had overcome polio to rise to the top of his firm; he would go on to chair the Malaysian Accounting Standards Board. I didn't know him well, but his father had worked closely with mine, as secretary of the National Operations Council in 1969. Like his father, he is serious and straight. But while his father was stern, Raslan is friendly and obliging.

KPMG was finding it hard to square the 1MDB accounts. The firm had already inserted a rare note of qualification into the previous year's accounts to make it clear they couldn't be sure of the value of some of the fund's key assets, including the money held by Bridge Capital. Raslan wasn't in a position to divulge the details; it would have been a breach of client confidentiality. But he said he was agonising over them again, and 1MDB's management wasn't being helpful. He wanted to know what I thought he should do.

I was alarmed and told Raslan to take his concerns to Najib. This was surely confirmation that something serious was amiss at 1MDB; if Najib heard this, I believed he would ensure something was done about it. I said I would mention it to my brother when I had the chance. The conversation left me feeling uneasy. A pattern was starting to establish itself: similar stories were emerging from several sources, including from concerned 1MDB staff.

As the worrying signs mounted, in November 2013, I instigated a meeting with my other brothers. As the youngest I was used to having to speak loudly to be heard, regarded as something of a family rebel or a drama queen, depending whom you talk to. We compared what each of us were hearing and decided it was time that we alerted Najib to the stories we were picking up about 1MDB. It was time we did so as a group. With a broad script agreed, Nazim requested a meeting with Najib without telling him who would be coming.

Late that month, along with Johari and Nazim – Nizam was overseas – I was ushered into the prime minister's office in the parliament building. Najib welcomed us with impeccable manners, joked a little, offered us tea and asked us why he was the happy recipient of this unexpected delegation. My brothers and I are close; but for us to go to see him together in his office was unprecedented.

Johari explained our concerns about what was happening at 1MDB. Nazim shared what he had heard. I referred to our previous conversations about 1MDB, pointed out that Raslan was a family friend, and urged Najib to take his concerns seriously. We were candid about our conclusion that something fishy was going on; if it wasn't dealt with, it could tarnish the family name and even bring down the government. Najib seemed genuinely surprised and concerned by what we told him. If what we were saying was true, the professionals on the 1MDB board should have alerted him, Najib said. He asked me to sit down with his chief of staff, Azlin, and Raslan to investigate further. As prime minister he had many things on his plate. It didn't seem unreasonable for him to be unaware of the details of what was going on inside the fund. I reminded him that credible professionals had already resigned from the board, which I suggested was now rather weak. He defended those on the board such as Lodin and Ismee, arguing that they had good track records.

When soon afterwards I contacted Azlin to arrange to discuss 1MDB, he chuckled knowingly. 'Are you sure he wants you to investigate this?' he asked. 'This involves Jho.' He was telling me that there were special rules for Jho. I told him it was a serious issue, and the prime minister had said he was concerned. I insisted the meeting with Raslan went ahead and, a few days later, I sat down with the two of them over breakfast in an alcove in the coffee house of the Hilton Hotel in KL Sentral. Raslan explained that he couldn't reveal too much because of client confidentiality. I told Azlin that he had to ask 1MDB to authorise Raslan to share the information with us, so we could verify whether there were problems so something could be done about it. Soon afterwards, something was done, but not in the way that we'd hoped.

A few days after that breakfast, 1MDB called KPMG to a meeting at which it was accused of breaching client confidentiality by talking to outsiders (by which I guess they meant me). Soon afterwards, KPMG was fired. A new firm, Deloitte, the smallest of the Big Four, duly and by all accounts, happily took its place.

Far from stopping the unfolding scandal I had succeeded in getting KPMG sacked (though Raslan must have been relieved to be off the job). Clearly, I couldn't leave the matter there. My initial concern had been that 1MDB was damaging the standing of the bond markets; now I was increasingly worried that it could damage much more. Private meetings to persuade Najib to do something hadn't worked. I figured that Najib needed to feel a proper pinch, and the best way to deliver that was to say something in public without being directly confrontational. He needed to know that I would go further on 1MDB because it could damage both the family and the country.

That is why on 14 January 2014, the thirty-eighth anniversary of my father's death, I published an article, 'Remembering My Father', which was carried by almost all major online and print news media. I used it to remind everyone of the high standards my father demanded of himself when in public office, and to which we were expected to live up. 'I have never wavered from being enormously proud of his selfless dedication to our young nation,' I wrote. 'I did not get the time to know him. But imprinted in me are the values he imparted, the integrity that he insisted upon above all. Yes, above all; including his family.'

The piece was a shot across my brother's bows, a public plea (publicity being the politician's currency) to live up to our father's values. I didn't mention him or 1MDB to make the point: I did not need to; Najib would know. The response online and in the press was overwhelmingly positive. My appeal for old-fashioned values of public service struck a chord.

The entire family met that night with close friends, as we did each year, at a *tahlil* prayers to mark my father's passing. That year we convened at the Ar Rahah mosque, which I'd had built in honour of my mother just a year before. Najib and I kept our distance until he was leaving, when he said icily: 'Interesting article.' Those were the only words he spoke to me. Two weeks later, retribution arrived.

Azlina and I were at home in Oxford, where she was studying at the university and our twins were at school. Out of the blue, Effendy Hamid, the head of communications at CIMB, started emailing me links to a string of posts on Facebook and obscure blogs attacking me, Azlina and even our children. It was a sudden torrent of fake news and innuendo. One photoshopped a picture of popstar Robbie Williams' house in Holland Park in London and claimed that the mansion belonged to me. Another used a photo of a luxury car showroom in Bahrain and claimed it was my private garage of expensive cars. Yet another accused Azlina of attending fashion shows in Paris and owning one of the largest collections of Birkin bags, a false and frankly ludicrous accusation to make of someone who spent most of her time perusing manuscripts at the Bodleian library in Oxford. The most vicious post of all targeted our children, claiming that they were profligate shopaholics and providing close-up photographs of them as well as the names and addresses of their schools. They were minors. To see your innocent children subject to vitriolic online abuse and have their safety compromised was distressing to say the least.

Azlina and I were really worried for their safety, just as the attackers wanted us to be.

Who was behind this orchestrated attack on our reputation? We concluded it could only be payback from my brother's camp for my article. We complained to the Malaysian Communications and Multimedia Commission but got little help. We obtained a court order against some of the posts, hired US lawyers and got Facebook to take down a number of sites. There isn't time and space to go into this here, but regulating social media so that it is not abused to spread rumour and fake news, sow division and even provoke conflict is one of the many issues we need to tackle together, internationally. Azlina, more feisty than me, wanted to point the finger of blame at Najib and Rosmah openly. I didn't want a public clash; instead, I called him. He denied knowledge of the attacks but conceded that they might have come from within his camp. People were angry with me, Najib explained, for writing the article.

Maybe they thought we would back off. If so, they miscalculated. The social media barrage had the opposite effect. It made the issue much more personal for us. It made us more worried about what was going on at 1MDB. The stakes were raised; we needed to redouble our efforts. Our opponents thought they could bully us into submission. They were wrong. We were only just getting started.

I immediately called my old friend Tong Kooi Ong to convince him that his weekly business publication *The Edge* had to pursue the 1MDB story more aggressively. 'There might be a financial scam of mighty proportions, and Jho Low is pulling the wool over Najib's eyes,' I told him. From then on, we began regularly comparing notes with a view to getting to the truth.

The international scale of 1MDB affair dawned on me in August 2014, when I met Louise Story, a *New York Times* journalist. Persistent and forensically precise, Louise was interested in who was buying apartments in the Time Warner complex in New York. Many of the purchasers were paying cash, she told me, using shell companies to ensure the ultimate owners remained unknown. The suspicion was that rich people were using these transactions to launder money. She was particularly interested in some purchases involving Malaysians linked to 1MDB. She'd heard about my opposition to 1MDB and was intrigued after reading 'Remembering My Father'. 'More what was between rather than in the lines,' she said.

Despite *The Edge*'s exposés and clamour from many quarters, the Auditor General of Malaysia had said on 12th November 2014 there was no reason for his office to audit 1MDB, since it had already been audited by a respected Big Four accounting firm, the recently installed Deloitte. The task would be 'very laborious', he explained.

By this stage 1MDB had gone through three of the Big Four accounting firms in five years. The accounts were routinely filed late and with qualifications, which cast doubt on their reliability. 1MDB had generated a surplus only because its assets were generously 'revalued' by its auditors. Between 2011 and 2014, 1MDB's auditors had revalued its assets, principally land, by a colossal RM4.9 billion.[83] If that amount was deducted from 1MDB's shareholders' funds of RM2.4 billion, the fund was in negative equity of RM2.5 billion: the technical term was 'balance sheet insolvent'. Moreover, a huge proportion of 1MDB's claimed RM16 billion cash and portfolio investments held abroad were classified as 'Level 3 assets': illiquid assets, the value of which could not be determined by observable measures. In other words, it was anyone's guess how much they were really worth. All this could be gleaned from a close reading of publicly available documents. Alarm bells should have been ringing in the offices of the various oversight bodies and regulatory authorities.

Early the following year, on 8 February 2015, the article Louise Story had been researching was published in the *New York Times*.[84] The piece, titled 'Jho Low, well connected in Malaysia, has an appetite for New York', focused on Jho Low's role in buying properties in the Time

Warner building but also described Rosmah's lavish spending. When the story came out, it sent shock waves across Malaysia, laying bare just how much money those close to Najib and Rosmah had been spraying around in New York. The obvious question was: where was the money coming from?

Shortly after the piece was published, Najib's office offered an answer, which only inflamed the situation.

A statement said the purchases were not unusual 'for a person of the prime minister's position, responsibility and legacy family assets'. This could only be meant to imply that the 'legacy family assets' came from our father. But that meant that Najib could have come by that kind of money only if the famously fastidious and honest Abdul Razak had been making money on the side. I was furious.

I 'pinged' my three brothers, Nizam, Johari and Nazim, on our group chat. It didn't take us long to agree that we had to respond in public. So we issued a statement from all of us, from my WhatsApp account, sent to all the journalists and commentators I knew. We were concerned about our father's reputation, we explained. Abdul Razak did not pass on any substantial 'legacy assets'. We concluded: 'We take issue with anyone who taints his memory, whatever the motive.'

Soon after we issued the statement, I got a call on my mobile from an unknown number. My other brothers, smartly, had switched off their phones. I answered and was immediately subjected to a barrage of angry invective from Najib. 'How could you guys do this to me, embarrass me in public?' he demanded. For Najib, personal loyalty was paramount, a tribal loyalty which meant putting aside everything for the sake of the leader. There was a limit to what I could put to one side.

Not for the first time, I pointed out that we were not trying to upset or harm him. On the contrary, we were trying to protect our father's legacy and our family name. We were not going to stand by and watch our father's name damaged now he was no longer around to defend himself. I added that I did not believe he could have written or endorsed that comment, so he should sack the officers who did so. He did not respond. Najib and I ended the call, each very annoyed with the other.

The prime minister's office blocked our statement from being carried in the mainstream media for a few days. The foreign media and blogs had a field day. It seemed to me utterly dismaying that a son would seek to censor his brothers' words in praise of their father. When our statement was eventually featured it included a quote from Najib praising Abdul Razak. I assume anyone who read it will have been quite confused!

By this stage I had more than enough reasons to be worried about 1MDB: the financial and the political, combined with the professional and the personal. 1MDB had flouted the norms of the bond market that CIMB had done so much to help develop. The fund was a GLC yet it had been exempted from the rules the rest of us worked by, and its antics could damage the image of GLCs as a whole. I was worried for my brother, Najib, who I feared was having the wool pulled over his eyes by unscrupulous advisors and associates. My own family had been subject to a vicious and concerted attack online after I had made veiled criticisms of my brother's handling of the affair. Then, to cap it all, my own father's good name had been dragged into it, his reputation potentially tarnished in an effort to throw people off the scent. To not press for the truth to come out would now be tantamount to turning my back on my own father, the principles of public conduct he upheld.

'EH, WE HAVE
A PROBLEM'

A band of people were now on the 1MDB case, among them the young lawmakers Tony Pua and Rafizi Ramli, who had been asking pointed questions in parliament, and the campaigning journalist, Clare Rewcastle-Brown, who had been examining its implications in her blog, the *Sarawak Report*. I was now working closely with Tong and *The Edge* chief editor, (Dato') Ho Kay Tat. We formed a strong bond over 1MDB during the next couple of years, though I remained largely behind the scenes; Tong and Ho took much more of the strain and the greater risks.

Tong had been a major corporate player in the mid-1990s. He turned from business competitor to a friend when I joined the Breakfast Club, an informal group of about ten youngish corporate figures who caught up over breakfast once a month to network and compare notes. Others in the club included Azman Yahya, (Tan Sri) Shahril Samsuddin (of Sapura Group), (Dato') Rohana Mahmood (a close advisor to Najib), Mirzan Mahathir (Dr Mahathir's eldest son) and (Dato') Sandra Wong (Halim Saad's right-hand lady). Tong had transformed his stockbroking company, PhileoAllied Securities, into a banking group, and launched *The Edge* business weekly. He was a close confidant of Anwar, and when the latter was sacked in September 1998, Tong was dragged down too. Compelled to sell his bank, he feared being arrested, so he exiled himself to Canada, where he again became a successful entrepreneur, this time taking over and adroitly turning around a building materials company.

After Badawi took over from Mahathir, Tong made his way back to KL. He became a successful property developer and dabbled in other businesses, but his first love was *The Edge*. He was extremely proud of its investigative journalism. The publication became almost evangelical when it believed there was an important story to be exposed. Ho was his perfect complement: Tong the extrovert, the ideas man; Ho the hardened, diligent newspaper editor.

The early months of 2015 were a turning point in the story for Tong. Between January and early February, a blogger known as ahrily90 alleged that *The Edge* was criticising 1MDB to undermine the government and drive down the ringgit so that Tong could make money by short-selling our currency. The ahrily90 attack made the issue personal for Tong. On 4 February none other than Dr Mahathir came to Tong's defence. Ahrily90 would go on to attack me and Mahathir too. Tong and I publicly accused Jho of being behind the blog, based on our intel, but of course there is not much you can do about anonymous slander without definitive proof.

In the autumn of the previous year, I had started an Instagram account mainly to mark family birthdays and holidays, CIMB events, and the comings and goings at Chelsea Football Club.[85] Now it proved the perfect vehicle for me to comment obliquely on 1MDB. A well-chosen picture, juxtaposed with the right caption, could make the point perfectly well without ever mentioning anyone by name. I started that year with a post quoting Razaleigh invoking the spirit of my father: 'We are reminded of how far we have deviated from the original path set out by our own founding fathers.' In February, I posted a picture from my mother's eightieth birthday celebrations back in 2013, at which my brothers and I had taken to the stage, complete with shades, to provide the backing vocals for my favourite singer, (Dato') Sheila Majid. The caption read: 'Trying to sing the same tune, not always easy.' Instagram provided me with a way to comment so that I could make a point in a subtle way. It wasn't a way to reach the masses; it was not meant to have any political impact, it just a way for me to express my own dissension, although my posts were often picked up by the media.

By this stage 1MDB was having to borrow money from banks to keep itself afloat. The mounting debts put the company into acute financial distress. Despite having raised about $7.5 billion from the bond market since 2009, 1MDB had taken out a commercial loan worth about $1bn in September 2014 to cover its cashflow. Repayment was due less than a year later. Since March 2014, when the fund's short-term liabilities had already reached $4.2bn, it had added a further $3.7bn in debt. Under a new CEO, Arul Kanda, 1MDB was talking about selling assets to pay down its debt, but once the assets were sold, the obvious question was: where was the income supposed to come from to pay back the original thirty-year bond?

At this point Tong decided to tell Najib in person everything he knew about the affair. Tong and Najib were close enough to have attended one another's social gatherings, and not only did Tong like Najib personally, he also respected his intellect and could live with him politically. He had thought carefully before chasing down the 1MDB story because he was aware that the political ramifications could be far-reaching.

Tong's meeting with Najib took place on 6 March 2015, at 10.45 p.m., at Najib's Jalan Duta home. It was evident to Tong that Najib didn't seem to understand the details of what was happening. Najib said the problem with 1MDB was that it had taken on too much debt and maybe it should be closed down. The turning point, according to Tong, was when he mentioned Jho Low and suggested Jho should be held accountable and prosecuted for what he had done at 1MDB. At that point Najib stood up, the meeting was declared over, and Tong was shown the door. The following day, 7 March, *The Edge* printed its most detailed exposé of what had gone on at 1MDB.

Soon afterwards, Tong's offices were raided by the Inland Revenue Department. Presumably, this deployment of the state apparatus was meant to scare him off. If so, it didn't work. Tong once said to me that how we react to our circumstances is what defines us – and the circumstances made him determined to fight back.

By then the network of people interested in 1MDB was abuzz with talk of a stash of documents detailing illicit transactions involving the fund. Tong and Ho had gone to Singapore in February 2015 to meet Xavier Justo, a disgruntled former employee of Petro Saudi, who was offering to sell a thumb-drive full of emails. Claire Brown was also at the meeting where he handed over the drive. There were hundreds of thousands of 1MDB-related emails that needed authenticating, Tong told me. He passed me a copy of the data for safekeeping and then set about laboriously analysing the contents.

A few days later, Tong called and said, 'Eh, we have a problem.' It was typical of him to start with 'eh'; it was also typical of him to get straight to the point. 'Najib might be more involved than we thought.' Our original premise had been that Jho, and the people around him, were abusing 1MDB without Najib's knowledge. The emails suggested the scam was even larger than we had imagined and that Najib had been more engaged than we thought (although he could not be sure what Najib actually knew and to what extent he was being manipulated).

Tong and I lobbied whoever would listen to look into 1MDB. I talked to two of Malaysia's nine rulers: eventually, in early October 2015, the Council of Rulers would issue a statement noting their concerns about 1MDB and pressing for the affair to be cleared up. I cannot be sure my lobbying had any bearing but it was an unprecedented intervention and about as far as constitutional monarchs could go. I had meetings with politicians from all sides of parliament; with Daim; with oversight bodies, including Bank Negara and the Securities Commission; and with ambassadors from the UK and US (in Singapore) to consider whether crimes might have been committed in their countries. Tension was mounting within UMNO. A clutch of back-benchers came to see me – (Dato') Aziz Shiekh Fadir, (Datuk Seri) Azeez Rahim and (Datuk Seri) Johari Ghani among others, officially to persuade me to openly show support for Najib, but it turned out that there were different motives; a couple of them told me in a whisper that some in the party were moving against him and I should try to persuade him to step aside and allow a full investigation.

The country's institutions, though, seemed to be finding their backbone. A task force had been set up in March 2015 comprising the heads of the Malaysian Anti-Corruption Commission, the police, the attorney general's chambers and Bank Negara. Pressure was growing for a proper public investigation and this culminated in an instruction from a reluctant prime minister to the auditor-general to conduct a public audit. The Parliamentary Public Accounts Committee (PAC) also started looking into 1MDB. Shortly afterwards, I posted a picture on Instagram of a US road sign to a town called Truth, captioned: 'I hope we are going to get it.' Could it be that our institutions were finally going to sort out the mess?

Tong and I were not so convinced, knowing the instruments of power at the PM's disposal. We resolved to fly to London for an extra-ordinary meeting with someone who would eventually bring the whole house of cards crashing down.

Since leaving office, Mahathir had built up a huge following as a blogger. He has a rare ability to convey a complex message in language the average Malaysian can easily grasp. He wrote his first blog about 1MDB in September 2014, based on some leaked emails he had been passed that showed that Jho Low wasn't a mere backroom advisor at the fund but was closely involved in investment decisions.

Tong and I sought Mirzan's help to get an appointment to see Maha-thir in April while he was in London. As we set off, we were both more than a little nervous. It was reminiscent of going to see the headmaster. To complicate matters, both Tong and I had history with "Dr M".

My previous meeting with him had been little short of traumatic. In September 2011, I invited former British Prime Minister Tony Blair to speak at the launch of the ASEAN Business Club (ABC) in Kuala Lumpur. ABC is a club I had set up to bring together the top business leaders and CEOs across ASEAN in support of economic integration. Days before the event was due to take place, I was informed that Mahathir was furious with me. He was about to stage a 'trial' of Blair and George Bush for war crimes in Iraq. Even though he had retired years before, Mahathir's views still mattered. Such was his aura that people still wanted to please him; it was almost ingrained in us. I didn't want him to be angry with me, so I went to his office to explain myself. He gave me an almighty dressing down for half an hour. I looked down at my feet in silence. It was like being told off by my housemaster at Oundle, who would always make you feel you had let yourself and the institution down badly. By the end, Mahathir seemed to be somewhat placated, probably out of pity.

Meeting Mahathir was even more emotionally charged for Tong. Back in 1998, Tong had been accused of helping manage a slush fund to support Anwar's bid to topple Mahathir. Apart from being compelled to sell his bank, he had his passport confiscated. He hadn't seen Mahathir since just after Anwar was sacked in 1999. When that last meeting had ended, Tong left him with the words: 'I am happy to support you, sir, but I need to tell you Anwar Ibrahim is a friend of mine and will always be a friend of mine.' Few people talk to Mahathir as forcefully as that and get away with it.

That is why there was a slight air of trepidation as we walked into No. 15 York House, the Malaysian government hospitality apartment near Kensington Palace. I'd stayed there several times with my mother when I was young, and what with the heavy flowery drapes and solid sofas, it didn't seem to have changed at all since the 1980s.

I opened by telling Mahathir that we believed billions of dollars had gone missing from 1MDB. It was Tong, though, who communicated the full scale of what we knew about the financial manoeuvres at 1MDB. Mahathir seemed to understand completely, which was surprising given their complexities, notwithstanding Tong's lucid, compelling account. I suspect Mahathir had already been briefed and was using this meeting to compare our assessment with others he'd already received. As the conversation unfolded, he grew more animated and, in due course, angry. After about an hour he looked at me and asked dumbfounded: 'Why is it me that has to do something about it? I'm retired.'

'Well, sir,' I replied. '*You* have to do something because you made him prime minister.'

The connections between our families went back decades. Abdul Razak had saved Dr Mahathir's career by bringing him back into the fold when he was an outcast from UMNO. Hussein had chosen Mahathir as his deputy prime minister purportedly because my father had indicated such a preference before he left for his last trip to Europe. That appointment put Mahathir in position to become prime minister after Hussein. Najib played a big part in keeping Mahathir in power when he threw his support behind him in the 1987 contest for the UMNO presidency. Mahathir in turn paved the way for Najib to become prime minister when he pushed Badawi to make him deputy prime minister in 2003. Mahathir's campaign against Badawi's lacklustre premiership led to Najib actually getting the top job. He then campaigned actively for Najib in the 2013 general election.

We left York House with no idea what would happen. Mahathir's views still carried huge weight but, with no organisation behind him, how much could the almost-ninety-year-old possibly do? We shrugged, shook our heads and vowed to press on. Little did we know. After our meeting in London, Mahathir went on the warpath.

It didn't take long for Najib to get hold of me. He wanted to know what I was up to, going to see Mahathir. I wondered whether I was being followed, or whether my phones were tapped. I didn't hide the topic of my meeting: there was no point. Najib warned me to be careful of Mahathir's motives. After I got off the call, I realised that in my case 'big brother' was indeed watching me.

Meanwhile, the multi-agency task force had been looking in detail at money flowing through 1MDB-related accounts inside and outside Malaysia. The report the task force eventually put together was the most comprehensive explanation of what had become of the billions 1MDB raised on the bond market. Someone, probably within the task force, decided the best way to make sure the information got into the public domain was to leak details to the *Wall Street Journal* and the *Sarawak Report*. On 2 July 2015, under the headline 'Investigators Believe Money Flowed to Malaysian Leader Najib's Accounts Amid 1MDB Probe', the *Wall Street Journal* reported that the task force had traced $1bn that had found its way into the prime minister's personal AmBank accounts between 2011 and 2014.[86] The largest payment was $681m, from a mysterious company called Tanore Finance Corporation. The inquiry wasn't able to establish where the money had originated. However, the task force had been able to trace in detail the route by which $42m had made its way from 1MDB through a company called SRC and into Najib's AmBank accounts.

When the story came out, I was on holiday with my family in Los Angeles. One morning, as I came down for breakfast in the hotel, I picked up a copy of the *WSJ*, and my eyes caught the headline key words 'Malaysia', 'Najib' and '1MDB'. I literally fell off my chair. I had been tracking 1MDB for almost six years at this stage but I was still stunned by what I read.

That *WSJ* piece became one of the most read articles that year, with more than a quarter of a million unique visitors. The 1MDB story now had a global audience. Its appearance, and the astonished reaction to it, provoked the leaking of yet more documents, which the paper also subsequently published. Mahathir called for Najib to stand down. Najib took to Facebook to warn that it was all a plot to unseat a democratically elected leader.

The difficulties that all of this created for me personally came home to me a couple of weeks later. Family is family, and on 15 July, I found myself at my brother's house for a Ramadan gathering. Since the social media attacks on our family, Azlina had declined to attend social events with my brother, so I was there on my own. It was a select, intimate affair. There were a couple of Sultans, some senior civil servants, staff from Najib's office, and, of course, the family. A spectacular spread of food was laid out in the ballroom of the prime minister's residence. Towards the end of the evening, I was chatting to Johari, and Najib came to join us. We shared the kind of banter we've engaged in since we were boys. Old habits die hard.

Out of the corner of my eye I spotted a woman with an unmistakeable head of hair bearing down on us. It was my sister-in-law Rosmah.

I first met Rosmah in my late teens. Najib's first marriage was traditional: his first wife was a member of the Kelantan royal family, tall and good-looking but not well-educated; nor was she particularly interested in world affairs. I sympathised with Najib for wanting a partner with whom he had more in common, for preferring a marriage of equals. I welcomed Rosmah as my senior sister-in-law and when I was a student, I was thrilled when the pair of them drove down to Bristol take me out to lunch. Najib would never have done that off his own bat: she must have put him up to it.

Unfortunately, the warm feelings didn't last. I soon began to worry that Najib's power was intoxicating for her. I recall being at a party at Najib's house to mark him being made minister of finance in September 2008. I told Rosmah I was worried that, as minister of finance, he would now have purview over GLCs and the financial sector and noted that this could create uncomfortable situations for us. She was irritated. In her view I was being a party pooper: I should be overjoyed that my brother now had the power to help us all. It may have been a throwaway line, but the sentiment unsettled me.

For Rosmah life was very simple: you were either with them or against them. There was no middle ground. Criticism was tantamount to betrayal. Now at the Ramadan party she grabbed Najib's hand and looking straight at me said, loudly: 'Don't talk to him! He's working against you and trying to topple you.'

People turned to look. Najib tried to calm her down and defend me. She was having none of it. Nor was she finished. She added, with more than a hint of venom: 'I know what you're up to. I have eyes. You had better watch out.'

I was taken aback to be threatened by my sister-in-law, in my brother's house, with my family and friends around us. I left immediately. I said nothing but I was seething. On the way home, I texted Najib to tell him that that would be the last event at his house I would attend since his wife was so openly hostile to me. To be fair, she was not entirely wrong, although my objective was to get to the bottom of what was going on at 1MDB, not to hurt Najib.

It wasn't just our family that was divided by 1MDB. Divisions were also opening up within government. Later that month, the home minister suspended *The Edge*'s publication license for three months on the grounds that its reporting on 1MDB could lead to public disorder. Rumours were circulating that the attorney general was preparing charges against Najib based on the task force investigation. There was also growing dissent within UMNO. Back in May, Muhyiddin had made a rousing speech to a closed session of UMNO party leaders, in which he speculated that the party's problems might be solved by dealing with all the people who had taken money from 1MDB. The speech was a barely veiled attack on Najib. 'We have to take a stand,' Muhyiddin told the gathering. I met Muhyiddin over dinner in Jakarta in late June, and he filled me in on his thinking: he could see that for the good of the party and the country the 1MDB affair needed to be confronted head-on.

On 26 July 2015, Muhyiddin made a speech in which he detailed the questions Najib must answer over 1MDB – which he described as a 'sovereign debt fund'. Muhyiddin and the attorney general were then seen talking to one another in the Bangsar Shopping Centre, a high-end neighbourhood mall, prompting speculation that Malaysia's institutions were about to take action and the deputy prime minister was being told to be ready to step up. Dark clouds were gathering over Najib.

The day after Muhyiddin's speech, a crowd of about 3,000 people descended on CIMB's Hari Raya (Eid) open-house event at the Hilton Hotel in KL Sentral. As usual the so-called VIP session, at which our senior staff mingled with government officials and our top clients, was to be held at dinner time. It was a badly kept secret that this was when the most influential people in town would be coming, so others poured in to rub shoulders with them. There was even more interest this year: all the talk was about the mounting tension between the prime minister and his deputy.

Muhyiddin was already sitting in his designated seat at the main dining table by the time Najib arrived. As Najib approached to take his seat opposite Muhyiddin he whispered to me: 'But I don't want to sit near that guy.' I insisted he had to, otherwise it would be seen as an open snub. The prime minister and his deputy endured forty-five minutes across the table from one another, silently glowering. They failed to exchange a word with one another. I was sat at the head of the table, trying to make small talk. A circle of journalists, photographers and onlookers surrounded the table as if they were watching a couple of prize fighters at the weigh-in before a fight. The scene was commemorated in an Instagram post I published a few days later with the caption: 'The last supper, one for the history books'.

Najib left early, saying he had work to do. Muhyiddin stayed on, and as he left, I walked him to his car. He asked if I knew when Najib was planning to reshuffle his cabinet. I told him I had no idea but added: 'Sir, I think your speech the other day brought the date forward.'

When Najib apologised that he had to leave early because he had work to do he wasn't kidding. He was planning a pre-emptive move to crush those who threatened his position. What followed was a master-class in the ruthless exercise of raw power.

On the morning of Tuesday, 28 July, the attorney general, (Tan Sri) Abdul Gani Patail, arrived at his office to find the doors locked and his way blocked by officers from the Police Special Branch. He was subsequently told he would be retiring on health grounds. (He did indeed have a chronic kidney complaint and was due to retire in three months anyway.) He was replaced by the judge (Tan Sri) Mohamed Apandi Ali. Later that morning, the head of the Police Special Branch was also replaced.

In a cabinet reshuffle that same day Muhyiddin was summarily dismissed as deputy prime minister. (Datuk Seri) Shafie Apdal, the second of UMNO's three vice presidents, was also fired for being crit-ical of 1MDB. (Dato Seri) Mukhriz Mahathir, Kedah's chief minister, and one of Mahathir's sons, followed swiftly for the same reason. The Public Accounts Committee, which had become increasingly critical of 1MDB, was thrown into disarray when its chairman was promoted to become a deputy minister, making it impossible for him to continue to lead the inquiry. Four of the other eight members of the commit-tee were also brought into government. A Najib loyalist from Pahang was brought in as the committee's new chair. At a stroke, the putative rebellion from inside UMNO's ranks was snuffed out.

I was forced to take emergency measures as well. I was warned that my name was on a list of people to be taken in for questioning under the sedition laws, on the grounds I was apparently party to an illegitimate attempt to unseat the prime minister. Tony Fernandes was asked to tell me to leave the country until the situation cooled down. Initially, I said I'd stand my ground, but Azlina was having none of it: she insisted I go, and I left her at the door looking concerned but, as ever, incredibly strong.

The crackdown all but extinguished moves to tackle 1MDB inside the system. Yet it also provoked a response from those from outside the system who were pushing for a clean-up. The leaders of the Bersih electoral reform movement – *bersih* means clean in Malay – announced they would hold a demonstration in Kuala Lumpur in late August. Despite numerous government attempts to stop the gathering on the grounds that it represented a security threat, it went ahead, and hundreds of thousands gathered in the centre of KL wearing yellow T-shirts or carrying yellow garments. The protests spread to other Malaysian cities and even to London. The Bersih protests were eventually dispersed but they left a lasting mark, not least because Dr Mahathir had attended, a signal that he was throwing his political weight behind them.

Slowly the critics began to regroup. *The Edge* started publishing again on 21 September after a High Court judge ruled its suspension illegal. The *Wall Street Journal* and the *New York Times* were still on the case. Switzerland announced it was suspending all 1MDB's accounts at its country's banks to allow for a full investigation. We knew that the FBI and the US Department of Justice were conducting their own inquiries. As for me I returned to Malaysia two days later after I was told that they had decided against rounding up anyone. They felt they had done enough and it certainly seemed so.

THE SYSTEM
IN QUESTION

The 1MDB scandal is a sorry tale on an epic scale: one of the largest financial scandals in world history. Yet, for me, this was a deeply personal drama because even my family's safety and my father's good name were at stake. Initially, my concerns were simply for the standing of the ringgit bond market. I then grew concerned that a GLC was being used and abused. The next stage was that I was motivated by a desire to protect my brother Najib. I wasn't trying to denounce him, still less to bring him down, but rather to save him from people around him who – I assumed – were abusing the trust he had placed in them. In time, I reluctantly had to recognise the pattern: I warned him, and my warnings were ignored. I objected, and my objections were put to one side. It became even more personal when my wife and children were subject to a barrage of social media attacks recycling falsehoods. Finally, there was an attempt to throw people off the scent by tarnishing my father's good name.

Navigating the affair drew me into difficult conflicts, including with myself. My father had instructed us to look after our good name, which meant caring about our public standing and reputation. He would not want his sons to a fall out in public, as that would be unseemly. Time and again during the 1MDB affair, these injunctions from my father came into conflict as I sought to stay loyal to my brother and protect the Razak name. But as I got deeper into it, I realised that there was a simple binary choice between right and wrong; there was no more grey. The question then was: what was the right way for me to oppose it, to try to stop it and to uphold the values my father stood for?

The moral maze of the 1MDB affair often left me feeling confused and frustrated. I took some wrong turns, no doubt. Perhaps I should have been more outspoken in my criticisms. I thought about all the options long and hard: each time I decided that acting more overtly wasn't possible for me. I discussed my options with many people whose opinions I value. Some said it wasn't my fight, walk away. Others said join the opposition.

Azlina and I discussed the issue at length but I did not adopt her advice. She was in favour of my stepping down as chairman of CIMB in order to support the PH election campaign. She was actively supportive of PH and was a significant sponsor of Pulang Mengundi (Go Home to Vote), an initiative to assist students and first-timers to vote.

In the end I listened instead to two ladies who both pointed out the important convergence of sticking by your principles and sticking by your family.

First, Ngaire Woods, dean of the Blavatnik School of Government in Oxford, where I was an advisory board member, said while she completely understood how strongly I felt and why I might want to be involved with the public opposition to Najib, I should remain in the background. 'Even the people who would back you now will never trust someone who could openly stab his brother. Ed Miliband never fully recovered from challenging his brother David.' And second, Rafidah Aziz, who would go on to fiercely campaign against Najib; she said I simply couldn't publicly go against Najib because 'it would break [your] mum's heart'. My mother had loved and supported me all her life – much of it as a widow and a single parent – and causing her such distress in her final years would be poor recompense for all her sacrifices.

I thought of just resigning from CIMB in subtle protest and discussed it with Azman at Khazanah, who was also very disturbed by 1MDB. We concluded that while 'Rome is burning, we should try to protect what we can for the rebuild that will come'. It was typically philosophical of him, and the point was correct: if we relinquished our posts and weak or compromised individuals took our place, then our institutions would get dragged into covering up the 1MDB financial mess. There was certainly institutional defending to do. I had been a member of the EPF Investment Panel for twelve years by 2015 and should have retired, but was asked to stay on 'to help the defence in case 1MDB comes', in CEO (Datuk) Shahril Ridzuan's words. Similarly, as a member of the Khazanah board, I found myself having to do the same; for instance we rejected requests for Khazanah to participate in 1MDB's Tun Razak Exchange (TRX) project. Ironically, being Najib's brother helped because his advisors would also have counselled that it wasn't good politics to have a public falling-out with a high-profile sibling.

So I stayed behind the scenes, nudging, prompting and encouraging our institutions and politicians into action. Had I done nothing I wouldn't be able to look myself in the mirror. Had I openly challenged my brother and split the family I wouldn't have been able to look my mum in the eye. Ironically, my loyalty to Najib came back to haunt me.

In March 2016, it emerged through the *Wall Street Journal* that the cheques I had cashed for Najib back in 2013 had been drawn from AmBank accounts into which money allegedly from 1MDB had been deposited.[87] It later emerged that the accounts were managed by Jho Low, and the cheques that came my way were part of a blizzard of cheques issued from the accounts. The realisation that money from 1MDB had probably gone through my accounts was deeply distressing and no doubt cast suspicions about my involvement in the whole saga. In the long list of recipients listed by *WSJ*, I was the only one who immediately acknowledged what had happened. But that was not good enough. I had to find a way of getting genuine independent affirmation that there was no impropriety on my part.

At the CIMB Annual General Meeting of shareholders on 18 April, rather dramatically I announced I would be taking leave as chairman while the board commissioned an independent inquiry. I was off work for thirty days. To ensure the inquiry was beyond reproach, the bank appointed independent advisors, lawyer Tommy Thomas and accounting firm Ernst and Young. Tommy was one of the fiercest critics of 1MDB, and after GE14, he would be appointed attorney general by the PH government. They investigated what transpired and checked through all transactions in all my bank accounts. The boards of both CIMB Bank and CIMB Group, totalling about fifteen respected local and foreign professionals, reviewed the findings and cleared my personal conduct, but found there had been some administrative shortcomings in how the bank had handled the funds. They reinstated me as chairman. Bank Negara then conducted its own investigations, on what transpired and the board's due process. CIMB handled the episode according to the highest governance standards – even Tommy said so – but it was never going to satisfy everyone. As usual the detractors would claim it was whitewashed because of my name. This episode remained there to be used against me in the future.

The 1MDB story involves many perpetrators and beneficiaries but also individuals who made the wrong decisions. There were lots of personal failings, moments in which people had the opportunity to do the right thing and failed to take it. In due course, the legal process will deal with the chief perpetrators and complicit beneficiaries. But the real failings are institutional. The big lesson for me is not so much about people as about the systems they work in and the culture systems create which shape how people make their decisions. 1MDB was the highly toxic offspring of two deeply flawed systems which came together with devastating effect. If we want to prevent similar scandals we have to sort out both of them.

The first was a financial system in which people were able to dodge responsibility for their actions. Too many people looked the other way as rules were bent and broken. The 1MDB scheme was engineered by a group of tricksters led by Jho Low; yet it also involved leading domestic and international banks, and professional advisors with sophisticated internal checks and balances and external oversight. The scam was facilitated by apparently respectable bankers and accountants who declined to ask difficult questions in case the answers got in the way of lucrative business. One measure of this failure is the sums involved in settling legal action taken against Goldman Sachs and AmBank for their role in the affair. Goldman eventually agreed to pay close to $3bn to settle a US legal action taken by the Department of Justice and $3.9bn to settle action in Malaysia. AmBank agreed a global settlement with the Malaysian Government for RM2.83bn. Malaysian financial system regulators didn't take opportunities to call it to a halt. A system in which regulators were unable to stand up to political power created the conditions in which Jho Low could get to work.

The culture of greed at the heart of the modern financial system found its wicked twin in Malaysia's flawed systems of politics and government. Power is more likely to be exercised well when those in power can demonstrate a strong thread of moral virtue connecting them to the people they serve. Good people, however, are never enough on their own; you can never guarantee having enough of them to hold the line. We need systems that ensure people will do the right thing even when they're not saints; when, like most of us, they are frail, vain, imperfect and sometimes selfish. Moreover good people can turn bad and someimes vice versa, often due to a change in circumstances rather than character.

We need independent institutions, the rule of law and effective enforcement, to help people adhere to the right values and principles. No politician can be above the law. Power turns bad when it becomes too concentrated in too few hands and can operate without checks and balances, challenge and contest. My brother inherited a government machine in which power was already too concentrated. Power turns bad when it is not subject to scrutiny from other institutions, when people with power can act with impunity. For too long, those involved in the 1MDB affair believed they could escape scrutiny by distracting, diverting, bullying and misleading institutions meant to check them and the PM. The scandal was brought to light only thanks to fearless reporting by *The Edge* and *Malaysiakini* as well as the likes of *Sarawak Report*, the *Wall Street Journal* and the *New York Times*, some brave individual leaders and ultimately the voters.

I do not in any way wish to underplay the magnitude of what went on at 1MDB. The scale of the sums involved, the blatancy with which the scam was carried out and the sophistication of its execution mean it is in a league of its own. Yet in many regards 1MDB was not too different from many of the financial scandals that had gone before, in which politicians, or their Rasputins, had used the power of government to source funds, ostensibly for campaigning purposes, only to siphon off or fritter away huge amounts. 1MDB took it to another level by using a GLC with implicit federal government financial backing and operating on an international scale.

1MDB was the clearest evidence yet that the system of politics, government and business, which could trace its roots back to my father, was now deeply flawed. Abdul Razak saw it as the means for the government to deliver for the people and build a nation. His successors came to see it as the means for them to finance their own grip on power first, and everything else after that. This left me, it seemed, with a fateful choice: to stand up for the values and principles of good government that my father believed in, I needed to repudiate what had become of the system he had created and call for its overhaul.

To this day I do not know what really transpired in the 1MDB saga, what Najib did or did not know at material times. I do know that the world's largest financial scam happened under my brother's watch and that 1MDB involved transgressions that could only have taken place with his authority being invoked (with or without his knowledge). The system should have held Najib to account with a thorough and impartial investigation back in 2015, which would have required him to step aside, at least temporarily. Instead, he purged his administration of critics and effectively brought investigations into 1MDB to a close. That he did so was his failing; that he was able to do so was a failing of the system.

The 1MDB matter is now in the courts. I expect that justice will now take its proper course. As his brother, I pray that Najib is able to clear his name. No matter the outcome I hope that in time we will be able to rebuild our fraternal relationship that has been damaged by this whole sorry episode.

For Malaysia's sake I hope we can reform our system of government, politics and business so that this is the last scandal of this kind we face. Working out how we can make that happen has been my focus since at least 2016. I see that as an obligation I am under from the true legacy that Abdul Razak left us, the legacy of values, principles and methods which underlie good power.

Democracy has many weaknesses, but it still exerts the most important discipline over power: the people can kick out a government they don't like. A citizenry of sheep encourages a government of wolves. Governments prefer passive, meek and ill-informed citizens. A society in which people live in fear of the state will tend towards bad power; a state which fears the people is more likely to use power for the public good. Powerlessness and passivity are bad for people. Democracy needs an active, skilled and knowledgeable public – and the people behind the 1MDB scandal thought they would get away with it because they assumed the Malaysian public could be ground into submission.

As we went into the fourteenth general election in May 2018, I had little optimism that the Malaysian people were ready to stand up for themselves. Malaysians are not inclined to rebel and revolt, to take power into our own hands. The sheep were cowering in front of the wolves. Or so it seemed. What happened next and what it means for Malaysia is the subject of the final section.

SECTION FIVE

CONVERSATIONS ON MALAYSIA

SWEET SORROW

The stunning victory of Pakatan Harapan, the coalition of opposition parties led by Mahathir, in the 9 May 2018 general election opened the way for a complete reset, for Malaysia and, without my anticipating it, for me as well.

I was excited by the PH victory. The people of Malaysia had risen up in a democratic rebellion to oust UMNO and the BN, to usher in a new ruling party for the first time in sixty-one years as an independent nation. It was a big step in Malaysia's democratic development, proof that the people could change the government by voting and that the transfer of power could take place peacefully. The victory marked the end of a political era that my father had inaugurated as the architect of the BN alliance. The system he helped to create was being overthrown, but despite my loyalty to him I felt the time had come for sweeping reforms. A new government had to be better than the one that had become so deeply mired in the 1MDB scandal. I was optimistic that the change would be good for the country, even though my academic research into what happens when a long-dominant coalition falls from power left me with a nagging worry that our new politics might not turn out to be better than the old. We were all in unfamiliar territory.

What I had not foreseen was that the change in government would affect my position at CIMB. Although we were a GLC, we were publicly listed, independently run by a board and not an instrument of government policy. The firm was on a strong footing. In April I wrote my annual letter to shareholders describing 2017 as the year 'we got our mojo back – we saw it in our share price, we read about it in analyst reports and the media, we heard it from customers and we felt it amongst staff'. Little did I know that it would be the last such letter I would write to them.

From what I had gleaned from PH's capacious manifesto, its main concerns were with government entities that had been mismanaged or abused, not those like CIMB that were well run. I understood that, as I was Najib's brother, many in the opposition would associate me with him. Yet many people at the heart of the new government also knew how much I had done behind the scenes to bring the 1MDB scandal to light. In my business dealings, I believed that I had always, visibly, been guided by professionalism, not just at CIMB but in my roles serving the nation on the board at Khazanah and as a member of the investment panel at the EPF. I had openly objected not just to 1MDB's conduct but to other questionable deals. Lim Guan Eng, the incoming minister of finance, made a point of inviting me to be the first private-sector figure to visit him at his new office, much to the astonishment of the MOF officials who saw me walk in. A few weeks later, I was given an audience with new Prime Minister Mahathir, where he shared his thoughts on the future and said he understood why I couldn't have done more than I did on 1MDB.

Nevertheless, rumours abounded that my contemporaries, Azman Mokhtar at Khazanah and Wahid Omar at PNB, and I were top of the list of people to be removed; quite why we had to go was never made clear. At the end of June, Wahid stepped down. At the end of July, Azman and the entire Khazanah board (including me) followed suit. All had been, not so subtly, prodded to do so. It took longer for my position at CIMB to become clear.

The shots were being called by the Council of Eminent Persons (CEP), a small high-level committee chaired by Daim to advise

Mahathir during the chaotic early phase of the new administration. The CEP had excellent credentials; other members were my father's old friend Robert Kuok; (Tan Sri) Hassan Merican, former CEO of Petronas; (Tan Sri) Zeti Aziz, former governor of Bank Negara; and the economist Jomo Sundaram. I could never though quite reconcile many of the decisions attributed to the council with my understanding of the majority of its members, all of whom I knew very well.

In mid-August, apparently the CEP made the decision: I was to go. My mentor Md Nor, who had once been Daim's advisor, was tasked with delivering the prod. It was a sad moment for both of us, given what we had been through together. He came to my house to deliver the news and was obviously pained doing so. But I told him it was better to hear the news from someone who I knew and respected. I agreed straight away that I would go; I had always told the CIMB board that the company should never be at odds with the government of the day. I did not ask for any compensation; my only request was that things should be done properly and with due regard to the interests of the company.

To that end I immediately met up with Shahril Ridzuan, who had just been installed as Azman's replacement at Khazanah. I knew Oxford-educated Shahril very well; we met almost every other week when I attended EPF Investment Panel meetings with him as CEO. I told Shahril that although the CEP wanted me to step down, the Council didn't have proper authority to instruct me to do anything. I requested that Khazanah, as the major shareholder, inform CIMB formally that it was no longer supporting my chairmanship. Shahril said he needed to consult the PM, as chairman of Khazanah. I was pleased that Shahril also wanted to follow due process, to do things properly.

A few days later, Shahril called me on his way back from seeing the PM to say that Mahathir wanted me stay on at CIMB and rejoin the Khazanah board. I was surprised but pleased because I wanted to see through CIMB's T18 project, help to prepare and launch its new five-year plan, 'Forward 23' and groom a successor before stepping down in August 2019, at the end of my term. I was also happy that I would be able to continue to help at Khazanah for some time. A clear decision had been made by the most powerful man in the country, so that had to be that. Or so I thought.

Two weeks later it was all changed: Shahril called once more to say that Mahathir had been advised to change his mind and I would have to leave after all. I was surprised and disappointed, but it was pointless to try to understand what was happening behind the scenes. Tommy Thomas's controversial memoir *My Story: Justice in the Wilderness*[88] has subsequently provided a graphic account of the chaotic and highly personalised decision making that characterised the inner workings of the heart of the PH government in the court around Mahathir. One thing I have learned is that every administration features Rasputin-like figures: they ingratiate themselves with the PM in order to pull the strings at court from behind the scenes and liberally use the PM's name to pursue agendas, often their own. Jho Low was just the most damaging of them. Thankfully, these people are never as clever as they think and usually come a cropper.

Shahril made it plain, in the nicest way, that he was worried that this administration's Rasputins could get quite nasty if I resisted this decision. I could not disagree so I just asked to be able leave at the end of the year in order to have time to wrap things up properly.

That was the announcement I prepared to make on 24 September 2018 as I made my way down in the lift at Menara CIMB and through a throng of staff gathered on the first floor. It was a speech I had always known I would one day have to make, although I hadn't imagined it would be in these circumstances. With a heavy heart, mixed feelings and much foreboding, I told the assembled CIMBians that at the end of the year I would be leaving the company I'd joined twenty-nine years earlier. Endings, when they come, can be quick and somewhat messy. At least I would have ample time to provide input for Forward 23 and say my goodbyes. Or so I thought.

Once more, my hope would not come to be. A few days later, Zulqarnain Onn, the Khazanah representative on the CIMB board, informed us that I should leave as soon as the Bank Negara approved a new chairman, not at the year end. Zul, a Harvard graduate, who had once worked for me at CIMB, made it very clear he was only carrying out instructions. The CIMB board had agreed that my designated successor was to be (Datuk) Nasir Ahmad, whom I had met in the early 1990s when he was an accountant in the finance division of Tenaga Nasional. We wanted an internal successor for continuity, but that also meant that Bank Negara's approval would come quickly.

So my official last day at the company I joined on Monday 11 September 1989 was Friday, 19 October 2018. It was an awkward, untidy end, but the board and management made every effort to give me a good send-off, including a farewell event in every major country that CIMB operated in. I really appreciated those memorable dinner parties with staff in Singapore, Bangkok, Phnom Penh and Kuala Lumpur. Unfortunately, I missed my own farewell party in Jakarta because when I got to KLIA to catch my flight I found that I was banned from travelling outside the country! It transpired that the authorities were investigating the alleged 1MDB funds that Najib put through my accounts back in 2013. I could accept that they might want to revisit matters even though CIMB and Bank Negara had already investigated, but I was shocked that they would deem me a flight risk. To ban me from international travel seemed vindictive. The only way I could make sense of it all was that people in very powerful positions were intent on making my life uncomfortable, for whatever reason. On reflection, perhaps there were several people with many reasons to want to make my life uncomfortable. Over the years I must have crossed a number of people who were now influential with Daim's return to power.

One thing Azman, Wahid and I shared was that we all played a role in the nationalisation of Renong and UEM in 2001 and their subsequent restructuring; maybe this was our comeuppance. The travel ban was lifted within days of it being imposed, but no one ever explained why it was warranted in the first place. Indeed, the persons in charge of the investigations into my matter seemed as perplexed as I was. The investigations would go on until January 2020, when I was informed that the MACC had closed the case.

The chaotic to-and-fro over my future showed that whatever we thought we had achieved to make GLCs more independent and professionally run, we had not insulated them from political influence. Despite all that, I had one huge consolation: my personal setback was a small price to pay for what appeared to be Malaysia's gain, the chance for a reforming government to overhaul a deeply suspect system. PH had campaigned on a manifesto promising substantial and far-reaching reforms – a fixing of all that was broken, a cleansing of all that was rotten, a healing of all that had been torn apart. After all, its *zeitgeist* was an all-encompassing vision of 'New Malaysia'. We all had a lot to look forward to, or so I thought.

SERIAL FAILURE

Despite the euphoria of the election victory and enormous goodwill on its side, PH did not come close to bringing a 'New Malaysia' into being. Understanding why PH failed to make good on the huge opportunity it had is vital if Malaysia is ever to stand a chance of creating a brighter future for all. The PH victory offered hope of system-wide reform; its failure underlined the deep-seated nature of Malaysia's challenges, particularly with regard to its political system.

The PH government seemed to get off to a good start. It tackled the 1MDB debacle with gusto and made a series of sound leadership changes to begin to repair key institutions. It drew on talent from across Malaysia's ethnic communities to fill key positions: non-*bumiputras* were appointed as minister of finance, attorney general and chief justice.

PH did not lack for ideas, aspirations and goodwill. On the economic front the PH government announced its agenda to bring about inclusive growth. The 'Shared Prosperity Vision 2030' launched in October 2019 said economic growth is being held back and shared unfairly.[89] Industry is still dominated by low-value-added activities. Monopolies are too powerful, allowing them to charge high prices. Meanwhile, too many businesses depend on low-wage, low-skilled workers so that there is little incentive to invest in new technology or automation. That in turn holds back productivity growth. Taken together, all these issues mean that disparities in income and wealth are widening. The SPV 2030 argued that much of the economy's dysfunctions stem from corruption which keeps these outdated structures in place and stifles growth. All good statements of course but there was a glaring absence of specifics.

PH did deliver some of its boldest promises like the removal of the unpopular Goods and Services Tax (GST) and successfully won cross-party support to lower the minimum voting age to eighteen years old. However, PH stalled on its most important structural reforms, including limiting the powers of the PM, rebalancing federal–state power, and repealing the Sedition Act. It set up an Institutional Reforms Committee (headed by (Dato) Ambiga Sreenevasan, founder of the Bersih reform movement) but refused to make either its findings or recommendations public, despite pleas by the committee members themselves to do so. It backed down on communally sensitive but relatively benign initiatives such as signing the International Convention on the Elimination of All Forms of Racial Discrimination (ICERD) and recognising the Unified Exam Certificate (UEC) for independent Chinese schools, which is already widely recognised outside Malaysia. It didn't even get to enacting 'Harmony' laws to regulate racially provocative and discriminatory speech and actions.

It was never clear how far PH really wanted to go to reform the system. PH came to power riding public anger against kleptocracy, corruption and patronage exemplified by the 1MDB scandal, but people drew different conclusions as to what that meant going forward. For some PH leaders the problems just lay with Najib's government, which needed to be cleared out. Others recognised that the problems lay deep in the system itself and advocated systemic reforms to varying degrees.

For his part, Mahathir was always an unlikely reformer of an over-centralised system which he, more than anyone, had built on top of the foundations that had been laid by my father. When pressed by journalists one day, Mahathir audaciously admitted that some manifesto promises were made because they did not expect to win. More ominously, guided by the CEP, the government made extensive personnel changes in government departments, its agencies and linked companies which confirmed that these were all political – rather than independent and professional – appointments. PH came to power campaigning against the politics of patronage but soon removed any ambiguity about the principal criteria for all government-related appointments – politics. Its successor government would follow this precedent with greater blatancy.

Despite its popular victory, PH was fragile and vulnerable from the outset. Its chances of enacting sweeping reforms were always slim; the odds were always stacked against it. It was a coalition of convenience brought together to defeat Najib, through the old adversaries, Mahathir and Anwar, burying their differences. Most observers understood there was a deal for Mahathir to become prime minister and then hand power to Anwar two years after taking office. It was always hard to reconcile the planned succession and the venom with which Mahathir had stated the case against Anwar succeeding him in the past. As the date for the handover approached, Anwar pressed his case, and the alliance became increasingly unstable.

At the end of February 2020, after only twenty-two months in office, a group of mainly Malay MPs from Bersatu and PKR broke away to form the Perikatan Nasional (PN) government, in partnership with UMNO, PAS and several parties that had been part of the old BN government with Muhyiddin as Malaysia's eighth PM. The short-lived experiment with a new coalition government promising sweeping reforms came to an end. Muhyiddin's government quickly became engulfed by responding to the Covid-19 pandemic. Lacking an electoral mandate of its own, and with a wafer-thin majority in parliament, Muhyiddin's government was equally vulnerable and unsteady from the start. Within months rumours were swirling that Anwar had mobilised a possible new coalition to take over the government. The game of musical chairs of leaders, parties and coalitions seemed set to continue without it leading to any fundamental change, feeding rancour and instability. In January 2021 HM the Agong declared a state of emergency and with it the suspension of Parliament, ostensibly to manage the Covid 19 pandemic. The music stopped with Muhyiddin in the chair. That was convenient for him and his party but the music will soon have to start again.

Why did PH fail to deliver us to a New Malaysia, and what are the lessons of that failure for those in Malaysia who believe the country needs far-reaching reform?

Of course, leadership, personalities and political infighting within the coalition played their role, but the real causes lie deeper, rooted in the nature of the political system itself and especially in the role that identity plays in political competition.

PH won the 2018 general election with less than 25% of Malay votes. The coalition's Malay component party, Bersatu, desperately needed to expand its Malay support to provide it with greater ballast. While Bersatu managed to persuade some UMNO MPs to cross over to it, its ability to appeal to the rural Malay public was hampered by being in government with the DAP, which had long been labelled by UMNO as Chinese chauvinists. For its part, the DAP struggled to maintain the support of its base because it had to moderate its position on communal issues for the sake of its place in the coalition. That provoked accusations that the party was not standing up for the Chinese community and ceding too much ground to its coalition partners. Meanwhile, the third main component party, multiracial PKR led by Anwar Ibrahim, was riven by tensions between its conservative (pro-Mahathir) and reformist (pro-Anwar) wings, as well as by personal rivalries within the leadership.

Although UMNO had been defeated, it was far from vanquished. Almost as soon as it fell from power, UMNO entered into an alliance called 'Muafakat Nasional' with PAS, featuring strong racial and religious overtones designed to rally the core Malay vote. A series of by-election victories for Muafakat Nasional put more pressure on fragile ties within the PH coalition which culminated in the "Sheraton move" named after the Kuala Lumpur hotel where Muhyiddin's new political grouping first gathered.

PH was not the first administration to promise major reforms, set high expectations and then fall very short. Ever since the Asian Financial Crisis in 1998, the need for reforms to strengthen national unity, promote economic competitiveness, improve educational outcomes, tackle corruption and strengthen institutions had been a consistent feature of government reports and party manifestos.

Both Badawi and Najib had positioned themselves as reformers. Both were extremely popular at the start of their administrations. Both were derailed at the ballot box and thrown off the reform course (or was it the other way around?). PH's rise and fall was not an aberration but part of a recurring pattern.

For almost two decades, Malaysia has suffered the recurring disappointment of governments coming to power telling people that fundamental change is required, only to fail to deliver it. The electorate is warned that the consequences of failing to effect radical change will be slow growth, widening inequality, mounting frustration and the fraying of the delicate social fabric which holds multi-ethnic Malaysia together. They vote for change, and yet the politicians charged with delivering that change quickly back off once they are in power. The one thing that has come true from all these bold plans is the warnings they issue about what would happen if Malaysia did not reform: investment would fall, the economy would slow, divisions would grow, and the country would drift into dangerous waters as politicians fight among themselves.

It is tempting to think the problem lies with leadership and that a better leader would be the solution. Perhaps we haven't found the right man or woman? And maybe – maybe – it's true that all Malaysia really needs is better leaders, inspired by a higher mission and prepared for the hard slog of enacting real change. Time and again, though, we've seen that even when governments come into power with a popular leader, a mandate for reforms and an apparent commitment to enact them, they fail to achieve change of real significance. The evidence suggests that it's not a question of *who* governs but of how our systems and institutions of democracy and government shape both the governors and the governed. If three different administrations with markedly different leaders – Badawi, Najib and Mahathir – have come to power on the basis of making fundamental reforms, and each has failed to deliver, then it must surely be time to acknowledge that we have a more systemic problem with deeper roots. Malaysian political culture is like a badly written play: it can't be improved by just casting different actors.

The Malaysian political landscape is littered with the wreckage of failed reform efforts. To understand how we can break through to a new phase of social and economic development in Malaysia, we need to understand the quagmire we are stuck in which prevents us from moving forward. That means confronting the monster at the heart of Malaysian politics.

THE THREE-HEADED MONSTER

A three-headed monster rules Malaysia: identity, money and centralisation of power. It is that combination which prevents us from carrying through reforms everyone agrees are needed. That monster stands between us and a better future. Each of the three heads needs to be dealt with, but we will fail if we try to deal with them in separation. We need to address how they work together to corrupt, distort and divert power from serving the public good.

First is the central role that identity plays in organising our politics. Politicians succeed and fail, rise and fall, primarily by delivering the ethnic core of their support base. As a result, compromise is seen as a concession to another group. Political competition organised along ethnic lines – the Malays versus the Chinese and the Indians – creates a divisive, distrustful culture which infects society as a whole.

Second is the corrosive and unrestrained role of money in politics. Politicians use money to win elections within their parties and their constituencies. To fund their politics, they raise money from individuals and businesses to which they feel compelled to offer favours and preferential treatment. Along the way there are also massive leakages of money into unintended hands. The 1MDB scandal was the most ambitious and sophisticated scheme to fund the Malaysian money politics machine but it was by no means the first. The past forty years is strewn with examples of how businesses and banks have been harnessed to service political ambitions. Not only does this lead to corruption, it has a disastrous long-term impact on the economy. The overbearing role of politics in making business decisions misallocates resources and dulls incentives to invest, innovate and take risks.

Third is the extreme over-centralisation of power which operates without proper checks and balances. As a result, vital decisions are too often taken behind closed doors, without proper clear criteria to make sure they serve the public good. Malaysian politics is a game in which the winners take all, which includes being able to change the rules to suit themselves and to control the referees who are supposed to be independent. The lack of effective oversight makes it far too tempting for those in power to use that power for their own sake rather than the public good. A good society needs an effective state. Some centralisation of power is almost a prerequisite for that. The question is how that power is held to account so that it acts for the public good.

This chapter sets out why we find ourselves battling this three-headed beast, the direct damage it does and how it holds us back from grasping the opportunities that lie ahead. I have seen each of these three factors at work in the course of my career and I can attest to the power they hold over people: It is hard to break free of their grip. Take the money. Stick with your kind. Do what you are told. This chapter explains why the grip of these destructive forces is so strong; the following chapter sets out a simple, bold and ambitious plan to tame the monster and break free.

IDENTITY

Modern Malaysia was a British creation. It was the British who fundamentally altered the peninsula's ethnic make-up by bringing in Chinese tin miners and Indian rubber tappers in their hundreds of thousands. The flood of immigrants became so great in the early decades of the twentieth century that controls and preferential policies were introduced to protect Malays from being overrun. In time new immigrants, and some of the sons and daughters of the miners, became shopkeepers, businessmen and bankers, while some of the sons and daughters of rubber tappers became doctors, accountants and teachers. But the two immigrant communities were kept largely separate from one another and from the Malays, who tilled the soil and cast their nets for fish, and whose elites dominated the civil service and the royal courts. The British ruled through long division. Which community and which spectrum of the community you came from determined what kind of job you did and what kind of life prospects you had.

When independence came in 1957, Malaya faced fateful choices. The immigrants, as they were seen by the Malays, were resident in such numbers and connected with such strong ties that they could not be shipped back to where their parents and grandparents had come from. For them Malaya was home. Yet the Malays feared they would be outnumbered in their own country and demanded they be given special protection and privileges. The constitution embodied a series of uncomfortable, yet inescapable, compromises: all citizens were equal, but Malays were to be given special status; the country would be secular and tolerant, but Islam would be its official religion. All citizens were to be assigned to an ethnic group at birth: a citizen could not just be a Malaysian, he or she had to nail his or her ethnic colours to the mast from the outset. You were conditioned to be Indian, Chinese or Malay first and Malaysian afterwards. That rigid categorisation profoundly shapes how we see ourselves and the political questions we debate.

Identity, based on race, quickly became the most obvious organising principle for political parties in a country with no experience of democratic elections. The suppression of left-wing political movements by the British after the war meant that ideology did not play that organ-ising role: left and right, conservatives and liberals, were not important poles of attraction as they were in Western developed democracies. The success of the Alliance Party's coalition of Malay, Chinese and Indian parties at the 1955 general election, and the multiracial IMP's dismal failure, entrenched race as the main basis for political allegiances. The DAP and Gerakan were both set up as multiracial parties, but neither could ever escape being caricatured as Chinese parties. The scene was set for parties to further the interests of specific ethnic groups even where they were part of a wider coalition.

It took a while for Malaya's new political system to face its first real test and yet promptly it failed – at GE3 in 1969. The 13 May race riots brought the country to the edge of an abyss, revealing just how dangerous competitive racial politics could be. It was out of the frying pan into the fire: Malaysia had gained independence but in the process acquired a dangerously unstable political system which threatened to pitch it into societal conflict.

Alvin Rabushka and Kenneth A. Shepsle explained the problem in their ground-breaking 1972 book *Politics in Plural Societies: A Theory of Democratic Instability*: 'Most independent plural societies fail to retain, over a sustained period, stable democratic politics. Free and open competition for people's vote is simply not viable in an environment of intense ethnic preferences. The demand-generating activity of ambitious leaders, the concomitant salience of primordial sentiments, and the politics of outbidding weaken commitment to national values.'[90]

Malaysia was not alone in facing these destabilising dynamics. Many former British colonies faced similar issues. In Sri Lanka polit-ical competition led to ethnic riots which turned to civil war. Plural societies, which comprise several ethnic groups, often fail to evolve into mature democracies because it is hard for them to sustain the kind of rational discourse needed for democracy to evolve. When there is a rigid conception of what serves group interests, proposed changes trigger fears – founded or unfounded – that the interests of one ethnic group are being promoted at the expense of another. Ethnicity is a powerful tool for those with vested interests to exploit to resist change. A sense of Malay vulnerability has always been close to the heart of Malaysian politics, an insecurity quick to be inflamed by any hint that the bogeyman – Chinese interests, the Christian church and so on – was gaining the upper hand.

In plural societies where identity defines political affiliation, political competition drives social division, pitting communities against one another: a gain for one party becomes a gain for its community and by definition a setback for the other party and its community. The system reinforces tribal loyalty, making it easy to flame discontent.

Malaysia's response to 13 May was to recognise that the Westminster system it had inherited was inadequate to the task of creating a stable democracy. The country recalibrated; it pulled back from the brink to develop a form of stable, managed democracy dominated by the Barisan Nasional grand coalition, which superseded the Alliance. BN's dominance ensured that a UMNO-led government had a working majority, which made the Malays feel safe, while the grand coalition meant that Indian and Chinese interests, as well as those of Sabah and Sarawak, were taken into account. The BN strategy was a classic example of the model of power sharing espoused by the political scientist Arend Lijphart, who argues that in multi-ethnic societies with race-based parties, broad-based coalitions are likely to emerge to provide a degree of stability to systems that become unstable when they become intensely competitive. Stable, broad-based coalitions would allow a wide representation of different interests and take the sting out of political competition based on ethnic groups. Conflicts tend to be moved to behind closed doors to be resolved by elite leaders.

That 1970s system survived for so long because for at least the first two decades of its life it delivered what most Malaysians wanted:

stability, social order, economic growth, poverty reduction and a degree of social mobility, especially for the Malays. From the turn of the millennium, however, the BN coalition, dominated by UMNO, came under growing strain not least because of voter frustration with the antics of the three-headed monster. Only Badawi's short-lived triumph in 2004 stemmed the loss of seats and votes. The 2018 general election seemed to mark a turning point, with the ousting of BN and the election of the PH coalition. There is no guarantee though that BN's fall would give rise to something better, or indeed something more democratic even. So far the ousting of the BN has opened the way to a game of musical chairs of shifting short-term coalitions, based on personalities more than policies. One could argue that this is a typically chaotic period of transition from a long and deeply entrenched rule by one party, but that would still beg the question: transition to what?

The distrust between Malaysia's communities is still deep-seated: witness the furore even among sophisticated and well-educated Malays at the PH's appointment of an eminently well-qualified Chinese finance minister and an Indian attorney general. It is far too easy for politicians bereft of ideas to turn this distrust into division and antagonism, to play the race and religion card to rally supporters. Even in my corporate career I saw the power of communal loyalties at play – in the takeover of Southern Bank and the abortive combination between AirAsia and Malaysian Airlines, amongst others. Politicians fear antagonising their own supporters by being seen to be weak on communal issues.

Indeed, while the end of BN was overdue, its demise has created unforeseen instability. Now there is competition among several Malay parties trying to outbid one another to be true political sons of the soil, as well as an array of Chinese and Indian parties, and multiracial parties such as the PKR. The establishment of Muafakat Nasional by PAS and UMNO to outflank Bersatu and PH shows how arch-rivals can unashamedly create alliances of convenience to exploit identity. The danger of ethnic outbidding for the Malay vote is that it could lead to ugly, chauvinistic Malay supremacism, with Malay politicians proving themselves by riding roughshod over the rights of minority groups. Or might democracy itself fall by the wayside? Either way, Malaysia would be far from the tolerant, open and consultative nation envisaged by its founders.

Even if we avoid that fate, our political system will not help us meet the challenges we face. The political system has already proven comprehensively unable to take on the big reforms required to take the country forward. The leaders of race-based parties have no incentive to tackle big shared challenges. They maintain their power by looking after their own ethnic groups.

It is naive to imagine that ethnic loyalties can, or should, be set to one side. These identities matter to people. It is utopian to imagine that in the space of a few years people would set aside the ethnic and cultural identities in favour of the national identity of being Malaysian. The Malaysian nation-building project was always going to take a very long time; perpetuating with race-based parties, prolonging affirmative action and growing religiosity have served to delay it even more. We need to be realistic that identity will remain a vital, powerful part of Malaysian politics for years to come. It is scant consolation that mature Western democracies are discovering how identity politics can so easily take centre stage.

We need to find a more effective, stable and creative way to work together, as a nation. CIMB became successful because we recognised diversity was our strength, and finding ways to work together to make the most of it was vital. I believe we need just such an agenda for Malaysia as a whole now. In the next chapter I set out ideas for how we can make a start by creating a more positive dynamic to our identity politics, one focused on the benefits of diversity and creativity.

MONEY POLITICS

Democracy requires resources, specifically money. That money has to come from somewhere, and if it does not come from state funding for political parties, it comes from individuals, businesses and other organisations, like trade unions and, in the US, Political Action Committees. Inevitably, in any system, that creates opportunities for corruption, as those donating the money ask for favours, and politicians keen to raise money push the boundaries of what is acceptable.

In its early years UMNO was at a profound disadvantage. As most private-sector businesses in Malaysia were owned and run by families of Chinese descent, the Malaysian Chinese Association was always well funded. My father would remark to colleagues that the only Malay business that UMNO could turn to for donations was a man who ran a petrol station. Tunku sometimes drew on his royal inheritance to support the party. The racial imbalance in the ownership of business threatened to translate into an imbalance in political influence if not power. It was hard for UMNO to be the flag bearer for the Malays when it depended on funding from Chinese business. Abdul Razak would lament the concessions he had to make to MCA and Chinese businessmen in order to raise money for UMNO.

That is why in the early 1970s Abdul Razak and Dr Ismail instructed a young Tengku Razaleigh to start investing funds for UMNO and develop businesses which could in turn fund the party. This led to the creation of the Fleet Group and other UMNO-linked business entities over the years.

At the same time Abdul Razak initiated a political fund which was set up under the sole authority of the president of the party that was not subject to the scrutiny of the Supreme Council for ease of administration and confidentiality. Instead, oversight was exercised by the deputy president and treasurer; proper processes and accounts were maintained, to begin with.

UMNO has since always been funded by a combination of returns from its own investments and contributions from businessmen. Membership subscriptions are rarely even collected. At the start it was all very proper and orderly. This is Musa Hitam's account of Dr Ismail's approach to fundraising: Ismail would declare up front that no donation could be made privately; every donation has to be made in front of witnesses and acknowledged accordingly.[91] He would tell donors to their face that they should neither expect nor hope for favours from the government, no licences or contracts or assistance from him in getting such favours. Each donor would be issued with a written receipt. There was to be no 'hanky-panky' on Dr Ismail's watch.

The combination of the power to make appointments and the political fund made the PM and UMNO president extremely powerful, and in due course the checks and balances provided by the party deputy president and treasurer, who was appointed by the party president, became ineffective. In time it also became more and more difficult to restrain politicians from using the power of ministerial positions to support UMNO's business interests and those of other donors too.

The Fleet Group became the behemoth that was Renong Group in all its pomp. Through a dense network of links between businesses and banks UMNO had assets held by the party, the president of the party and in trust by individuals on its behalf. Under the NEP government contracts, licences and permits could easily be awarded to businesses that belonged to, supported or were proxies of the party. Those contracts could be used as collateral to raise money from banks and push up share prices on the stock exchange. At the heart of this dense system of clientelism and patronage, with business, government and ruling party working hand in glove, sat some very powerful people. Daim Zainuddin was the best known; for a while he was simultaneously party treasurer and minister of finance, while also tacitly controlling the Renong group. This system was not designed for corruption, it just got too easy and tempting to resist, and the lines between accelerating *bumiputra* wealth creation, protecting UMNO's hegemony and corruption became very fine. Ultimately, it was the foundation for a baroque edifice of vested interests determined to protect and preserve the system that benefitted them so handsomely. It was that edifice that came crashing down, causing such damage during the Asian Financial Crisis.

As UMNO grew more dominant, positions within the party became more and more valuable. The political scientist Barry Wain paints this picture of the party's way of doing business: 'What had been little more than a free lunch and junket habit escalated dramatically with the 1984 clash for deputy presidency between Musa and Razaleigh. That contest set an example that was followed in all subsequent elections and for all positions from branch leaders to party president. In the divisive 1993 party elections in which Anwar deposed Ghafar, Anwar's team of vice presidents (Najib, Muhyiddin and Taib) outpolled opponents, reputedly spending hundreds of millions.'[92] That was the election in which Ghafar was said to have been 'electrocuted' because Anwar's team distributed the right to buy shares in the lucrative Tenaga Nasional flotation, in which I played a minor role at the outset of my banking career.

During the 1993 party election campaign, there was rampant distribution not only of gifts, watches, pens and travel packages but also of cash. Delegates were shamelessly passing on bank account numbers to the campaign teams of the candidates. On the eve of the voting day, delegates found envelopes of cash slipped under the door of their hotel rooms. I can recall one delegate jovially describing the night's events as a 'carpet bombing of cash'.

In 1994, Mahathir decided to try to combat money politics within UMNO by passing resolutions that banned 'rewards, gifts and valuable returns of any form' and gave the Supreme Council power to enforce the new rules. In the 1996 party elections all campaigning was banned, and in 2001 a disciplinary board was formed. Several leaders accused of trying to buy votes were suspended; but all too often they made their political comebacks quite soon. Amongst the delegates money politics just wasn't the abhorrent practice that it needed to be. Despite the various attempts to curb its influence, money politics remained rampant in UMNO. Patronage became the principal currency, and even where candidates avoided the crudest cash payments, there are plenty of other forms of largesse available, especially when one is in office.

The scale of the financial resources in the hands of the UMNO president can be gleaned from Mahathir's remark that in 2003 he handed the party presidency to Badawi with total assets of RM1.2bn of which RM200m was in cash.[93] And that was just the official coffers. Well before 1MDB was dreamed up, UMNO presidents were well endowed with cash.

The rot created by this system still ails Malaysia despite repeated attempts to clean it out. The 1MDB affair was the most blatant, extreme and ambitious example of the kind of corruption the system could generate. But it did not come out of the blue; far from it. This was a well-established pattern which I saw myself in the Bakun dam debacle; the way that share allocations in public flotations were decided by politicians; the dire state of Bank Bumiputra; and so the list goes on.

Democracy in mass societies requires resources, namely money, to organise parties and to fight elections. There isn't a political system that is totally impervious to the influence of money. The ability to raise and effectively deploy money is in itself a competitive edge for politicians and political parties everywhere. Yet as money is so important to politics it requires effective regulation, and in Malaysia there is barely any. Political parties are not obligated to disclose donors, are allowed to own businesses and do not have any income or expenditure ceiling. The Election Offences Act 1954 limits spending by candidates during elections, yet there is no oversight over what they do before they are nominated and after they are elected. Attempts to regulate political funding, during Najib's administration most notably, have failed because they invariably involve greater transparency in a system where there is a lack of trust in the independence of oversight institutions.

The malign, unrestrained role of money in politics creates three major problems for Malaysia which we need to tackle to move forward.

It is the breeding ground for endemic corruption. Money oils the wheels of power. Party delegates and communal leaders expect gifts to win their votes. Politicians expect money from businesses that they are in a position to reward (and hurt).

The role of money in deciding political outcomes undermines democracy. There is an inherent tension between democracy and money. Democracy works on the principle of one-person-one-vote. Money politics works on the principle of dollars-per-vote. A democratic system in which the big decisions are all actually made by who has the most money is a sham. Democracy depends on civil servants and politicians being insulated from the influence of money, so they think about the interests of citizens rather than rich donors.

The economy becomes deeply distorted because too often business has to follow political imperatives rather than economic ones. In Malaysia the entanglement of business, government and politics has meant far too often businesses have been favoured, contracts and licences awarded, to serve political ends rather than to raise productivity, encourage innovation or make profits. The lines between political parties, business and government have become dangerously blurred. Far too often, short-term political calculations trump long-term economic and social ones. The result is that the economy underperforms and its structure, which businesses prosper and which struggle, is determined by political favours. The undue and capricious influence of politics inevitably deters investment and strangles entrepreneurship.

Money politics breeds corruption, undermines democracy and distorts the economy. We have to sort it out for Malaysia to have a future. In the next chapter I set out how we can make a start on that task. Again, it is a task that may never be finished, a continual battle, which is why we have to make a start now.

Identity and money are two of the beast's three ugly heads. Over-centralisation of power is the third one.

OVER CENTRALISATION

The colonial administrators who ruled for the first half of the twentieth century were only interested in government and public service in so far as it served colonial interests: they built roads and ports to export tin and rubber; defended the borders and the seas to enable trade and ensured law and order, in part by keeping the different ethnic communities apart and cracking down hard on dissent. This was a highly centralised yet very limited state. Even after independence in 1957, and the creation of Malaysia in 1963, there was considerable continuity. The Anglophile Tunku pursued a largely laissez-faire approach; business remained largely in foreign and non-Malay hands, and the state restricted itself to maintaining order, although the hand of government was quite active in rural development and by the late 1960s having to respond to demands of Malay groups for business opportunities.

As the state needed to become more powerful it also became more centralised. That happened in two stages, the first relatively benign and the second much more troubling. The state needs to have power to be able to work for society. A degree of centralisation is required for the state to act effectively. The question is how to hold that power to account, to make sure it works for the public good.

The first turning point of state activism came after the race riots of 1969, when it became obvious that the limited, laissez-faire state would never do enough to address the deep-seated economic and social imbalances which held back the Malays. Malaysia would need a much more active, capable, dynamic state, to drive national economic and social development through education, rural development and the NEP. This was the social democratic, reforming and modernising state envisaged and enacted by my father and his peers. The state was society's problem solver. It trained professional civil servants and organised them with detailed plans to lift up the Malays especially. It built health centres and schools, paved roads and laid electricity cables, opened universities and set up state-owned enterprises. It was a state infused with public purpose within a framework of democratic accountability.

When a new generation of politicians took over in the 1980s, they started with the foundations of a much stronger state and a much richer society. Over the next two decades power was markedly centralised around the office of the prime minister and the personality of Mahathir. After he survived Razaleigh's challenge for the presidency, by a whisker, he fortified the position of UMNO president and PM; it became impossible to oust the incumbent (except via a general election, as we would find out later). From the mid-1980s his highly trusted, long-time collaborator Daim Zainuddin was finance minister. When they fell out in 2001, Mahathir took on both jobs: prime minister and minister of finance. His successors – Badawi and Najib – inherited the dual role and were happy to keep things that way. The prime minister's office became the government within the government.[94]

There might have been good reasons for such centralisation. Governments can be destabilised and diverted by infighting, especially if that involves the people doing the two top jobs – the fraught relationship between Tony Blair and Gordon Brown is a case in point. My father recognised governments can drift all too easily; civil servants can opt for the quiet life. Drive, dynamism and ambition imparted from the centre are often needed to jolt a sleepy system into action. Mahathir was nothing if not audaciously ambitious and extremely impatient. He wanted power to drive the rapid progress he thought was necessary for Malaysia to become a developed nation. To him, "the Doctor" knew best.

Malaysia was not alone in centralising power in this period. There are no doubt times when decisiveness and fear work well as a recipe for ruling. But I contend that the costs of the centralisation, and the personalisation of power it allows, are enormous. Power that is unaccountable to parliament or the people is open to favouritism and cronyism; all too often obedient lip servants and hangers-on rise to the top. When power is centralised in a few hands it becomes dangerous to challenge or question decisions; as a result the debate that is needed to make good decisions, to test assumptions, does not happen. Authoritarian leaders, who hold the power to confer good jobs on those who do as they are told, get used to riding roughshod over legitimate criticism. The rule of law and due process can give way to a my-way-or-the-highway, bullying style of government. Getting the prime minister's support becomes more important than going through due process. Checks and balances depend on independent institutions, which do not rely on the support of the prime minister to do their job. When power and appointments become centralised in the hands of the prime minister and his advisors, that independence is undermined. All too easily the power to drive change for the good of society becomes the power to protect favourites, cronies and vested interests. Then the pomp of state becomes arrogance; the detachment needed for good judgement becomes indifference to the fate of others; status becomes an excuse for self-indulgence.

Over-centralisation is a recipe for power to turn bad. From my own experience I learned that it is dangerous for one person to spend too long in a powerful position. I had been chief executive of CIMB for fifteen years when I resigned in 2014, in part because I felt people had become too deferential, and my decisions were almost never challenged. Imagine what would happen if one were prime minister for twenty-two years.

So in conclusion, Malaysia is tackling a three-headed monster: identity politics, money politics and power centralisation. Competition between race-based political parties drives division, breeds distrust, inflames tensions and undermines democracy's ability to foster rational debates between policy options. Rampant, unrestrained money politics means too many elections are decided by which candidate has spent more rather than by who is the best candidate, with the best policies. Money politics, the intimate, entangled relationship between business and politics, breeds corruption while also distorting the economy, dulling incentives for innovation, investment and entrepreneurship. Centralised, unaccountable power means decisions are made by a handful of people without checks and balances to hold them to account, to test their assumptions and evidence. If Malaysia faced just one of these threats it would be serious. But it faces all three, and they are working together in a vicious cycle in which politics becomes a game of musical chairs to occupy the one chair which bestows the power to punish enemies and reward supporters, while the tunes are provided by a mix of identity and money politics.

Malaysia will never close the gap with more developed economies by becoming a more entrepreneurial economy driven by innovation and knowledge while it has an economic and political system driven by short-term calculations, money politics, competition between ethnic groups and power held in the hands of the tiny coterie who become the rulers in Putrajaya. Indeed, it is much more likely that Malaysia will go backwards in the decade to come as political infighting and instability deters investment and does nothing to reverse the brain drain of Malaysian talent overseas. If that happens, growth will slow even more, competition between ethnic groups will intensify, and politicians lacking any long-term vision for the nation will resort to yet more cash handouts to their supporters to win elections. That is a recipe for more vote buying, more corruption, more distrust and woeful government. That is an all too plausible future. We must avoid it. The question is how?

RECALIBRATING
THE SYSTEM

There is no room for complacency: Malaysia is drifting. If economic growth slows in the next decade, as many economists expect, the competition over who gets a share of that growth will become more intense. Politicians, lacking a big shared vision, could be drawn to populist slogans and cash giveaways to win support. Inequality and social division could easily be whipped up into social conflict. Meanwhile Malaysia remains badly prepared for the challenges – and the opportunities – of the Fourth Industrial Revolution, climate change and the rising tensions between China and the US. All too easily we could find ourselves adrift, without a rudder or a working engine, in very threatening seas.

As we've seen, it is not that our political leaders do not recognise the need for sweeping reform; they do. Their manifestos over the last two decades are eloquent testimony to their ability to analyse the problems. The trouble is that they lack the courage of their convictions to take on systemic reform. A system so sorely in need of reform will not take on the job itself, just as turkeys will not vote for Christmas. Incumbents generally are not inclined to change the system through which they won power. Democracy can be very poor at reforming itself.[95]

Malaysians are not alone in growing disenchanted with a deficient political system. All over the world voters have stopped turning out in elections, and when they vote they are turning to parties from the margins rather than the mainstream. A late 2020 report by the Centre for the Future of Democracy at Cambridge University, drawing on hundreds of studies conducted over the previous twenty-five years, found that faith in democracy had been declining virtually everywhere since the late 1990s.[96] Democracy flourished after the fall of the Berlin Wall but quite soon went into long-term decline as people became increasingly frustrated with growing inequality and detached elites who did too little for the average voter.

Some people see all this as grounds for adopting a more decisive, authoritarian approach to governance. There are plenty of strongman leaders to look to as examples from Putin and Erdoğan to Duterte and Modi. That would be a mistake for Malaysia, a profound one. Our system is failing because it is already over-centralised and at times it has been far too authoritarian and personalised for its own good.

We need to acknowledge democracy's failings and limitations but use that as a spur for democratic innovation, to find new and more effective ways for democracy to work. In business, when you sense the market is shifting and a complete change of strategy is needed, you need to embrace discontinuity with open arms and create a widespread acknowledgement of the need for major change. The same should apply to politics. Sadly, political systems, not just in Malaysia, have proven well behind the curve: resistant to change, bereft of imagination and oddly conservative when they should be open to radical ideas.

Where should we look for ideas to recalibrate our political and economic system, to rewrite the rules of the game? In Malaysia we are lucky. We have radical *old* ideas that can be drawn on to open our way into the future. There is a Malay saying *Sesat di hujung jalan, balik ke pangkal jalan*, which means that when you are stuck you should retrace your steps to find a new way forward. I believe we can find inspiration by going back to learn from the generation of reformers who created modern Malaysia, my father included. In particular to renew our democracy and recalibrate our political and economic systems, we should look again at the role the National Consultative Council played in Malaysia's response to the crisis of the 1969 race riots which threatened the very future of the country. The NCC saved Malaysia by recalibrating the system; perhaps we can do the same again.

Abdul Razak was ruling by decree following the riots, when he set up the NCC in January 1970, made up of sixty-seven people from political parties, communal groups, NGOs, religious groups, professional bodies and businesses from across society to 'establish positive and practical guidelines for interracial cooperation and social integration for the growth of a Malaysian identity'.[97] By all accounts, frank and sometimes fierce debates were encouraged in pursuit of a convergence towards agreed solutions.

The NCC endorsed: the NEP to eradicate poverty and increase the Malay and indigenous share of the economy; limits to public discussion on communally sensitive issues; the Rukun Negara as a set of guiding National Principles to help imbue a sense of Malaysian nationhood. The NCC also laid the ground for the founding of the BN grand coalition. The Council brought Malaysia back from the brink, and its reforms underpinned years of peace and stability, albeit at the cost of some limitations to democracy.

The NCC was a success because it brought together people from every political party (other than the DAP, which set as a precondition for its participation the release of its leader from detention) and every faith and community. The vast majority of Malaysians could look at its members and identify with one or more of them.

The Council members were encouraged to debate the most important issues facing the country. Aware of the dangers of his absolute powers, Abdul Razak wanted to hear criticism and challenge, recognising that unless issues were aired, it would be impossible for the right decisions to be made. My father appears to have been the ideal chair of such a body, content to listen and reflect on what he was being told and able to synthesise a response from the different strands of debate. The NCC avoided getting bogged down in small issues; nor did it focus on just one issue. It took on a realistic yet ambitious agenda which allowed the different communities to trade off compromises in one area with benefits in another. To put it crudely, the Council allowed deals to be done between the different communities to create a way forward to which all could sign up. We need to engage in that kind of creative deal making now to reset our course.

There would be no Malaysia as we now know it – stable, peaceful, educated, affluent – without the NCC. Malaysia could easily have turned towards dictatorship or fallen into prolonged civil strife. The country avoided those outcomes largely because the NCC laid out a path for shared development across all of Malaysia.

Could a modern version of the NCC help Malaysia undertake the national recalibration that is needed now? I am sure it could, because, without realising it, we convened the forerunner for such a body back in October 2016.

As Najib was clamping down on dissent in Malaysia, Azlina and I convened a group of twenty-five thinkers and public leaders at the Blavatnik School of Government in Oxford to discuss the country's future.[98] It was a measure of the appetite for the discussion that we attracted a stellar cast (we did not invite any active politicians). There was former Deputy Prime Minister Musa Hitam and former minister Idris Jala. Jomo Sundaram attended, as did Marina Mahathir, the social activist, Zainah Anwar, the head of Sisters in Islam, and Cynthia Gabriel, head of C4 Center to Combat Corruption and Cronyism (C4 Center). There were people who would go on to important roles in the rise of the PH and PN governments: Maszlee Malik, who became the PH education minister, (Datuk) Dr Marzuki Mohamed, who became PM Muhyiddin's chief of staff, Wan Saiful Wan Jan, who co-wrote the PH manifesto, and (Tan Sri) Jemilah Mahmood, founder of Mercy Malaysia and later public health advisor to PM Muhyiddin. There were newspaper editors, representatives of NGOs, academics and businesspeople, including Wong Choon Wai (Star), (Tan Sri) Sheriff Kassim (G25), Ben Suffian (Merdeka Centre), Dr Nungsari Radhi (Khazanah) and (Tan Sri) Yong Poh Kon (Selangor Pewter).

Our gathering – 'Conversations on Malaysia' – confirmed how much can be achieved when a group of people with diverse views deliberate in a safe space, unshackled from prior allegiances and focused on a shared goal. The setting encouraged us to look for common ground rather than sticking to our communal or political allegiances. We were trying to understand each other and find solutions that worked for everyone. The urgent issue at the time was the Malaysian system's abject failure to deal with the 1MDB scandal, but everyone agreed the problems ran deeper. We needed to address the system's shaky foundations, not merely the ins and outs of what happened at 1MDB. We considered every major issue facing the country from the future of education, to the role of religion, the social safety net and the need for stronger independent institutions of government.

Of course, we did not agree on everything. There were sharp exchanges, for example, over the role of vernacular schools. But the important thing was that we were able to have those exchanges without falling out: we could agree to disagree having aired our views and having been listened to with respect.

We concluded our deliberations by reaching the common view that 'Malaysia faces daunting challenges which must be addressed holistically given their complexities and interdependencies.'[99] When we returned to Malaysia, we tried to take those ideas forward through a proposal to set up the second National Consultative Council (NCCII), which won support from across the political spectrum and civil society, including several BN leaders. Najib, however, was not among them; he was having nothing of it. After a public dressing-down, targetting me and Choon Wai, by a well-known unofficial spokesperson for the prime minister's office (otherwise known as an attack dog) on primetime television, one of Najib's would-be Rasputins told me in no uncertain terms to drop the idea or suffer the consequences.

I never did drop the idea. Over the years since I have been quietly nurturing it by learning more about why it is needed and how it might work. Indeed, I am now more convinced than ever that Malaysia needs something like the NCC to reset its system.

Interestingly since our initial prototype in Oxford the case for this approach, known as deliberative democracy, has gained traction in both theory and practice across the world. Many commentators believe deliberative discussions could play a critical role in helping society address issues which are structural in nature and too nuanced and complex for the rough and tumble of everyday party political debate.[100]

Democracy should mean more than people periodically having a vote; it should encourage joint deliberation among citizens on what should be done. According to Aristotle, democracy in classical Athens did not mean voting, it meant practical reasoning conducted in public, in the agora, where citizens came together to air their views. Modern variants of deliberative democracy stem from this root.

Deliberative democracy forums enable citizens to engage in open-minded, reflective, well-informed discussion with a representative mix of people who treat one another with mutual respect. Participants must listen carefully to what others have to say as they try to justify their position in front of their peers. This should improve the quality of decision making in several ways.

Decisions should be more legitimate if a representative group of citizens has been directly involved in making them. Better, more knowledgeable decisions should be made because citizens are informed by experts as well as calling on their own varied experiences and insights. Direct, face-to-face discussions among citizens builds trust. When people with different opinions engage with one another directly they are far less likely to disagree, and even if they do disagree, they are much less likely to distrust one another. Deliberative democracy can create legitimacy, enable knowledge to be shared and deepen trust: we need all of that to avoid polarisation, populism and pessimism shaping our future.

These deliberations can take many forms. James Fishkin's America in One Room, based in the Center for Deliberative Democracy at Stanford University, for example, convenes groups of randomly selected citizens for a weekend of 'deliberative polling' on contentious issues like gun control and immigration.[101] Participants often arrive with quite entrenched views but soften their stance after listening to their fellow citizens. Other deliberative forums include citizens' juries, which have been used in the UK to assess the case for genetic screening of embryos and participatory budgeting. The OECD recently reported on the lessons from 289 cases of deliberative democracy around the world, covering a wide range of topics from urban planning and transport, to health and the environment. The OECD concluded that deliberative democracy is good for tackling complex, long-term issues which involve difficult trade-offs over fundamental values, such as freedom, equality and identity: these are precisely the kind of issues that face Malaysia.[102]

The most impressive example of how democratic deliberation can open up a new way forward for a country comes from the 2016 Irish Citizens Assembly, which tackled the hugely contentious issue of abortion, which had divided the nation for decades. One hundred ordinary citizens convened for deliberations over several weekends.[103] They were informed by experts, and their discussions were chaired by a respected judge. Most MPs were surprised by the Citizens' Assembly's final recommendation to allow largely unrestricted access to abortion. Yet at the consequential national referendum, the proposition was supported by 66% of voters, an indication of how detached the elected representatives can be from the electorate they represent. The Irish Citizens' Assembly was very carefully designed so that informed deliberation among citizens paved the way for a debate in Parliament, which turned a proposal into legislation by the government, which was then voted on in a referendum. Deliberative, representative and direct forms of democracy all worked together to find a solution to a huge, contentious and difficult matter, but it was the deliberations of citizens that unlocked the issue.

How could we turn these ideas into a practical reality in Malaysia to convene democratic deliberations to comprehensively reset the system?

If another National Consultative Council, let's call it NCCII, were to be set up by the government of the day its independence would be questioned, and it is unlikely the body would survive a change of government. For that reason, I think the NCCII has to have strong involvement of other institutions and civil society. It could also be initiated by the Rulers' Council with a view to submitting recommendations to Parliament for its consideration. How would it gain the momentum needed to succeed? The NCCII should have three parallel strands.

It needs a high-level body, a bit like the original NCC, to deliberate on a National Recalibration Plan (NRP). This is where the heavy lifting would be done to devise a plan that could be put to the nation. The core group would be large enough to allow for diversity but not too large to be unwieldy. They would be respected figures from all walks of life, including past politicians, people from business, academia, the professions, civil society and all religious faiths. This group should, as far as possible, have impeccable credentials, expertise and experience beyond reproach.

It would be too much to expect ordinary citizens to be involved in this lengthy and detailed process of policy deliberation. However, it is not too much to expect them to be able to debate and give feedback on the proposals. That is why the second strand to the process would be a series of dialogues with groups of citizens across the country. These discussions would be vital to ensure that citizens at large were able to feed into the deliberations over the NRP.

The original NCC was not a talking shop; it turned ideas into action. The third strand of NCCII would ensure implementation. To make real change the NCCII has to work with, not against, the institutions of representative democracy, to show it can tackle, and solve, issues that politics-as-usual cannot. The NCCII does not need the government's endorsement to get going but it does need the executive and parliament to move forward its recommendations, perhaps to a referendum or directly to policies and legislations.

It is not for me to prejudge what the NCCII should discuss. But I think it would first need to set some red lines, issues which are considered already enshrined such as Islam as the official religion, our commitment to multiculturalism and preservation of the monarchy. It should start with a reaffirmation (or otherwise) of the principles of nationhood as contained in the constitution and the Rukun Negara to set the parameters for reforms in the various facets of the political system, economy and society. And then it can begin thrashing out detailed proposals for reform.

The preceding chapter made clear my view that three linked issues hold Malaysia back: the role of identity and money in politics and the over-centralisation of power in government. The NCCII cannot clear the way for a national recalibration unless it is confident of tackling this three-headed monster and boldly reconfiguring and rebalancing our system.

As former US Secretary of State Condoleezza Rice writes in *Democracy: Stories from the Long Road to Freedom*, finding the right balance is critical to effective democratic decision making and so to progress: 'Democracy requires balance in many spheres: between executive, legislative, and judicial authority; between centralized government and regional responsibility; between individual and group rights; and ultimately, between state and society. In functioning democracies, institutions are invested with protecting the equilibrium. Citizens must trust them as arbiters in disputes and, when necessary, as vehicles for change.'[104] We need a comprehensive rebalancing of the relationships between the key parts of our political system so that they function effectively and work together while also standing up against one another when necessary.

With that in mind, we need to break up the concentration of power around the prime minister and strengthen the capacity of independent institutions to keep a check on that power. We should limit the tenure of the prime minister and prohibit the prime minister from also being the minister of finance. Changes such as this may not be sufficient however if the prime minister is still in total control of the executive branch. We would need to tilt the balance of power away from the executive branch by removing the power of appointment of the agencies that referee political competition from the prime minister. Until then our political system appears to be one where the winning team is in control of the referee. Needless to say, the most important function of the referee is to control the role of money in politics.

The PH manifesto recommended that the power to appoint the chiefs of Malaysian Anti-Corruption Commission and the Election Commission, agencies which oversee political competition, be moved to a parliamentary select committee. But, given that the ruling party tends to dominate the, legislature this would not be robust enough in my view.

History has shown that the legislature and the judiciary have too often been found to be deferential of the executive (and with that the prime minister). We need to be bold and find our own Malaysian balance, the Westminster one has not worked. One option to consider is to shift the role of refereeing political competition to a unique Malaysian institution: the revolving monarchy.

Malaysia is fortunate to have a unique system of a revolving monarchy in which the Agong is elected by the Council of Rulers for a five-year term. Our monarchy is more democratic than other constitutional monarchies. Indeed in 2018, the Council demonstrated its ultimate power by persuading HM the Agong to step down early; it is unambiguous that the Agong holds his position at the discretion of the Council of his brother rulers. The Sultans themselves hold their positions for life and succession is hereditary (or at least kept within certain families); as a result, the Council is more insulated from undue influence by the executive branch. The rulers must not interfere in politics, they must stand above the fray; from that position they can make sure political competition is fair and above board.

The monarchy already has some powers to arbitrate politics; it is the monarch's prerogative to appoint the head of the executive (state and federal governments), but his choice must be the person who is most likely to command the support of the majority in the assembly. Strengthening the powers of the Rulers Council by giving it the power to appoint the heads of the MACC and the EC could be a highly productive combination of the old and the new. The support of the Rulers Council would give these bodies much-needed independence as well as roots in the traditional power structures of the country. A stronger constitutional monarchy could become the institution responsible for ensuring free and fair political competition. The rulers sit in an elevated position and yet they have deep roots in Malay tradition and culture. They are familiar and respected.

Expanding the role of the Rulers Council will no doubt provoke controversy. At the time of independence, Tunku disagreed with conferring more powers to the Rulers Council, as it would encroach on the powers of the Agong. Expanding the powers of the monarchy would be seen as regressive in liberal circles. It isn't a perfect solution, I admit, but if we agree that we need an effective referee to ensure political competition is fair is there a better alternative? There may be other variants of the idea I have suggested that should be considered; perhaps a Rulers Council 'plus' to include other eminent individuals. The most important objective is to have an independent, effective referee to bring money politics under control and ensure that politics and politicians serve the interest of the people.

The search for a new balance applies just as much to our identities as to our institutions. We need a stronger sense of national identity in Malaysia to balance the identities bestowed on us by our ethnic heritage. When Italy was unified in the late nineteenth century, Massimo d'Azeglio, the Italian statesman, declared: 'We have made Italy, now we must make Italians.' That is still a work in progress in a nation made up of Venetians, Sicilians and Romans, amongst others. Creating a stronger, embracing Malaysian identity is a long cultural work in progress as much as a political one. Bringing people together face-to-face, whether through politics, education, culture, business or sport, will be central to that.

It also requires us to rebalance the fundamentals of the implicit social contract between communities as embodied in the constitution and conventions. The key tenets and tensions managed by that contract are, of course, around language and education; the balance between the secular and Islamic state; affirmative action and special position of the Malays; the role played by race-based political parties. We need a new social contract that works for today's Malaysians and the challenges they face. That does not mean casting aside the identities that matter so much to people. It does mean changing the way we feel about our ethnic and national identities.

At the NCC's second meeting in February 1970, its deputy chair, Dr Ismail, declared that 'the problems that give rise to racial conflict' were rooted in different interpretations of the constitution's position on Malay special privileges. He made it clear that, whatever the short-term solutions might be, the ultimate goal was to build a Malaysian Malaysia.

The NCCII should start from the same aspiration. In recent years, Malaysia's communities have become more separate and divided. Identity, race and religion touch almost everything from education to business and welfare. That means we have a very wide agenda to work on. It also means we have to be realistic. We cannot expect people to leave their communal, ethnic identities behind. Yet that does not mean we should accept simplistic, one-sided accounts of who we are which reduce our identity to our ethnic roots, especially when those crude simplifications are peddled by politicians competing for power.

We should develop better ways to make sure that our strong and legitimate communal identities do not lead to growing division and conflict. We need to revitalise frameworks which help pull us together, to show how our diversity can be a strength, promoting innovation and creativity. Many grand initiatives such as Mahathir's Bangsa Malaysia (contained in Vision 2020) and Najib's 1Malaysia all sounded good but largely failed by being mired in contradictory policies and decisions driven by racial outbidding that the current electoral system tends to encourage.

To further safeguard against the politicisation of race and religion the NCCII should look to redesign the electoral system. Our Westminster-inspired 'first past the post' electoral system incentivises politicians to exploit race and religion as their rallying cry. It is not communal identity that threatens our democracy but an electoral system that does too little to encourage finding of common ground, creates an all-or-nothing, 'winner takes all' politics and leaves too many people feeling unrepresented. Any number of alternatives can create more collaborative dynamics, from the mixed constituencies used in Germany, to the Australian alternative vote system and the mixed group constituencies in Singapore in which voters elect mixed team candidates. All these alternatives involve proportional representation, which encourages parties to cooperate as well as to compete on the common ground in the middle of the political spectrum. Indeed, political scientists are quite consistent in arguing that plural societies are better off with proportional representation. Stating the obvious, another word for proportional is – fair.

I have given no more than an outline of how the NCCII could help to address the nation's big challenges and shared some ideas on how to slay the three-headed monster – by empowering a new institutional referee to political competition, revitalising the national integration project and introducing proportional representation. More detailed planning would be needed to turn this into a reality, but it is well within reason to think we could establish such a body in Malaysia quite quickly. NCCII would not start with a blank sheet but it can be a fresh start, a *re*calibration of the Malaysian system. Our goal is no different from that of Abdul Razak and Dr Ismail: the unfulfilled mission to develop a strong nation of Malaysians.

MALAYSIA RENEWED

We need to engage our collective imaginations to create a better Malaysia. That Malaysia is tantalisingly close. If we act concertedly, we could achieve that in my own lifetime, especially if we map out the right path. As my father showed, it is a question of combining big leaps with small steps, being consultative to bring everyone along to make bold moves which create a step change in national progress.

I imagine a nation where every child has the best possible start in life, one which is rooted in belonging based on traditions and culture but combined with a strong sense of being Malaysian. Children will be equipped with the languages and skills to make a contribution to society and a difference to the world: speaking at least Malay, English and Mandarin; they will also be adept in the language of artificial intelligence as well as maths and science, literature and history. Culture and ethnicity will be vital to who they are, the food they eat, the customs they observe, the faith they follow; but this will coexist in balance with a Malaysian identity based on citizenship, rights, duties and obligations. Most Malaysians will be Muslims, tolerant and respectful of other faiths. There will be no benefit to politicians in raking up the battles of the past by making people feel insecure and threatened. We will need to work continuously at integration, to promote diversity and inclusion rather than bias and prejudice. We will be at ease with one another, able and willing to trust and collaborate to solve problems both big and small. We will engage confidently with the rest of the world, deploying our combined intelligence, our capacity for collaboration and action.

The future will depend not on what we individually know but what we can do with our shared knowledge; that means making the most of our diversity. We will have to be capable of learning fast as the world shifts around us as the Fourth Industrial Revolution unfolds, and we use that abundant technology to bring climate change under control and to create new ways to work. Young Malaysians will be inquisitive and bold, outward-looking and curious, unafraid of using new technologies to tackle opportunities and challenges in business and society.

Our economic and social outcomes will not just depend on the amount of rubber, tin or palm oil, cars, televisions or microchips we produce but on the quality of the ideas and technologies we create, and how we apply them to tackle our challenges and take the new emerging opportunities. Success will hinge on how we govern ourselves, politically and economically: how we frame incentives, acknowledge performance, set standards for behaviour, build trust and distribute rewards. We will only become a dynamic, diverse country if we are confident as citizens, entrepreneurs and creators; if we find a way to take power into our own hands rather than relying on the conformist, passive, top-down approaches of the past.

Young Malaysians will have to learn how to remake themselves time and again as technology, markets and the environment shift. Malaysia will become an ideal stage for entrepreneurs, problem solvers, makers and creators. For those who find it hard to make a living in an increasingly volatile, uncertain and unpredictable world or who suffer other misfortunes, there will be a modern safety net based on need and potential rather than ethnicity and identity. One sign of Malaysia's renewed dynamism will be the steady flow of educated, talented Malaysians returning through KLIA, drawn not only by culture, food, family and opportunities, but also by the framework of good government.

Made up by changing coalitions, the government will be held to account by voters in a new proportional voting system, by an invigorated free press and by stronger checks and balances between institutions. It will be impossible for power to be centralised and personalised as it was in the past. Our system will have a new balance of roles, responsibilities and power between the federal executive and legislature, the judiciary and the Rulers Council, state legislatures and state governments. Deliberative democracy platforms will be built into the system to allow for constant reflection. Corruption will be largely eliminated from the political system by a strict referee enforcing fair competition, backed by the Rulers Council. It won't be perfect – political systems never are – but it won't be fundamentally corrupt; it will be trustworthy and accountable and capable of adapting through deliberation. Elections will not be an opportunity for politicians to bribe voters or to outbid with appeals to ethnic pride; instead, the currency of Malaysian politics, as in Malaysia's culture and daily life, will be a search for a creative and productive common ground.

Such a system will encourage us to do more together rather than less. We will build on the easy-going everyday democracy of Malaysian life, in which people find a way to rub along, to create a stronger, vibrant and creative nation. Malaysia has an incredible opportunity to show the world that we are a genuinely integrated, inclusive, tolerant and creative multi-ethnic society. We will have to stick together through uncertain and challenging times, with respect for our diversity as the basis for both our cohesion and our competitiveness. By turning to one another, we will be able to shape the future. It is finally time for Malaysians to assert ourselves to trust what we can achieve together, to believe in our joint future. For Malaysia to be a success we now have to become Malaysians.

First however we need to recalibrate our nationhood – what it means and how it works – to get back on the path to becoming truly a nation of Malaysians.

POSTFACE

What's in a Name began as a quest to understand the name I inherited and the man I inherited it from, so I could make better sense of what I have done in my life. Whenever people ask whether my achievements were due to my family's standing, my answer is that I could only play the hand I was dealt. In the course of writing this book, my understanding of the cards that hand comprised, however, has changed quite a lot. Family is the guiding thread of this book. What I really cared about in my career was not money, but my family (past, present and future); my people at CIMB, the large extended corporate family I was part of; and my country, Malaysia, in all its confounding and wonderful diversity. I am committed to my family, the people I work with and the country which I come from. I owe a duty of care to all of them. This book is about how I have sought to make good on those commitments and what I have done when they have come into conflict with one another.

I misunderstood and underestimated my inheritance from my father, both its value to me and the obligations it placed me under. My understanding of what my family name meant was superficial for most of my life perhaps because I got to know my father mainly through stories told by family and friends, from books and photographs. I never felt I ever got to the heart of the kind of person he was.

I have learned that the most important inheritance I received was the values that were imparted to me, which found expression in who I cared about, what I was committed to and how I behaved towards others. I have always wanted to imagine my father being proud of me.

I have always tried to follow the subconscious codes of behaviour I inherited from him. I have always felt a duty to *jaga nama baik*, to uphold the good name he gave me.

Three aspects of Abdul Razak's work are extremely relevant to us today.

Abdul Razak was completely committed to the Malay cause but he worked for the whole nation, not just a part of it. He is best known to all of us as the nation's master builder, The Father of Development, doing much of the heavy lifting to drive rural development, define independent Malaysia's identity and set the foundations for educating Malaysians, before stabilising society after the 1969 riots and creating the new platform for a high-growth economy and social integration. He and his contemporaries had a big shared mission: to build a new nation from the rubble left by a retreating empire, in the teeth of a communist insurgency and in the wake of a world war which brought the nation to its knees. We need to rekindle that sense of shared mission today because the nation is far from built and the system he put in place has run its course.

My father believed that the shared mission to build the new nation required the power of a capable state, well-run government and first-class public services. He was not squeamish or naive about using power. He understood how power worked just as an engineer under-stands steel and concrete. However, he also understood that for power to work for the public good it needs to be held to account, by checks and balances, the rule of law and the practice of democracy. Without those checks he knew that power had a tendency to turn bad. We need to relearn that lesson today in Malaysia.

Abdul Razak knew that, while public power had to be constrained by a system of independent institutions, the people in power running those institutions needed to abide by the very highest standards of integrity. He never laid out those personal values in a credo; they were evident in how he behaved and how people talk about him even now. He showed people equality of respect whatever their background. He never talked down to people. He listened to what they had to say respectfully. He behaved with an absolute, binding integrity, especially with public money. That was the basis on which people put their faith in him as he moved the country forward. We need leaders in Malaysia who embody these values.

Even though he never explicitly instructed me in these values, his code of behaviour had a strong subconscious influence upon me. Only looking back now do I realise how much my work was influenced by my father's approach. What I learned about the application of those values to my career provides these key lessons.

Persistence and tenacity count for a lot.
I did not plan to stay at the same bank for twenty-nine years. I stayed for as long as I thought I was good for the company. There are many different ways to make a contribution to achieving something significant. But more often than not it takes real persistence: the rewards go to people who stick at it.

Work for a powerful shared mission.
Achieving something significant almost always requires working with other people who are committed to the same cause. It's easier to be persistent if you are part of a team, willing one another on. The thing I am most proud of at CIMB is the way people worked together to build an institution they were proud of and to make a difference to the lives of their customers and communities. People work hard for many different reasons, but having a shared mission, a sense of obligation to others, to provide a sense of direction is critical. I discovered that dedication to a shared mission regulates people's actions and demands and encourages compromises for the greater good.

The best teams and organisations are diverse.
Solving complex problems involves teamwork. Creativity comes from throwing ideas around with people who bring different insights to the

table. Most people feel comfortable with people who are like them; but we get new insights from people who are different from us. Learn to embrace that difference rather than being frightened of it.

Always look forward.

The possibilities of the future are always more interesting than defence of the past for its own sake. We only learn by reflecting on what we have done. But in this world of tumultuous, uncertain upheaval and change one constantly has to step into the future, welcoming its uncertainty as a marker of its potential. Uncertainty can be troubling; it can also be surprising, exciting and inspiring. Learn to love it because uncertainty and creativity go hand in hand.

Take big leaps as well as small steps.

Life is about knowing when each of these is appropriate. There were plenty of times when CIMB needed to take small steps, to improve what it did bit by bit. But there were other times when it needed to make big bold leaps of faith. Timing the right move, anticipating when conditions are going to change is vital to this.

As my career unfolded, I became ever more aware of the growing conflict between my father's values and what had befallen the system he created, from the legacy of the NEP to the dire state of legacy institutions such as Bank Bumi when we took it over to what I regard as the culmination of the conflict, the 1MDB affair. The obligations and values which come with my family name explain why I could not let go of the 1MDB affair; it touched everything that mattered to me, the standing of my family, my company and my country. 1MDB eventually led me to a choice I long wanted to avoid: between standing up for my father's reputation and being loyal to my brother. Eventually I felt compelled to choose between what had become of my father's system of power and the code of values he imparted to us. I chose the values.

I do not pretend that the choice is an easy one. Far from it. It can be painful and it's rarely black and white. In the course of my own career I made compromises and accommodations. That is the real world. None of us is perfect, and we work in imperfect conditions. If you want to be a saint, live in a monastery. If you want complete certainty, do not leave the house. We discover our values partly through inner reflection on who we are but also through testing them in practice, learning where we draw the line in the sand, often in conditions of radical uncertainty in which it is hard to know for certain how things will turn out. If we make mistakes, and invariably we do, then we should face up to them, learn from them and make amends. If we make compromises, which we all do, then learn to make good compromises that we can live with.

Malaysia too has big choices to make. After the May 1969 race riots, Abdul Razak realised sweeping change was needed in the Malaysian social, economic and political system. No one knew if that new system would work. It was a bold step into the unknown. The NEP helped to restore peace and stability while correcting some of the ethnic imbalances built into the economy from colonial times. It was meant to last only twenty years. The fact that it remains in place fifty years after its inception means that things have not gone according to plan. My father would have fully expected the NEP and other aspects of the 1970s system to be reviewed and reformed in time and for different times.

That system now needs a sweeping recalibration. Having the right people at the helm while important will never be enough. This has been true for many years; the longer we put it off the more frustrated Malaysians will become. For too long Malaysians have been told the country needs fundamental reforms only for those efforts to falter almost before they got going. Going into a much more uncertain future we cannot afford to be ruled by caution and complacency, what more vested interests.

Abdul Razak's legacy offers Malaysia a path to follow as we go about systemic national recalibration: we should set up the National Consultative Council II in a form best suited for today's challenges and today's Malaysians. That prospect of Malaysians from all communities and walks of life coming together to deliberate on the future of the nation should excite and inspire us to hope for a better future. Such deliberation will lift us above the divisive politics of race, identity and money as we create together a sense of shared national mission to carry us all forward. We need to be consultative yet bold, as my father was in his time.

My name came with a sense of obligation, a duty of care and an expectation of service. The legacy of my father's values explains why, as I went from corporate finance rookie to building one of the biggest banks in Malaysia, to digging into 1MDB and campaigning for NCCII, I was never content to just be a banker. I could never see myself as a politician, yet I have always sought to contribute to public life, building CIMB, helping to shape the capital market, spearheading deals that reshaped the corporate scene, trailblazing in ASEAN and setting up the CIMB foundation.

In its own small way, I hope this book is also a service to the nation and the generations that will make its future. I want this book to help young Malaysians understand how we have become trapped on the wrong path and to provide a way to find a better path into the future, one on which we can make the next Malaysia.

When I completed the final draft of this book, I realised that I have just begun to have lived for longer than my father, who passed away two months short of his fifty-fourth birthday. That was a poignant realisation. I am so thankful that, unlike Abdul Razak, I have been able to pen these reflections from my own journey, about the name that I inherited and the name that I pass on to Arman and Marissa.

APPENDIX:
HONORIFIC TITLES

Malaysia has a complicated federal and state system of honorific titles, as listed below, which can seem complicated to those unfamiliar with it. To simplify matters, in the text we provide a person's most up-to-date title with their name when they are first mentioned in the book. Thereafter their name appears without their title. The following is a simplified explanation of these naming systems to help the reader.

HM the Agong His Majesty the King, constitutional monarch and head of state of Malaysia also known as the Supreme Head, elected every five years by the Rulers Council made up of the nine sultans

Datin Seri Accorded to the wife of a male Dato' Seri or Datuk Seri.

Dato' A state title conferred by the state ruler – a sultan or the governor in states with no sultan

Dato' Seri, Dato' Sri or Datuk Seri is the highest state title conferred by the ruler – a sultan or governor in states with no sultan.

Datuk the third most senior federal title conferred by HM the Agong. Also the second most senior title conferred by the state ruler – a sultan or a governor in states with no sultan.

HM the Permaisuri Agong, Her Majesty the Queen, wife of HM the Agong.

Puan Sri Accorded to the wife of a male Tan Sri

HRH Sultan Malay ruler of a state.

HRH the Sultanah, wife of HRH the Sultan.

Tan Sri The second highest federal title conferred by HM the Agong

Tengku It can mean 'Prince' or 'Princess'. It is spelled this way in the states of Pahang, Selangor, Kelantan and Terengganu. Other states may spell it as 'Tunku'

Toh Puan, Accorded to the wife of a male Tun

Tun the most senior federal title conferred by HM the Agong.

Tunku It can mean 'Prince' or 'Princess'. It is spelled this way in the states of Kedah, Johore and Negeri Sembilan. Other states such may spell it as 'Tengku'.

ACKNOWLEDGEMENTS

Despite many people having suggested that I write a book, I agonised over the idea for a very long time. I was lucky to decide to work with Charles Leadbeater, because he was so sure from the start that I had a story that should be told and was persistent in telling me so. It has been a huge pleasure co-authoring this book with Charles over many more months than we expected. His writing skills, experience, insights and ideas have been invaluable especially for an ambitious novice who wanted his first book to make a difference.

We met and interviewed so many people for this book, and I apologise for being unable to name every one of my family members, my father's friends, my friends, CIMB colleagues and corporate contemporaries. Thank you all for spending your time and sharing your precious memories and insights with us.

Over the course of the project, we were supported by a number of young and energetic researchers, including Arinah Najwa, Norziana Mohd Ainon and Nazran Johari, and aided by generous sharing of source documents by Datin Kalthom Taib Andak and Datin Rossaya Mohd Nasir.

I owe a debt of gratitude to the many people who dedicated their time to reviewing the manuscripts in part or in whole, namely my wife Azlina Aziz, my brothers Johari Razak and Nizam Razak, HRH Sultan Nazrin Shah, Professor Ngaire Woods, Professor Eugene Rogan, Tan Sri Azman Mokhtar, Dato' Lim Chee Wee, Effendy Shahul Hamid, Dato' Tong Kooi Ong, Dato' Ho Kay Tat and Ung Su Ling. Thanks also to those who read the manuscript and provided wonderful endorsements: Tun Musa Hitam, Tan Sri Andrew Sheng, Professor Kishore Mahbubani, Dato Hussamuddin Yaacub, Joydeep Sengupta and Tharma Pillai.

I would also like to apologise to all those people who we should have engaged with but were not able to, for one reason or another, and the many individuals who deserved to be mentioned in this book but were not due to my oversight or to keep the text to a manageable length.

Nazir Razak
Kuala Lumpur
March 2021

SELECT BIBLIOGRAPHY

We drew on a wide range of sources in researching this book. This is a selected list of those we have drawn on most.

GENERAL

Zsuzsanna Chappell, *Deliberative Democracy: A Critical Introduction*, Palgrave, 2012.

Francis Fukuyama, *Identity: Contemporary Identity Politics and the Struggle for Recognition*, Profile Books, 2018.

Edmund Terence Gomez and Jomo Kwame Sundaram, *Malaysia's Political Economy, Politics, Patronage and Profits*, Cambridge University Press, 1997.

Sophie Lemière (ed.), *Illusions of Democracy, Malaysian Politics and People*, vol. II, Strategic Information and Resesearch Development Centre, 2017.

Sophie Lemière (ed.), *Minorities Matter: Malaysian Politics and People*, vol. III, Strategic Information and Research Development Centre, 2019.

Arend Lijphart, *Democracy in Plural Societies: A Comparative Exploration*, Yale University Press, 1977.

Mahathir bin Mohamad, *The Malay Dilemma*, Times Books, 1970.

Alvin Rabushka and Kenneth A. Shepsle, *Politics in Plural Societies: A Theory of Democratic Instability*, Longman, 2008.

Rehman Rashid, *A Malaysian Journey*, Rehman Rashid, 1993.

Rehman Rashid, *Peninsula: A Story of Malaysia*, Regana Kuala Lumpur, 2016.

Andrew Reynolds, *The Architecture of Democracy: Constitutional Design, Conflict Management, and Democracy*, Oxford University Press, 2002.

Sultan Nazrin Shah, *Striving for Inclusive Development: From Pangkor to a Modern Malaysian State*, Oxford University Press, 2019.

Jomo Kwame Sundaram and Wee Chong Hui, *Malaysia @ 50, Economic Development, Distribution, Disparities*, Strategic Information and Research Development Centre, Petaling Jaya, 2014.

Michael Vatikiotis, *Blood and Silk: Power and Conflict in Modern Southeast Asia*, Weidenfeld & Nicolson, 2017.

SECTION 1: TUN RAZAK, HIS ERA AND HIS LEGACY

Azam Ismail Bakri and Suziyana Natasya, *Suatu Pengkisahan*, Orlaith Inc. Sdn Bhd, 2013.

Ooi Kee Beng, *The Reluctant Politician: Tun Dr Ismail and His Time*, Institute of Southeast Asian Studies, Singapore, 2006.

Joseph M. Fernando, *The Making of the Malayan Constitution*, Malaysian Branch of the Royal Asiatic Society, 2002.

Edmund Terence Gomez and Johan Saravanamuttu (eds.), *The New Economic Policy in Malaysia: Affirmative Action, Ethnic Inequalities and Social Justice*, Strategic Information and Research Development Centre, Petaling Jaya and National University of Singapore Press, 2013.

Musa Hitam, *Frankly Speaking*, Pelanduk, Petaling Jaya, 2016.

Nik Anuar Nik Mahmud, Muhammed Haji Salleh and Adb Ghapa Harun, *A Biography of Tun Abdul Razak, Statesman and Patriot*, Penerbit Universiti Kebangsaan Malaysia, 2012.

R. S. Milne and Diane Mauzy, *Politics and Government in Malaysia*, Institute of Southeast Asian Studies, University of British Columbia Press, Vancouver, 1978.

Rajah Rasiah and Kamal Salih (eds.), *Driving Development: Revisiting Razak's Role in Malaysia's Economic Progress*, University of Malaysia Press, Kuala Lumpur, 2018.

Tun Abdul Razak, *Dedikasi & Integriti*, The New Straits Times Press (M) Bhd, 2013.

Strategy for Action: The Selected Speeches of Tun Abdul Razak, Malaysian Centre for Development Studies, 1969.

Yayasan Run Razak (ed.), *Tun Adbul Razak: A Personal Portrait*, Utusan, Kuala Lumpur, 2005.

Paridah Abd. Samad, *Tun Abdul Razak: A Phenomenon in Malaysian Politics*, Affluent Master, Kuala Lumpur, 1998.

Tun Ahmad Sarji, *My Recollections of Tun Abdul Razak*, MPH, 2016.

William Shaw, *Tun Razak: His Life and Times*, Longman, 1976.

Jomo Kwame Sundaram, 'Malaysia Incorporated: Corporatism à la Mahathir', *Institutions and Economies*, vol. 6, no. 1, April 2014.

Kobuka Suwannathat Pian, *Tunku: An Odyssey of a Life Well-Lived and Well-Loved*, University of Malaya Press, Kuala Lumpur, 2017.

Kalthom Taib, *Taib Andak: In a Class of His Own*, MPH Group Publishing Sdn Bhd, 2009.

Kalthom Taib, *The Shafee Yahya Story*, Kalthom Taib Publishing, 2010.

Daim Zainuddin, *The Creation and Implementation of the New Economic Policy: Successes and Failures 1970–2008*, University of Malaysia Press, 2019.

SECTIONS 2 AND 3: INVESTMENT BANKER / UNIVERSAL BANKER

Zuraidah Omar, *Of People and Principles: The Commerce Asset Story*, Commerce, Kuala Lumpur, 2003.

Most of the material in these sections is based on recollections and interviews with participants, augmented by information from the relevant CIMB Annual Reports and official documents along with judicious use of press reports from the time.

SECTION 4: 1MDB

Clare Rewcastle Brown, *The Sarawak Report: The Inside Story of the 1MDB Exposé*, Gerakbudaya, Petaling Jaya, 2018.

Tom Wright and Bradley Hope, *Billion Dollar Whale: The Inside Story of Jho Low and the 1MDB Scandal*, Hachette, 2018.

We also drew on extensive and detailed reporting on 1MDB by *The Edge*, the *Wall Street Journal* and the *New York Times*.

SECTION 5: CONVERSATIONS ON MALAYSIA

Daron Acemoglu and James A. Robinson, *Why Nations Fail*, Random House, 2012.

Andrew Arato, Jean L. Cohen and Astrid von Busekist, *Forms of Pluralism and Democratic Constitutionalism*, Columbia University Press, 2018.

Andrew Bachtiger, John Dryzek, Jane Mansbridge and Mark Warren (eds.), *The Oxford Handbook of Deliberative Democracy*, Oxford University Press, 2018.

Amy Chua, *Political Tribes*, Bloomsbury, 2018.

John S. Dryzek, *Foundations and Frontiers of Deliberative Governance*, Oxford University Press, 2010.

David M. Farrell and Jane Suiter, *Reimagining Democracy: Lessons in Deliberative Democracy from the Irish Front Line*, Cornell Selects, 2019.

James S. Fishkin, *Democracy When the People Are Thinking: Revitalising Our Politics Through Public Deliberation*, Oxford University Press, 2018.

Patrick Fournier et al., *When Citizens Decide: Lessons from Citizen Assemblies on Electoral Reform*, Oxford University Press, 2011.

Geoff Mulgan, *Good and Bad Power: The Ideals and Betrayals of Government*, Penguin, 2007.

Diana Mutz, *Hearing the Other Side*, Cambridge University Press, 2006.

John Parkinson and Jane Mansbridge (eds.), *Deliberative Systems*, Cambridge University Press, 2012.

Condoleezza Rice, *Democracy: Stories from the Long Road to Freedom*, Hachette, 2017.

Graham Smith, *Democratic Innovations: Designing Institutions for Citizen Participation*, Cambridge University Press, 2009.

Henry Tam (ed.), *Whose Government Is It: Renewal of State–Citizen Cooperation*, Bristol University Press, 2019.

Juan Ugarriza and Didier Caluwaerts (eds.), *Democratic Deliberation in Deeply Divided Societies: From Conflict to Common Ground*, Palgrave Macmillan, 2014.

Barry Wain, *Malaysian Maverick: Mahathir Mohamad in Turbulent Times*, Palgrave Macmillan, 2009.

Bridget Welsh (ed.), *The End of UMNO: Essays on Malaysia's Former Dominant Party*, Strategic Information and Research Development Centre, Pataling Jaya, 2018.

Bridget Welsh, James U. H. Chin (eds.), *Awakening: The Abdullah Badawi Years*, Strategic Information and Research Development Centre, 2013.

NOTES

1   My response to my personal brush with prostate cancer was to initiate a campaign OnlyMenCan.com to highlight the need for men and the rest of society to take the illness more seriously.

2   A note on the complex names of Malaysians. We come from many different religions and communities, so we have names that reflect the traditions of the Malay Peninsula, Indonesia, India, China and the Middle East. A Malay name consists of personal names, in my case Mohamed Nazir followed by a patronym, Abdul Razak. If Osman had a son called Musa, the son would be called Musa Osman. In my case my full name is Mohamed Nazir bin Abdul Razak. I am most commonly known as Nazir Razak. When addressing one another Malays always use one of the first names, rather than the last name, as it would be impolite to address someone using their father's name.

3   The main published sources we drew on are to be found in the Bibliography.

4   The state secretary is the second most senior civil servant in the colonial administration after the chief minister of a state.

5   Dr Ismail had died suddenly in August 1973. He was replaced as Deputy PM by Hussein Onn, who was the eldest son of Onn Jaafar, the first president of UMNO.

6   Interview with the author.

7   This statistic and many others about the population and economy of Malaysia are drawn from Sultan Nazrin Shah's outstanding book *Striving for Development*, Oxford University Press, 2019.

8   This story is recounted in detail in William Shaw, *Tun Razak: His Life and Times*, Longman, 1976.

9   Ibid.

10   A History of Malaysia by Barbara Watson Andaya dan Leonard Y. Andaya.

11   *The Making of the Malayan Constitution* by Joseph M.Fernando: Malaysian Branch of Royal Asiatic Society January 2002.

12   *Alliance Ad Hoc Political Committee Meeting Minutes*, 3rd April 1957.

13   Education Ordinance of 1957, Section 3.

14   "Collection of Tun Razak's Speeches 1971, National Archives".

15   https://www.nam.ac.uk/explore/malayan-emergency.

16   "The Greatest Safeguard Of Our Sovereignty" A speech by Tun Abdul Razak when he addressed delegates at the opening of the Afro-Asian Seminar on National Development in Kuala Lumpur on 28th October, 1966.

17   Interview with the author.

18   https://www.parlimen.gov.my/files/hindex/pdf/DR-27011968.pdf.

19   Limited accounts of the working of the NCC can be found in: Shaw, *Tun Razak*; Yayasan Tun Razak (ed.), *Tun Adbul Razak: A Personal Portrait*, Utusan, Kuala Lumpur, 2005; Ooi Kee Beng, *The Reluctant Politician: Tun Dr Ismail and His Time*, Institute of Southeast Asian Studies, Singapore, 2006. We have reconstructed its working through interviews and by drawing on contemporary press reports and speeches in the National Archive.

20   Chapter 1, Second Malaysia Plan (1971-1975). Available at: https://www.pmo. gov.my/dokumenattached/RMK/RMK2.pdf

21   Speech by Tun Razak, during the Declaration of Rukun Negara on 31 August 1970. Referenced by HM the Agong in this speech: https://www.utusanborneo. com.my/2019/10/06/didik-graduan-dengan-nilai-rukun-negara-agong

22   Second Malaysia Plan (1961-1965), Government or Malaysia

23   The New Economic Policy remains to this day one of the boldest and most controversial set of measures. For measured assessments of the impact of the NEP see Sultan Nazrin Shah, *Striving for Inclusive Development: From Pangkor to a Modern Malaysian State*, Oxford University Press, 2019; Jomo Kwame Sundaram and Wee Chong Hui, *Malaysia @ 50, Economic Development, Distribution, Disparities*, Strategic Information and Research Development Centre, Petaling Jaya, 2014.

24   Interview with the author

25   Tun Razak and Malaysia's New Economic Policy, Jomo Sundaram, in Driving Development: Revisiting Razak's Role in Malaysia's Economic Progress, ed Rajah Rasiah and Kamal Salih, University of Malaya Press, kuala Lumpur 2018.

26   Interview with the author.

27   http://lib.perdana.org.my/PLF/Digital_Content.

28   Interview with the author.

29   https://news.stanford.edu/2005/06/14.

30   Time out with Friends, Tan Sri Robert Kuok, in Tun Abdul Razak : A Personal Portrait compiled by Yayasan Tun Razak, Utuasan Publications & Distributors Sdn Bhd, Kuala Lumpur 2005.

31   Interview with the author.

32   https://www.nst.com.my/news/2016/01/122250/full-text-hishammuddin-hussains-speech-special-commemorative-seminar-tun-razak.

33   Interviews with the author.

34 https://ir.lib.uwo.ca/cgi.

35 Much of the history of the banks that came together to create Commerce Group is told in Zuraidah Omar, *Of People and Principles: The Commerce Asset Story*, Commerce, Kuala Lumpur, 2003. Most of the material in these sections about CIMB is based on my own recollections along with interviews with participants, augmented by information from the relevant CIMB Annual Reports and official documents for from Bursa Malaysia along with judicious use of press reports from the time covering key deals and announcements.

36 Clayton Christensen, *The Innovator's Dilemma*, Harvard Business Review Press, 1997.

37 https://data.worldbank.org/indicator.

38 https://www.theedgemarkets.com/article/drawing-foreign-interest-back-local-equities.

39 Telekom IPO Prospectus, 1992.

40 https://www.nytimes.com/1992/04/21/business/worldbusiness.

41 http://psasir.upm.edu.my/id/eprint.

42 http://www.columbia.edu/cu/thai/html/financial97_98.

43 See 'Crisis and Recovery in Malaysia, The Role of Capital Controls – Prema-Chandra Athukorala', https://www.e-elgar.com/shop.

44 https://www.wsj.com/articles/SB870371714342497000.

45 http://edition.cnn.com/ASIANOW/asiaweek/97/0704/biz4.html.

46 https://www.iuj.ac.jp/mlic/EIU/Report/Brunei/April_1997_Main_report.pdf.

47 https://www.wsj.com/articles/SB105765305279258800.

48 Philip Augar, *The Death of Gentlemanly Capitalism*, Penguin, 2008.

49 https://www.wsj.com/articles/SB856727773415695000.

50 https://www.theedgemarkets.com/article/special-report-truth-2001-sale-renonguem-finally-coming-out.

51 https://www.wsj.com/articles/SB971949341143257281.

52 CIMB Annual Reports 1999, 2000, 2001.

53 The book value of a company is just what the accounts say it is worth based on its physical tangible assets, such as property and the cash it has in the bank. It is the most conservative way to value a company as it takes no account of its brand and reputation, or research and development.

54 CIMB Annual Reports 2003, 2006.

55 https://www.economist.com/asia/2004/03/25/bravo-badawi.

56 "Rent Seekers" or Real Capitalists?: The Riddle of Malaysian Capitalism by Peter Whitford Searle.

57 https://www.theedgemarkets.com/article/cover-story-bigger-not-best-yet.

58 Conversation with the author.

59   New Economic Model, Part 1, by the NEAC March 30 2010, pg 6.

60   New Economic Model, Part 1 by the NEAC March 30 2010, pg 15.

61   https://policy.asiapacificenergy.org/sites/default/files/ETP.pdf

62   Rozali stood down as CEO of Commerce in January 2006. Shukri Hussin took over the reigns for a short period, until I took over in November 2006.

63   AEC document

64   https://www.thestar.com.my/business/business-news/2008/06/03/bank-niaga -and-bank-lippo-to-merge.

65   CIMB Annual Reports 2008–2012.

66   CIMB Annual Reports 2008–2012.

67   CIMB Annual Reports 2008–2009.

68   https://www.bloomberg.com/news/articles/2013-05-16/asian-pay-television- said-to-raise-1-1-billion-in-singapore-ipo.

69   CIMB Annual Report 2013.

70   Ibid.

71   Ibid.

72   Ibid.

73   CIMB Annual Report 2014.

74   https://hbr.org/2013/03/long-ceo-tenure-can-hurt-performance.

75   https://www.theedgemarkets.com/article/china-galaxy-buys-50-cimbs-overseas- securities-business.

76   https://www.cimb.com/content/dam/cimb/group/documents/investor-relations/ annual-reports/2017/CIMB-Annual-Report-2017-180413.pdf.

77   CIMB Annual Reports.

78   https://www.theedgemarkets.com/article/1mdb-update-besides-jho-low-who- made-millions-big-flip-2009.

79   https://www.theedgemarkets.com/article/1mdb-update-besides-jho-low-who- made-millions-big-flip-2009.

80   The story of 1MDB, its inception and collapse, is told in detail in: Tom Wright and Bradley Hope, *Billion Dollar Whale: The Inside Story of Jho Low and the 1MDB Scandal*, Hachette, 2018; Clare Rewcastle Brown, *The Sarawak Report: The Inside Story of the 1MDB Exposé*, Gerakbudaya, Petaling Jaya, 2018. Throughout this section we have drawn on extensive and detailed reporting on 1MDB by *The Edge*, the *Wall Street Journal* and the *New York Times*.

81   https://www.aljazeera.com/news/2020/7/28/timeline-how-malaysias-1mdb- financial-scandal-unfolded.

82   https://www.sarawakreport.org/2015/10/furious-1mdb-board-demanded-back- jho-lows-us700-million-five-days-after-jv-was-signed-major-exclusive/.

83 https://www.theedgemarkets.com/article/cover-story-cheap-land-bails-out-1mdb-its-negative-cash-flow.

84 https://www.nytimes.com/2015/02/08/nyregion/stream-of-foreign-wealth-flows-to-time-warner-condos.html.

85 https://www.instagram.com/nazir.razak/.

86 https://www.wsj.com/articles/malaysian-investigators-probe-points-to-deposits-into-prime-ministers-accounts-1435866107.

87 https://www.wsj.com/articles/malaysian-leader-spent-millions-on-luxury-goods-1459383835.

88 Tommy Thomas, *My Story: Justice in the Wilderness*, Strategic Information and Research Development Centre, 2021.

89 https://en.wikipedia.org/wiki/Shared_Prosperity_Vision_2030.

90 https://scholar.harvard.edu.

91 Interview with the author.

92 https://en.wikipedia.org/wiki/Malaysian_Maverick.

93 https://www.malaysiakini.com/news/307126.

94 Edmund Terence Gomez has written extensively on the financial links between corporate and political institutions in Malaysia. See especially *Minister of Finance Incorporated: Ownership and Control of Corporate Malaysia*, Palgrave Macmillan, 2017; https://www.icgn.org/professor-dr-edmund-terence-gomez.

95 David Runciman, *How Democracy Ends*, Profile Books, 2018.

96 https://www.cam.ac.uk/stories/dissatisfactiondemocracy.

97 Malay Political Leadership, Anthony S. K. Shome Routledge Curzon 2002.

98 The story of this gathering was eventually told in 2018 after the fall of the BN government.

99 Conversations on Malaysia report, unpublished.

100 Andrew Bachtiger, John Dryzek, Jane Mansbridge and Mark Warren (eds.), *The Oxford Handbook of Deliberative Democracy*, Oxford University Press, 2018. In this section we have drawn on a wide range of books and studies of deliberative democracy which are noted in the Bibliography.

101 https://www.thestar.com.my/news/nation/2018/06/10/towards-a-more-mature-democracy-two-years-ago-a-group-of-prominent-malaysian-figures-gathered-in-oxf.

102 https://www.oecd-ilibrary.org/governance/innovative-citizen-participation-and-new-democratic-institutions_339306da-en.

103 David M. Farrell and Jane Suiter, *Reimagining Democracy: Lessons in Deliberative Democracy from the Irish Front Line*, Cornell Selects, 2019.

104 Condoleezza Rice, *Democracy: Stories from the Long Road to Freedom*, Hachette, 2017, https://www.goodreads.com/book/show/31934469-democracy.

INDEX

NR indicates Nazir Razak